CU-C03BPG-302

UNIVERSITY PARTNERSHIPS FOR ACADEMIC PROGRAMS AND PROFESSIONAL DEVELOPMENT

INNOVATIONS IN HIGHER EDUCATION TEACHING AND LEARNING

Series Editor: Patrick Blessinger

Recent Volumes:

INNOVATIONS IN HIGHER EDUCATION TEACHING AND
LEARNING VOLUME 7

UNIVERSITY PARTNERSHIPS FOR ACADEMIC PROGRAMS AND PROFESSIONAL DEVELOPMENT

EDITED BY

PATRICK BLESSINGER

*International HETL Association, New York, USA;
St. John's University, New York, USA*

BARBARA COZZA

St. John's University, New York, USA

Created in partnership with the
International Higher Education Teaching and Learning Association

https://www.hetl.org/

United Kingdom – North America – Japan
India – Malaysia – China

Emerald Group Publishing Limited
Howard House, Wagon Lane, Bingley BD16 1WA, UK

First edition 2016

Copyright © 2016 Emerald Group Publishing Limited

Reprints and permissions service
Contact: permissions@emeraldinsight.com

No part of this book may be reproduced, stored in a retrieval system, transmitted in
any form or by any means electronic, mechanical, photocopying, recording or
otherwise without either the prior written permission of the publisher or a licence
permitting restricted copying issued in the UK by The Copyright Licensing Agency
and in the USA by The Copyright Clearance Center. Any opinions expressed in the
chapters are those of the authors. Whilst Emerald makes every effort to ensure the
quality and accuracy of its content, Emerald makes no representation implied or
otherwise, as to the chapters' suitability and application and disclaims any warranties,
express or implied, to their use.

British Library Cataloguing in Publication Data
A catalogue record for this book is available from the British Library

ISBN: 978-1-78635-300-9
ISSN: 2055-3641 (Series)

ISOQAR certified
Management System,
awarded to Emerald
for adherence to
Environmental
standard
ISO 14001:2004.

Certificate Number 1985
ISO 14001

INVESTOR IN PEOPLE

CONTENTS

LIST OF CONTRIBUTORS

Rick J. Arrowood	Northeastern University, Boston, MA, USA
Inese Berzina-Pitcher	Michigan State University, East Lansing, MI, USA
Cathy Bishop-Clark	Miami University, Middletown, OH, USA
Patrick Blessinger	International HETL Association and St. John's University, New York, NY, USA
Wendy Bloisi	London Metropolitan University, London, United Kingdom
Laura J. Carfang	Babson College, Wellesley, MA, USA
Sherri Cianca	Niagara University, Lewiston, New York, NY, USA
Barbara Cozza	St. John's University, New York, NY, USA
Beth Dietz	Miami University, Middletown, OH, USA
Kathleen C. Doutt	Immaculata University, Immaculata, PA, USA
David Dunbar[†]	Cabrini University, Radnor, PA, USA
Elizabeth Faunce	Immaculata University, Immaculata, PA, USA
S. Giridhar	Azim Premji University, Bengaluru, India
Gerwin Hendriks	HU University of Applied Sciences Utrecht, Utrecht, The Netherlands
Leslie Hitch	Northeastern University, Boston, MA, USA

Adrian Huang	LASALLE College of the Arts, Singapore
Rutger Kappe	Inholland University of Applied Sciences, Haarlem, The Netherlands
Doris Kiendl-Wendner	FH JOANNEUM – University of Applied Sciences, Graz, Austria
Dominic Mahon	Nazarbayev University, Astana, Kazakhstan
Anabella Martinez	Universidad del Norte, Barranquilla, Colombia
Hazel Messenger	London Metropolitan University, London, United Kingdom
Punya Mishra	Michigan State University, East Lansing, MI, USA
Marjon Molenkamp	Rotterdam University of Applied Sciences, Rotterdam, The Netherlands
Elizabeth Moy	Southeastern Pennsylvania Consortium for Higher Education, Radnor, PA, USA
Leslie Myers	Chestnut Hill College, Philadelphia, PA, USA
Rachel Niklas	Nazarbayev University, Astana, Kazakhstan
Iddah Aoko Otieno	Bluegrass Community and Technical College, Lexington, KY, USA
Tom Otieno	Eastern Kentucky University, Richmond, KY, USA
Judith Parsons	Immaculata University, Immaculata, PA, USA
Anne Peirson-Smith	City University of Hong Kong, Kowloon Tong, Hong Kong
Jill Alexa Perry	Carnegie Project on the Education Doctorate and University of Pittsburgh, Pittsburgh, PA, USA

Natascha Radclyffe-Thomas	University of the Arts London, London, United Kingdom
Ana Roncha	University of the Arts London, London, United Kingdom
Thomas Schmalzer	FH JOANNEUM – University of Applied Sciences, Graz, Austria
Alia Sheety	Cabrini University, Radnor, PA, USA
Zuke van Ingen	Inholland University of Applied Sciences, Haarlem, The Netherlands
Jaap van Zandwijk	Leiden University of Applied Sciences, Leiden, The Netherlands
Digby Warren	London Metropolitan University, London, United Kingdom
Olof Wiegert	Amsterdam University of Applied Sciences, Amsterdam, The Netherlands
Domien Wijsbroek	The Hague University of Applied Sciences, The Hague, The Netherlands
Debby Zambo	Carnegie Project on the Education Doctorate, Phoenix, AZ, USA

SERIES EDITOR'S INTRODUCTION

The purpose of this series is to publish current research and scholarship on innovative teaching and learning practices in higher education. The series is developed around the premise that teaching and learning is more effective when instructors and students are actively and meaningfully engaged in the teaching-learning process.

The main objectives of this series are to:

(1) present how innovative teaching and learning practices are being used in higher education institutions around the world across a wide variety of disciplines and countries,
(2) present the latest models, theories, concepts, paradigms, and frameworks that educators should consider when adopting, implementing, assessing, and evaluating innovative teaching and learning practices, and
(3) consider the implications of theory and practice on policy, strategy, and leadership.

This series will appeal to anyone in higher education who is involved in the teaching and learning process from any discipline, institutional type, or nationality. The volumes in this series will focus on a variety of authentic case studies and other empirical research that illustrates how educators from around the world are using innovative approaches to create more effective and meaningful learning environments.

Innovation teaching and learning is any approach, strategy, method, practice or means that has been shown to improve, enhance, or transform the teaching-learning environment. Innovation involves doing things differently or in a novel way in order to improve outcomes. In short, Innovation is positive change. With respect to teaching and learning, innovation is the implementation of new or improved educational practices that result in improved educational and learning outcomes. This innovation can be any positive change related to teaching, curriculum, assessment, technology, or other tools, programs, policies, or processes that leads to improved educational and learning outcomes. Innovation can occur in institutional development, program development, professional development, or learning development.

The volumes in this series will not only highlight the benefits and theoretical frameworks of such innovations through authentic case studies and other empirical research but also look at the challenges and contexts associated with implementing and assessing innovative teaching and learning practices. The volumes represent all disciplines from a wide range of national, cultural and organizational contexts. The volumes in this series will explore a wide variety of teaching and learning topics such as active learning, integrative learning, transformative learning, inquiry-based learning, problem-based learning, meaningful learning, blended learning, creative learning, experiential learning, lifelong and lifewide learning, global learning, learning assessment and analytics, student research, faculty and student learning communities, as well as other topics.

This series brings together distinguished scholars and educational practitioners from around the world to disseminate the latest knowledge on innovative teaching and learning scholarship and practices. The authors offer a range of disciplinary perspectives from different cultural contexts. This series provides a unique and valuable resource for instructors, administrators, and anyone interested in improving and transforming teaching and learning.

Patrick Blessinger
Founder, Executive Director, and
Chief Research Scientist,
International HETL Association

PART I
CONCEPTS AND PRINCIPLES

INNOVATIVE APPROACHES IN UNIVERSITY PARTNERSHIPS: AN INTRODUCTION TO UNIVERSITY PARTNERSHIPS FOR ACADEMIC AND PROGRAM DEVELOPMENT

Barbara Cozza and Patrick Blessinger

ABSTRACT

The chapters in this book focus on how university-school partnerships can be used to foster academic and program development. The introductory chapter is oriented around three key questions: How do we define innovative international university partnerships? Do these innovative international university partnerships really work? What factors contribute to the success of these collaborations? In addressing these questions, this chapter presents a framework that addresses a taxonomy for innovative programs, elements to develop partnerships, ideas for sustaining collaboration, and challenges that might surface during implementation. In this volume a range of perspectives is presented using case studies and empirical research on how university partnerships are being implemented

University Partnerships for Academic Programs and Professional Development
Innovations in Higher Education Teaching and Learning, Volume 7, 3–17
Copyright © 2016 by Emerald Group Publishing Limited
All rights of reproduction in any form reserved
ISSN: 2055-3641/doi:10.1108/S2055-364120160000007001

internationally. These findings suggest that university partnerships have great potential to enhance and even transform colleges and universities.

Keywords: Innovative; partnerships; university; academic; program development

INTRODUCTION

The purpose of this chapter is to establish a framework for this volume and to present an overview and introduction to all the chapters. We begin with an understanding of the concepts and principles that guide and connect a rationale of why these university partnerships for academic and program development should be encouraged on an international basis. These partnerships are receiving increasing attention in higher education and other public sectors based on the belief that individuals and organizations can achieve more by working together in a collaborative setting (Dhillon, 2009). This chapter presents frameworks for innovative university partnerships for academic and program development in the following areas: taxonomy for innovative programs, elements to develop partnerships, ideas for sustaining collaboration, and an agenda that outlines obstacles that might surface during such actions.

CONCEPTS AND PRINCIPLES

When considering innovative approaches in university partnerships on an international level, three questions surface: How do we define innovative international university partnerships? Do these innovative international university partnerships really work? What factors contribute to the success of these collaborations?

Firstly, we must define what innovation means. Innovation is the process of building on existing research, knowledge, and practice through the application of new ideas to solve problems. It is important for organizations to nurture a culture that continually introduces new ideas and translate those ideas into action (Setser & Morris, 2014). The term innovation refers to a new approach that positively alters the processes of services, programs, and administration. These innovative programs stress risk-taking in order to achieve improvement and reformation. Programs that consider innovations emphasize uniqueness, dissemination, creativity, organizational improvement, and knowledge-building (Reviere, Berkowitz, Carter, & Ferguson, 1996). Carnegie Foundation's (2016) concept of innovations within community engagement partnerships emphasize the development of mutually beneficial collaborations based on reciprocity and exchange. The Carnegie Foundation confirms that institutional approaches are different based on the political, economic, cultural, demographic, and historical context.

Secondly, we must ask the question: do these partnerships really work? "Governance" in these international institutions drives all partnerships. This governance approach recognizes and embraces a global perspective. It involves integrating stakeholders and communities to resolve university problems, and it ultimately recognizes that new methods (e.g., contracts, grants, joint initiatives) are required for gaining success for these international partnerships. Many supporters (Salamon, 2002) suggest that the governance approach is a natural progression to assist with improving international universities and these institutional arrangements are indicative of trends toward integrating innovative ideas that will help to solve institutional problems and encourage global communication and collaboration among partnership groups. The governance paradigm stresses the importance of a synergistic partnership (Martin, Smith, & Phillips, 2003; Salamon, 2002) that connects all partners. The governance model focuses on a win-win situation where social issues and problems are targeted but where all partners benefit from the exchange of ideas.

Thirdly, research tells us that there are critical factors that lead to successful innovative international university partnerships (Blackwell, Tamir, Thompson, & Minkler, 2003; Cozza & Blessinger, 2015; Dugery & Knowles, 2003; Howell & Blessinger, 2012). Such factors include the following: funding, communication, synergy, measureable outcomes, and dissemination of findings, organizational compatibility, and simplicity. Funding is central to the success of the relationship. Government agencies and foundations are usually willing to provide funding to international university partnerships that focus on research and collaboration (Blackwell et al., 2003). However, there is a growing need for greater support for academic partnerships abroad that go beyond the scholarly grants to individuals. Funding agendas should target good quality partnerships that consider a need for deepened collaboration across national, cultural, and language barriers. Partnerships with higher education institutions abroad enable US universities to strengthen their curricula and research, provide students and faculty with opportunities to learn about other countries and cultures, and cooperate in addressing common problems. The integration of such innovative higher education partnership cultures may lead to the emergence of a third educational environment that focuses on caring and nurturing collaborative partnerships (Eisler, 2002).

In addition, communication should be in the form of frequent meetings between partners to discuss expectations and develop professional relationships. The effectiveness of communication is based on the following elements (Partnership Index, 2004): program objectives, effective collaborative groupings, clarity of decision-making, clarity of accountability in assignments, putting the right person and skills in the appropriate place of the partnership, credible leadership, and responsible ways of working on projects. This international partnership synergy means that successful university partnerships allow various stakeholders to treat all stakeholders involved as full partners. The interaction of multiple participants in the partnership stimulates more significant change than individuals acting separately on the same problem. All stakeholders should have buy-in to the partnership. Partnerships need specific results that demonstrate success.

Therefore, early in the development of the international university partnership, members need to construct measurable objectives that integrate with the partnership agendas. Partnerships do not exist in a vacuum and should disseminate data and results to a wider audience. This can be done by having academics publish articles, chapters in books and present at professional conferences. Technology also plays a significant role in dissemination of information of the partnership. Websites and blogs can provide a clear illustration of the international partnership, the stakeholders involved and recent program components. Organizational compatibility connects to the governance concept where power and decision-making are connected in a shared community. All stakeholders should compromise when and where necessary and hold an equal role as "expert" in the partnership. Simplicity is important to consider when investing time into the partnership. Successful partnerships should be made simple by including explicit goals and objectives, common definitions, and achievable outcomes.

THEORETICAL FRAMEWORK

Long-term higher education collaborations are often integral to university-university, university-community or university-school agendas. These collaborations all focus on goal setting, sharing common perspectives, capacities, and resources in order to make positive changes (Dhillon, 2009). These organizations encourage a shared community that embarks upon a transformational partnership. Transformational partnerships in these higher education communities are often connected to inspiring educators that commit to a shared vision and goals while challenging the members of the partnership to be innovative problem solvers (Bass & Riggio, 2006). A transformation partnership has a moral dimension in which the collaborators work towards with common purpose and create institutional growth and change through mutual interaction while applying available resources to address complex problems (Brown et al., 2006). Transformational leadership is portrayed as having leaders who set challenging expectations and in doing so motivate other stakeholders in a partnership to do more than they intend or thought possible (Bass & Riggio, 2006; Butcher, Bezzina, & Moran, 2011). The engagement of professionals in transformational social change of a partnership demands perseverance, self-discipline, and innovation (Rodin, 2005). Success in this transformational program draws on the long-term goals that demand a deep commitment by all partnership stakeholders or obvious problems will surface such as "burn out" and high turnover of partnership members with an outcome of lack of continuity in the program (Strier, 2014).

SYMBIOTIC AND ORGANIC PARTNERSHIPS

Goodlad (1994) argued that the essence of higher education and community partnerships are markedly different cultural entities which need to be symbiotically joined in order to bring about renewal in the partnership organizations. Symbioses agendas depend on (1) distinctive differences between the parties in the partnership, (2) structures to compliment differences that exist in the partnership, (3) strategies that surface through partnership experiences based on shared commitment and effort, and (4) adding additional resources and enhanced status within the partnership. Catelli, Padovano, and Costello (2000) encourage symbiotic relationships, a partnership where two parties work together in order to satisfy their mutual self-interests, and add that an organic relationship, where the two parties in a partnership function in an interdependent fashion in order to achieve a set of common goals, is also a necessary perspective. In these authentic partnerships, the partners need to agree to work closely together over time toward a common goal. During this process, the organizations share physical resources, funding, personnel, and administrative decision-making.

REASONS FOR COLLABORATION

There is research on how to enable higher education institutions conduct collaborative partnerships (Duffield, Olson, & Kerzman, 2013; Kezar, 2005), but there is a fair amount of literature that discusses partnerships within higher educational institutions, between higher education and outside entities such as community organizations, businesses and K-12 school systems (Duffield et al., 2013). Internal and external factors encourage entities to collaborate in partnerships. Internal factors include resources, pooling expertise of employees, common goals, and solving challenging issues (Eddy, 2010; Scherer, 2009). External factors include requirements of collaboration agendas for funding, accreditation and state purposes that call for collaboration on assessment, and encouragement by employers that support collaborative efforts (Kezar, 2005). The decision to create a partnership should consider internal and external factors and be thoughtful and strategic – the partnership should make sense and be a good fit, sharing common values, goals, and objectives (Creamer, 2003; Gajda, 2004).

TAXONOMY OF INNOVATIVE UNIVERSITY PARTNERSHIPS

In this volume, reasons for innovative university partnerships fall under a taxonomy of seven categories (OUP, 1999):

1. Major institutional change initiatives: agendas that bring about internal organizational change in the areas of changes in mission, and academic and program offerings.
2. Service learning: an initiative designed to engage students in community learning and service tasks in coursework and extracurricular activities.
3. Service provisions: initiatives that involve faculty and students in coordinating, sustaining long-term projects in a community.
4. Faculty involvement: faculty members become involved in partnership activities for research and sharing expertise.

5. Student volunteerism: students engage in community tasks separate and apart from service learning initiatives.
6. Community in the classroom: initiatives that involve the design of university courses that enhance community building and community capacity.
7. Applied research: initiatives involve university administrators, faculty and/or students in data collection, analysis, and research to report on innovative program implementation.

DEVELOPING A PARTNERSHIP

Partnerships often take a long time to build and it is assembled in stages (Amey, Eddy, & Ozaki, 2007). The partnership should be supported. Once the partnership begins, it requires the development of common mission and goals, the nurturing and building of relationships, establishment of governance body, and the definition of the roles and agendas that drive the partnership. The elements to consider when developing a partnership are the following:

- Types of partnerships: The partnership can have a central governing body that consists of representatives from all the partners or have a partnership with a lead partner with several less involved partners. A partnership can be transactional, operating on a superficial level or transformational level, encouraging shared leadership with a goal for systematic change (Butcher et al., 2011).
- Relationships in the partnership: The establishments of relationships are the most important elements of a partnership. Members of the partnership should get to know one another during the development stage and during meetings. The partnership is more apt to be successful if the identification of roles is established early in the collaboration process (Baumfield & Butterworth, 2007).
- Building trust: Trust is essential for a partnership to be successful. Meetings face-to-face and through virtual platforms allow colleagues to keep an open communication system to help to sustain the partnership and build mutual trust relationships.
- Governance: The governance of the partnership is determined by the partnership's goals, decision-making process, and accountability. The partnership should also have at least one champion of the partnership

that can influence other to feel deeply about the collaboration (Amey et al., 2007).

SUSTAINING A PARTNERSHIP

In order to sustain a partnership relationships need to be nurtured and the responsibilities of the collaboration need to be stated clearly from the onset of the partnership. It is recommended that monitoring of the collaborative relationship be ongoing. It is effective if partnerships provide opportunities for cross-institutional work that promotes interdependence and urges accountability by the organizations (Peterson, 2007). Formalized agreements and clarifying roles and responsibilities and commitments by all partners will help to make the partnership an effective and sustaining agenda. Partnerships need to be dynamic (Amey et al., 2007) to meet the needs of the members and the collaboration purpose, to avoid stagnation. When everyone benefits, the partnership is more likely to endure (Duffield et al., 2013).

However, longevity is not necessarily the main indicator of a quality partnership rather it could be a sign of unhealthy situations that surface (Bringle & Hatcher, 2002). A partnership should be beneficial to all partners if the collaboration is worth sustaining. To allow for an organization to support sustainable engagement systemic relationships with communities need to be established. There are four primary characteristics (Barnes et al., 2009; Ostrander, 2004): partnerships are grounded in meaning, they focus on community capacity building, they encourage long-term relationships, and they create collaborative networks between the partners.

OBSTACLES

The main obstacles for partnerships often show that there are unequal power relations, institutional tensions, conflicts of interest, bureaucratic constraints, poor planning and implementation, and lack of ongoing evaluation process. Sometimes there is competition over resources and recognition among staff which generates uncertainty about the viability of the partnership purpose and outcomes (Gray, 2004). Sometimes there is a challenge of contradictory goals and differing priorities that can lead to disagreement. A final challenge is the resistance from staff. Through partnerships, each group is vulnerable to outsider observation and evaluation. These evaluations might result in concerns of each partner's legitimacy to the collaboration (Barnes et al., 2009). It is important that stakeholders' explain collaborative successes and failures on an ongoing basis and continue to communicate how the partnership is moving along on agenda items.

CHAPTER SUMMARIES

In "Internationalization: A Strategic and Complex Approach," by Laura J. Carfang, the author explores, via a bounded rationality framework, the complex decision-making processes involved in internationalizing university campuses. In this study, university presidents describe their experiences of complex decision-making. The findings that emerged from this study suggests that this type of decision-making requires a strategic approach which empowers these leaders to navigate more effectively through the complex factors that impact decisions. Within this context, this chapter explores the real-world complexity of how decisions are formulated in a university setting, presents strategies and best practices, and offers recommendations to university leaders as they embark on their own internationalization initiatives.

In "The Centrality of the Faculty Role in Transnational Partnerships: A Research Agenda," by Rick J. Arrowood and Leslie Hitch, the authors discuss how international partnerships in higher education often focus on the strategic importance of the partnership to the institutions involved and the administrative challenges and intricacies of negotiating across languages and cultures. Of particular important of such partnership are the financial benefits to be gained by each party. They note that some scholars discuss the importance of developing global citizens as a result of partnerships yet research is limited on the role that faculty play in such partnerships. This chapter offers insight into how faculty can play a key role in forming sustainable and profitable partnerships.

In "Inter-Institutional Collaboration through Non-Positional Leadership: A STEM Higher Education Initiative," by Sherri Cianca, the author discusses how a non-positional faculty member led an inter-institutional STEM initiative. The chapter traces how one idea developed into a vision and how that vision morphed into a joint STEM concentration. The initiative centered on the idea of leading organizational change through an awareness of multiple lenses. The faculty member led to the formation of a committed STEM team who then set an agenda and pursued cross-campus collaboration to implement the initiative. The author discusses the challenges and setbacks the team experienced in developing and implementing the initiative.

In "Interinstitutional collaboration in Dutch professional higher education," by Rutger Kappe, Domien Wijsbroek, Marjon Molenkamp, Olof Wiegert, Gerwin Hendriks, Zuke van Ingen and Jaap van Zandwijk, the authors describe the development and running of an interinstitutional research group started by five large universities of applied sciences in the Netherlands. The topic of this research group was the study success of ethnic minority groups. A dedicated research team set out to address several unresolved research questions. This chapter examines board level and strategic level (directors of education policies) study success-related topics such as new legislation and diversity issues. This chapter provides readers with insights on effective working methods, challenges and achievements of this collaboration. The authors provide ten factors for success in establishing such interinstitutional collaborations.

In "The evolution of a foundation program: Reflections on the five year partnership between University College London and Nazarbayev University," by Dominic Mahon and Rachel Niklas, the authors analyze the five year partnership between University College London (UCL) and Nazarbayev University (NU) in Astana, Kazakhstan. These authors discuss interviews with key members of staff from both institutions and they offer their reflections on the successes and challenges of the partnership. The authors used critical case sampling of key staff members from UCL and NU who were involved in the establishment and running of the program. Also, a sample of four participants from UCL and NU were interviewed. The results of the data analysis provide the basis for a set of recommendations for those entering into transnational higher education partnerships.

In "Cross-country faculty learning community: An opportunity for collaboration around the Scholarship of Teaching and Learning," by Anabella Martinez, Cathy Bishop-Clark, and Beth Dietz, the authors discuss how they led a faculty learning community (FLC) on the scholarship of teaching and learning (SoTL). The chief aim of the FLC was to increase faculty members' knowledge of SoTL. The FLC facilitators worked in the United States and the co-facilitator and the participants worked at Universidad Del Norte in Colombia, South America. The facilitators in the US spoke English whereas the participants spoke Spanish. While the technology that was used was at times problematic and the translation difficult, the authors deemed the learning community a success in meeting its goals.

In "Home and Away: a case study analysis of a learning and teaching program supporting the development of a "transformative" partnership with a private higher education institution in Sri Lanka," by Hazel Messenger, Digby Warren, and Wendy Bloisi, the authors discuss how transnational arrangements between different types of higher education institutions provided a unique partnership. The authors emphasize that successful partnerships both learn and work together and can be mutually transformative, requiring both organizations to build a good working relationship and trust. This approach focused on the development of a new hybrid organization characterized by mutual benefits, communication, competence, and trust. The authors use multiple sources of data to identify practical characteristics associated with developing a culture of transformative partnership.

In "By Design and by Chance: The Story of One International Partnership," by Inese Berzina-Pitcher, Punya Mishra, and S. Giridhar, the authors discuss how emerging economies have become less reliant on funding from foreign agencies and that one result of this is the formation of more self-funded international partnerships. This chapter describes a partnership between two institutions of higher education – one in the United States and the other in India. It describes the context of the partnership through Sakamoto and Chapman's functional model for the analysis of cross-border partnerships to analyze the key factors involved in the development of the partnership. The chapter focuses on the short-term professional development visits to the United States for educators from the Indian institution. The authors make recommendations to establish international university partnerships.

In "Community College-University Cross-Border Partnership through Faculty Exchange," by Iddah A. Otieno and Tom Otieno, the authors discuss how higher education institutions are increasingly facing new challenges as a result of a fast changing educational landscape brought about by increased competition and internationalization. One strategy colleges and universities have adopted is the formation of strategic partnerships with other institutions locally and globally. The authors examine a faculty exchange based strategic partnership between an American community college and a public university in the Republic of Kenya, East Africa. The authors discuss the rationale for the partnership despite their differing missions, the partnership formation process, and program activities, outcomes and challenges. The authors make several recommendations useful when considering starting a cross-border faculty exchange program.

In "Small is Beautiful – How a Young University Can Successfully Establish University Partnerships – The Case of FH JOANNEUM

University of Applied Sciences," by Thomas Schmalzer and Doris Kiendl-Wendner, the authors discuss how a relatively new university located in a small town in central Europe has been able to establish networks and international collaborations with universities and industry. This case study focuses on one university department, the "Institute of International Management". Despite budget limitations and a geographical disadvantage compared to large urban universities the authors discuss the program's success by way of an approach that combined teaching activities (study abroad, project classes, joint degrees, quality assurance, massive open online courses, and more) and research and development. This case illustrates how small or new or financially limited universities can build sustainable international partnerships to the benefit of students, faculty, and other stakeholders.

In "University Partnerships for Academic Program and Professional Development Building Faculty Capacity for 21st Century Teaching and Learning," by Alia Sheety, Elizabeth Moy, Judith Parson, David Dunbar, Kathleen Doutt, Elizabeth Faunce, and Leslie Myers, the authors discuss the collaborative relationship between eight private colleges and universities located in the Greater Philadelphia region through the Southeastern Pennsylvania Consortium for Higher Education (SEPCHE). SEPCHE's institutions are small to mid-sized colleges and universities that are characterized by diminished growth in enrollment, reduced funding, and greater demand for accountability. The authors discuss the role that SEPCHE plays in the professional development of the faculty working at these institutions. The authors examine faculty perspectives and institutional support to improve teaching, learning, and research outcomes.

In "Creative Cross-cultural Connections: Facebook as a Third Space for International Collaborations," by Natascha Radclyffe-Thomas, Ana Roncha, Anne Peirson-Smith, and Adrian Huang, the authors discuss how students need to become competent with cross-cultural collaboration, yet current curricula often remain focuses on the local culture. The authors discuss the experiences of the teachers and students involved around the issues in internationalizing the curriculum. Tutors created a shared private Facebook group to connect London College of Fashion students with students at City University of Hong Kong and LASALLE College of the Arts, Singapore. Students worked on separate but aligned briefs that mirror contemporary working patterns and allowed for the co-creation of educational outcomes. The Facebook platform provided a third space for co-creation of learning: a global classroom.

In "The Carnegie Project on the Education Doctorate: A Partnership of Universities and Schools Working to Improve the Education Doctorate and K-20 Schools," by Jill Alexa Perry and Debby Zambo, the authors discuss how the Doctorate in Education (Ed.D) has been surrounded with some confusion regarding its purpose and distinction from the more traditional PhD. In response to this, the Carnegie Project on the Education Doctorate (CPED), a collaborative project consisting of 80+ schools of education located in the United States, Canada, and New Zealand, was formed to take a critical examination of the Ed.D and to develop it into the degree of choice for educators who want to generate knowledge about practices and policies of the education profession. This chapter explains the origins of the education doctorate and how CPED has improved the focus and distinction of the Ed.D.

CONCLUSION

In this volume, we have presented a range of perspectives, case studies and empirical research and theories on how innovative higher education partnerships are being implemented. These findings suggest that the innovative higher education and community partnerships have great potential to enhance and transform the higher education and community organizations.

REFERENCES

Amey, M. J., Eddy, P. L., & Ozaki, C. C. (2007). Demands for partnership and collaboration in higher education: A model. *New Directions for Community College, 139*, 5–14.

Barnes, J. V., Altimare, E. L., Farrell, P. A., Brown, R. E., Richard Burnett III, C., Gamble, L., & Davis, J. (2009). Creating and sustaining authentic partnerships with community in a systemic model. *Journal of Higher Education Outreach and Engagement, 13*(4), 15–29.

Bass, B. M., & Riggio, R. E. (2006). *Transformational leadership* (2nd ed.). Mahwah, NJ: Lawrence Erlbaum.

Baumfield, V., & Butterworth, M. (2007). Creating and translating knowledge about teaching and learning in collaborative school-university research partnerships: An analysis of what is exchanged across the partnerships, by whom and how. *Teachers and Teaching: Theory and Practice, 13*, 411–427.

Blackwell, A., Tamir, H., Thompson, M., & Minkler, M. (2003). *Community based participatory research: Implications for funders*. Oakland, CA: Policy Link.

Bringle, R. G., & Hatcher, J. A. (2002). Campus-community partnerships: The terms of engagement. *Journal of Social Issues, 58*, 503–516.

Brown, R. E., Reed, C. S., Bates, L. V., Knaggs, D., McKnight-Casey, K., & Barnes, J. V. (2006). The transformative engagement process: Foundations and supports for university–community partnerships. *Journal of Higher Education, Outreach and Engagement, 11*(1), 9–23.

Butcher, J., Bezzina, M., & Moran, W. (2011). Transformational partnerships: A new agenda for higher education. *Innovative Higher Education, 36*, 29–40.

Carnegie Foundation for the Advancement of Teaching. (2016). *Community engagement elective classification.* Retrieved from http://nerche.org/index.php. Accessed on March 20, 2016.

Catelli, L. A., Padovano, K., & Costello, J. (2000). Action research in the context of a school-university partnership: Its value, problems, issues and benefits. *Educational Action Research, 8*(2), 225–241.

Cozza, B., & Blessinger, P. (2015). *University partnerships for community and school* system development. Bingley, UK: Emerald Group Publishing.

Creamer, E. G. (2003). Exploring the link between inquiry paradigm and the process of collaboration. *The Review of Higher Education, 26*, 447–465.

Dhillon, J. K. (2009). The role of social capital in sustaining partnership. *British Education Research Journal, 35*(5), 687–704.

Duffield, S., Olson, A., & Kerzman, R. (2013). Crossing borders, breaking boundaries: Collaboration among higher education institutions. *Innovative Higher Education, 13*, 237–250.

Dugery, J., & Knowles, J. (2003). *University and community research partnerships.* Charlottesville, VA: University of Richmond Press.

Eddy, P. (2010). Partnerships and collaborations in higher education. *ASHE Higher Education Report, 36*, 1–115.

Eisler, R. (2002). Partnership education: For the 21st century. *Encounter: Educational for Meaning and Justice, 15*, 5–15.

Gajda, R. (2004). Utilizing collaboration theory to evaluate strategic alliances. *American Journal of Evaluation, 25*, 65–77.

Goodlad, J. I. (1994). *Educational renewal: Better teachers, better schools.* San Francisco, CA: Jossey-Bass.

Gray, B. (2004). Strong opposition: Frame-based resistance to collaboration. *Journal of Community and Applied Psychology, 14*, 166–176.

Howell, B., & Blessinger, P. (2012). Coventry university: Good international partnerships start at home. *Guardian Higher Education Network.* Retrieved from http://www.theguardian.com/higher-education-network/higher-education-network-blog/2012/jul/11/coventry-university-international-partnerships

Kezar, A. (2005). Redesigning for collaboration within higher education institutions: An exploration into the developmental process. *Research in Higher Education, 46*, 831–860.

Martin, L. L., Smith, H., & Phillips, W. (2003). Why are innovative university-community partnerships important? *The Innovation Journal: The Public Sector Innovation Journal, 10*(2), 1–16. Retrieved from http://www.innovation.cc/volumes-issues/martin-u-partner4final.pdf.

Office of University Partnerships (OUP). (1999). *University-community partnerships: Current practices* (Vol. 3). Rockville, MD: US Department of Housing.

Ostrander, S. A. (2004). Democracy, civic participation, and the university: A comparative study of civic engagement on five campuses. *Nonprofit and Voluntary Sector Quarterly, 33*(1), 74–93.

Partnership Index. (2004). *Making public private partnerships work.* Retrieved from www.partner ingintelligence.com

Peterson, L. M. (2007). Articulating the future through collaboration. *New Directions for Higher Education, 2007*(138), 95–102. Retrieved from http://onlinelibrary.wiley.com/doi/10.1002/he.260/abstract

Reviere, R., Berkowitz, S., Carter, C., & Ferguson, C. (1996). *Needs assessment: A creative and practical guide for social scientists.* New York, NY: Taylor & Francis Ltd.

Rodin, J. (2005). The 21st century urban university: New roles for practice and research. *Journal of American Planning Association, 71*, 237–249.

Salamon, L. (2002). *The tools of government: A guide to the new governance.* New York, NY: Oxford University Press.

Scherer, J. (2009). Understanding the role of partnership configuration in NSF MS program. *Journal of Educational Research & Policy Studies, 9*, 1–21.

Setser, B., & Morris, H. (2014). So you think you want to innovate? Emerging lessons and a new tool for state and district leaders working to build a culture of innovation. *2 Revolutions Educause.* Retrieved from http://www.2revolutions.net/news/2Rev-TLA_Assessing_Culture_of_Innovation.pdf. Accessed on March 18, 2016.

Strier, R. (2014). Fields of paradox: University-community partnerships. *Higher Education, 68*, 155–165.

INTERNATIONALIZATION: A STRATEGIC AND COMPLEX APPROACH

Laura J. Carfang

ABSTRACT

This chapter presents findings from the author's qualitative descriptive phenomenological dissertation and explores the complex decision-making processes inherent to internationalizing college and university campuses through the framework of bounded rationality. By capturing the essence of how college and university presidents describe their experiences of complex decision-making, a notable finding that emerged from the author's study suggests that complex decision-making requires strategic decision-making approaches. Applying other decision-making strategies in complex situations empowers the decision-maker to mindfully maneuver through the intricate factors that impact choice and drive action. This chapter explores the complexity of how decisions are formulated from a strategic mindset, presents strategies and best practices, and offers recommendations that can be implemented as higher educational leaders embark on their own internationalization initiatives.

Keywords: International; partnerships; phenomenology; decision-making; university

University Partnerships for Academic Programs and Professional Development
Innovations in Higher Education Teaching and Learning, Volume 7, 19–35
Copyright © 2016 by Emerald Group Publishing Limited
All rights of reproduction in any form reserved
ISSN: 2055-3641/doi:10.1108/S2055-364120160000007009

INTRODUCTION

The higher education landscape compels college and university leaders to adopt innovative and strategic practices in order to remain sustainable in a highly competitive environment (Butt, More, & Avery, 2011; Marginson, 2006; Martinez & Wolverton, 2009). One of the ways in which higher education institutions respond is through the internationalization of their curriculum, faculty, student body, and campus (Altbach & Knight, 2007; Finkelstein, Walker, & Chen, 2013; Kehm, 2007). There are a variety of models higher education leaders may adopt in order to internationalize there campus (DeWitt, 2009; Knight, 2004; Teichler, 2004). However, with numerous choices, the decision-making process can no longer be understood as a simplistic, linear, cause and effect logic model, with one correct outcome. Instead, the complicated nature of internationalization requires higher education leaders to explore multiple opportunities with the understanding that an optimal solution may not be available. As a result, decision-makers are required to select among satisficing options, and make good decisions based on incomplete information within the context of unknown and dynamic variables.

Globalization has placed university leaders in a unique role as both key actors as well as spectators (Edwards, 2007, p. 374), and has given them the opportunity to engage in the complex decision-making processes associated with internationalizing one's campus in the 21st century. Research shows that the internationalization of higher education institutions has become a strategic priority among senior leadership (Bartell, 2003). These initiatives have permeated mission statements (NAFSA, 2012; Stromquist, 2007) and visionary plans (Stohl, 2007) across 71% of U.S. higher education institutions (Childress, 2009). Evidence from the literature point to the multifaceted approaches scholars have taken to understand internationalization (Deardorff, 2006; Knight, 2001; Norris & Gillespie, 2009; Stella & Gnanam, 2004; van Damme, 2001). Higher education institutions are being held accountable for producing "global graduates" (Robson, 2011, p. 622) who are prepared to work in today's global economy. Public accountability has positioned internationalization under the microscope and has paved the way for research through the prism of quality (Knight, 2001; Stella & Gnanam, 2004; van Damme, 2001) and assessment (Deardorff, 2006; Norris & Gillespie, 2009). Additionally, other researchers have studied internationalization through the lens of motivation (Altbach & Knight, 2007; Friesen, 2013), strategy (Childress, 2009; Harris & Wheeler, 2005), and policy (Gul, Gul, Kaya, & Alican, 2010; Lee, 2014), while other seminal authors have explored the opportunities and challenges brought about by these international initiatives (Edwards, 2007; Lee, 2014; van der Wende, 2007). Interestingly, as evidenced by the literature, research has shown that there is not a one model fits all approach to internationalizing a campus (Chan & Dimmock, 2008) and the intricacy of the situation is further complicated by the myriad definitions of internationalization found within the literature (Knight, 2015; Marginson & Sawir, 2011; Whitsed & Green, 2014).

While internationalization may be understood within the construct of transformative and innovative organizational change (Robson, 2011; Rudzki, 1995; van der Wende, 1999; van der Wende, Beerkens, & Teichler, 1999), and investigated from a variety of perspectives (Deardorff, 2006; Knight, 2001; Norris & Gillespie, 2009; Stella & Gnanam, 2004; van Damme, 2001), there continues to be a limited amount of research that explores how college and university leaders make complex decisions in the context of internationalization (Carfang, 2015). One of the key findings from Carfang's (2015) study suggests that complex decision-making may not be a stand-a-lone decision-making model in and of itself; the author proposes that the attributes of complex decision-making require the utilization of other decision-making processes and frameworks. The following sections articulate Carfang's (2015) methodology, findings, and concludes with recommendations.

METHODOLOGY

Phenomenological research acknowledges that there is a need for understanding a particular phenomenon to improve practice. Because complex decision-making is an abstract phenomenon, and cannot be explored directly, it is through open-ended questions and in-depth, one-on-one interviews with college and university presidents who have experienced making complicated decisions in terms of internationalization, that an understanding of the phenomenon was able to be revealed. Unlike alternative forms of phenomenology, descriptive phenomenology recognizes that the account of the phenomenon needs to be described exactly as it appears. Descriptive phenomenology provides a deeper understanding of lived experiences by making evident the taken-for-granted assumptions of the phenomenon (Starks & Trinidad, 2007).

A constructivism paradigm was also applied to Carfang's (2015) study to complement the qualitative phenomenological approach; constructivists,

"hold that reality is constructed in the minds of the individuals [the college
and university presidents], rather than it being an externally singular entity"
(Hansen, 2004, as cited in Ponterotto, 2005, p. 129). Thus, it is through the
interactions between the participant and their relationship to the phenomenon (i.e., complex decision-making) that meaning unfolds and that complex
decision-making incorporates other decision-making practices.

Carfang's (2015) study utilized a purposeful sampling technique in order
to identify qualified participants. Critical sampling allowed the researcher
to identify exceptional cases (Creswell, 2012) where colleges and universities
have been nationally recognized for their internationalization efforts. The
criterion for selecting participants was as follows:

- Participants consist of college and university presidents.
- The researcher drew from institutions that have been recognized for their
  internationalization efforts by adhering to one, or more, of the following
  requirements:
  o A commitment to internationalization as articulated in the institution's
    mission and visionary statements.
  o A commitment to internationalization by demonstrating a high percen-
    tage of students who study abroad, or, by the percentage of interna-
    tional students studying at the U.S. institution, based on Institute for
    International Education's (IIE) Open Doors Reports.
  o A recipient and/or nominee of the NAFSA: Association of
    International Educators – Simon Award for Comprehensive Campus
    Internationalization.
  o A recipient and/or nominee of the "Senator Paul Simon Spotlight
    Award" for a specific international program or initiative that contri-
    butes to comprehensive internationalization.
  o A recipient and/or nominee of the Institute for International
    Education (IIE) Heiskell Award for Internationalizing the Campus.
  o An institution that has set up branch or satellite campuses and/or
    operations across borders.

The goal of phenomenological research is to achieve a level of understanding by extrapolating the essence of a central phenomenon through
in-depth, one-on-one interviews and learning about participants' unique
and individual experiences. In line with a qualitative descriptive phenomenological methodology, a small sample size was adopted and six qualified
presidents were interviewed.

The following section articulates and presents the mined data and analysis, while telling the story of Jerry, Rich, Zach, Cindy, Margo, and Stephen,

as they experience the complexity of internationalization and the critical decisions that need to be made.

STRATEGIC DECISION-MAKING IN COMPLEX SITUATIONS

One of the ways in which college and university presidents make sense of the complex task of internationalizing one's campus is through a series of strategic tactics. Labib, Read, Gladstone-Millar, Tonge, and Smith (2014) posit that strategic decision-making entails planning and making decisions across the whole organization. In order to drive internationalization across the campus, participants described the process of strategic decision-making in terms of being financially driven, resource conscious, and innovative in their approach.

FINANCIAL DRIVERS

Financial considerations played a large role in the way in which some of the college and university presidents navigated decisions. However, the nuanced ways in which financial drivers became a catalyst for decision-making varied across participants.

Some participants' experiences of financial and strategic decision-making strategies stemmed from adopting a student-centered mindset. Both Zach and Rich articulated a strong commitment to providing students with opportunities to participate in international programs. While colleges and universities are able to expand their global offerings, Lien (2007) encourages higher education institutions to eliminate financial constraints so that more students have the opportunity to partake in offshore programs. In working toward developing these opportunities, Zach and Rich identified the financial barriers that were inhibiting their students from taking advantage of the various global programs and set out to eradicate such obstacles.

Financial concerns are a critical factor that directly impact a student's choice for engaging in international programs. While Rich saw that in some cases, paying for a semester abroad in certain parts of the world was a cheaper, and a more economical choice for students, Rich's dilemma was that these opportunities were not available to *all* students, only the select few who could afford it. The culture, Rich explains, was that students wanted to study abroad but recognized the financial implications for doing so. As a result, merit-based and need-based scholarships have emerged as a popular incentivizing practice (Lien, 2007) and has become an enabler for assisting students to study aboard. Rich saw the lack of financial support as a significant barrier to students going overseas. The strategic decision of awarding financial aid to students and eliminating monetary barriers became one of the biggest factors in how Rich was able to internationalize his campus.

Similarly, Zach saw an opportunity to scale a domestic educational program by offering the program globally. In the process of implementing this initiative, Zach was met with resistance by students who feared that the global opportunities to gain experience abroad would favor those students who could afford it. Parallel to the culture at Rich's institution, Zach was able to hear more implicitly that the students were not questioning the scalability of the program, but rather, wanted to ensure that they had access to participate in it. Zach recognized that the choice to internationalize a domestic program was a step in the right direction. Like Rich, the participants did not want to marginalize students, and therefore, made the strategic decision to reallocate financial aid and scholarship in an effort to support students who were interested in going overseas.

Alternatively, other participants such as Margo, Cindy appeared to experience strategic decision-making associated with the internationalization of their campus in terms of describing their financial responsibility. Strategies like expanding an institution's international reach may enhance enrollment and prestige, propel the reputation of colleges, generate additional revenue streams, and enhance student learning (Coryell, Durodoye, Wright, Pate, & Nguyen, 2012). Another approach to internationalization resides in the ability to diversify sources of revenue and build international relationships. Margo's institution is engaged in a variety of global initiatives that are decentralized across the campus. Depending on the project, some of Margo's initiatives provide monetary benefits to the college and can be understood as revenue generating partnerships. Altbach and Knight (2007), identify the realities of generating profits as a strong motivation behind internationalizing one's college or university. Moreover, Qiang (2003) posits that global initiatives provide economic enhancements and competitiveness, and promotes "income generated from educational products and services" (p. 255).

In some instances, internationalization of higher education has become a reaction to the unintended consequences of student mobility and international cooperation between institutions (Knight, 2004). However, for Margo, the decision to internationalize her institution and forge international relations are not ad hoc relations, but rather, strategic partnerships met with great intentionality grounded on the institution's core mission.

Cindy appears to ask the pointed questions of whether or not an internationalization initiative was feasibly and realistically affordable. Cindy's experience with complex decision-making is strongly rooted in exerting fiscal responsibility. While it is in the best interest of her institution to have a very well thought out international strategy, Cindy feels strongly that "until we can fund that, we can't do it". As a result, Cindy's experience appears to be a question of, "what strategic commitments are we going to make, and can we afford them? We're not going to do them if we cannot afford them".

It is critical for the decision-maker in complex environments to understand not only the action of such decision, but also the consequences of strategic decision-making. Rich wanted to confirm that eliminating one financial obstacle would not create another fiscal challenge and that the institution would still be able to recuperate revenue when students went overseas. As such, the implicit meaning alluded to by the participant illustrates that the success of internationalization can bear new fiscal challenges as well as bring about new opportunities to increase enrollment and fill spots in terms of room and board.

RESOURCES

In addition to finances, participants described strategic decision-making in terms of resources. This theme took on a variety of forms as participants described staff development and increasing human capital, to recognizing the need for infrastructure and support structure to enhance the student experience. To assist with implementing a comprehensive internationalization strategy across an institution, Brennan and Dellow (2013) suggest that presidents hire a chief international officer (CIO), someone who has a full appreciation for the complexities of implementing an internationalization plan and understands the value of building human capital in times of transformational change.

Stephen describes the decentralization of international activity as something that is not very well coordinated across his university. When benchmarking against other institutions, the participant noticed the lack of human resource support and that there was not a chief figure responsible for international strategy and coordinating global activities.

Similarly, Rich's experiences mirror those of Stephen's in terms of strategic decision-making and the need for human capital. Rich's description starts off by noticing what other institutions were doing in terms of internationalization and then realizing that he would need to make resource related strategic decisions if he wanted to compete in a similar market.

In addition to human capital, physical space became a resource that entered in the strategic decision-making process. Stephen advocates the need for resources in terms of physical space. While Stephen was thinking long term about the physical plant and the need for operational space, Rich had space available, and strategically decided to move the study abroad office across the hall from the President's Office. This was a bold and tactical move which sent a message across campus that international education was important. Therefore, resources like human capital and operational space were strategic decisions for both Stephen and Rich in an effort to help propel their international agenda.

Jerry describes strategic decision-making in terms of "opportunity cost". Working in a small private institution makes Jerry acutely aware of the balance between quantity and quality. While most of Jerry's international partnerships are grounded in research, Jerry knows that he cannot stretch his faculty and staff too thin. Jerry asserts that he is working with lean resources in terms of human capital.

Zach's approach to human capital was slightly different relative to the other participants. Zach appeared to already have the personnel and the infrastructure in place. However, for him, it was a matter of staff development and training. Using the admissions office as his primary example, Zach's success story initiates with the expansion of international students on campus; Zach was able to increase the international student population from 3% to 17%. For Zach, this was "easier said than done". One of the obstacles Zach noticed was that "the staff that were supposed to do it [recruit international students] were not global. They didn't travel overseas". Zach empowered his admissions team by providing them with opportunity to travel abroad.

Cindy also points out, like Jerry, that she too is working "with limited resources" in terms of personnel, and because of this limitation, the decision-making process is not simple. Cindy is aware of the importance of moving the institution's international agenda forward over the next five years, and is committed to revamping the way in which international programs operate, including international student enrollment.

For Stephen, Rich, Zach, Jerry, and Cindy, strategic decision-making in terms of resources means acknowledging the role human capital plays in moving the international agenda forward; this can be illustrated in the hiring or training of personnel and developing a strategy that can work within those boundaries without over taxing the faculty and staff.

INNOVATION

Innovation emerged as a key component to complex and strategic decision-making. Labib et al. (2014) suggest that complex decisions require both innovative and productive approaches in order to garner stakeholder support and drive decisions. Stephen described the process of developing a university wide strategy as something that has never been done before (it was only ever done at a departmental level); Stephen was willing to try something new in order to accomplish his agenda.

Similarly, as Cindy was trying to generate buy-in among her campus community, she too decided to engage in an innovative experiment. For Cindy, experimentation allowed all of the stakeholders to learn about a process without committing to taking on too much risk. Since complex decisions typically have multiple goals, it is possible that stakeholders encounter conflicting objectives (Labib et al., 2014) and therefore adopting an experiential venue to test criteria allows for the decision-makers to evaluate outcomes before embarking on a decision.

Internationalization provided Rich with an opportunity to be innovative in the sense of redesigning the undergraduate core curriculum. Transforming the curriculum, according to Raby (2007) could be at the individual level where students acquire new knowledge, or at an institutional level where there college educational reform (Raby, 2007). For Rich, this redesign embedded global perspectives into course content and focused on enhancing student learning outcomes such as intercultural competence. Pedagogically, internationalizing the curriculum prepares students live, work, and engage in a global and interconnected world (Raby, 2007). However, this innovative strategic decision became the "biggest and thorniest" decision with which Rich was confronted. Despite the challenges, Rich's original ideas allowed him and his team to "rethink what we are trying to do [and] rethink our pedagogy".

For Stephen, Cindy, and Rich, innovation and experimentation allowed the presidents to embrace new and creative ways of addressing complex decision-making in terms of internationalization. While Cindy and Rich described their experiences as challenging, all three participants were able to utilize innovation as part of their strategic decision-making process to successfully advance their internationalization agenda.

DECISION-MAKING THROUGH THE LENS OF BOUNDED RATIONALITY

Rationality is defined as "a style of behavior that is appropriate to the achievement of given goals, within the limits imposed by given conditions and constraints" (Simon, 1972, p. 161). Rational choice theory assumes that people always make prudent and logical decisions in an effort to achieve the greatest benefit, value, or satisfaction. Bounded rationality postulates that people weigh the likely positive benefits against likely negative consequences and subsequently base their decision on the likely costs and benefits (Scott, 2000). According to Simon (1979), rationality becomes bound when it can no longer be considered omniscient. For example, time restraints may preclude the decision-maker from obtaining all of the necessary information prior to making a decision, as a result, parameters such as time can become a factor by which the decision-maker is bound.

The two central concepts of Bounded Rationality lay within the search and satisficing features. This theory is revealed in the findings as participants described aspects of the decision-making process in altruistic terms thus contemplating the benefits of the decisions against their challenges and negative consequences. The participants engaged in various methods for seeking out available alternative choices and described the strategic factors that allowed them to arrive at the critical moment of choice and the commitment to take action. Within the framework of Rational Choice Theory, decision-makers must calculate the unknown outcomes of a selected course of action and determine which alternative is best (Scott, 2000).

While aspirations for these participants may start off at an optimizing level, real-world scenarios become over-simplified to a degree that the decision-maker can manage. As the decision-maker continues to examine the available strategic choices, the individual may ultimately arrive at a realistic end, yielding a satisfactory response due to various constraints, or boundaries, that is, financial, human capital, physical space. Carfang's (2015) findings suggest that balance was a critical component that factored into how college and university presidents arrived at their decisions and, as Rich asserts, "none of us got everything the way we wanted it, but we really worked to get to the point where I felt like this is much better than what we had". In this example, the complex decision-making process resulted in the decision-maker seeking out alternatives, understanding the factors which impacted the decision-making process and was able to arrive at the best available option.

Optimizing decision-making emphasizes the formal and calculated process involved in evaluating and detecting the best possible outcome while mitigating as much uncertainty as possible (Simon, 1972). Through strategic processes, participants developed criteria to help them navigate the complex decision-making process. As participants described their practice of sorting through the various alternative choices, they often would refer to a guiding framework such as their institution's mission or strategic plan to help them evaluate their available options. To this extent, optimization complements rationality asserting that decision-making is a fully rational process.

Most notably, rationality cannot be understood within a global context. That is to say, the complexity of a situation may be too large in scope and unmanageable, and the decision-maker is required to simplify the circumstances in order to drive a realistic scenario to which one is able to arrive at a decision. Therefore, limitations such as the lack of information, the cognitive limitations of one's mind, and/or the finite amount of time one has to make decisions, Simon (1972) argues, are elements by which the rational decision-making processes are bound. While limitations are grounded in reality, boundaries based on assumptions are critical because they establish limitations in which to apply theory (Bacharach, 1989).

THE ESSENCE OF COMPLEX DECISION-MAKING

Participants reveal that complex decision-making involves a variety of strategies and tactics which allow the decision-making agent to commit to a decision and select an available alternative. These attributes range from managing internal and external influences such as budgets, resources, stakeholder expectations, and the competitive environment of higher education, to relying on strategy, mission, and core values to filter through the numerous and available choices. This is significant because the essential structure of complex decision-making incorporates elements of other mature and well-established decision-making models. Therefore, it begs the question of whether or not complex decision-making, at its root, is different than other types of decision frameworks?

Harrison (1996) asserts that strategic decisions are highly complex because of the copious and dynamic variables involved in the process. Strategic decisions deal with the long-term health of the organization (Bass, 1983, as cited in Harrison, 1996) and, in an effort to assist leaders make successful strategic decisions, Shirley (1982) identified a five-step decision-making process as outlined by the following sequence:

1. The decision must be directed toward defining the organization's relationship to the environment.
2. The decision must take the organization as a whole as the unit of analysis.
3. The decision must encompass all of the major functions performed by the organization.
4. The decision must provide constrained guidance for all of the administrative and operational activities of the organization.
5. The decision must be critically important to the long-term success of the total organization (p. 46).

Kotler and Murphy (1981) look specifically at strategic planning within the higher education space, and similarly, assert that strategic decision-making involves an analysis of the environment in terms of both the organization's internal landscape (within this context, trustees, administrators, and faculty) as well as the external market environment (i.e., traditional/non-traditional students, alumni, sources of funding, and competition). In a more recent study, Dooris, Kelley, and Trainer (2004) suggest that strategic planning is rooted in intentionality and when successfully implemented, will be able to advance and transform colleges and universities. Furthermore, decisions associated with strategic plans and visions shape the organization, and as a result, situating strategic decision-making within the context of organizational behavior (Eisenhardt & Zbaracki, 1992).

Six participants revealed that when making complex decisions they incorporated numerous strategic decision-making elements in their process which includes, but are not limited to, assessing their environment, elevating decisions to university wide levels, gathering information, sorting through the alternative choices, bearing in mind the long-term health and sustainability of their organization and implementing a decision.

Participants surveyed the environmental landscape of higher education, both domestically as well as internationally, as they addressed the competitive nature of higher education, and the need to make strategic decisions in order to sustain and strengthen their presence in the market-place. Participants engaged in benchmarking and examined external environments which prompted procedural and strategic decisions-making processes as they internationalized their respective campuses. Participants were able to cognize the financial, economic, and socio factors impacting higher education and therefore, were able to identify the best available options for how they were going to internationalize their campus.

Scholars have gone on to advance the work of Simon (1972, 1979) and have suggested that complex decision-making involves the interplay between two cognitive systems (Stanovich & West, 2002). The first system is most often associated with emotion, or the immediate automatic gut feeling one experiences when making decisions (Stanovich & West, 2002). The second system is more deliberate and requires additional effort in order to make a decision. These two systems are what Kahneman (2012) has developed into the framework described as "thinking, fast and slow" which provides another lens in how leaders navigate the complex decision-making process.

CONCLUSION

Carfang's (2015) research provides new insights into the complex decision-making arena. This chapter allows the readers to garner a deeper understanding of how institutional leaders experience decision-making in complex environments. Through the lens of bounded-rationality, decision-makers are able to address a set of underlying assumptions and set limitations for how s/he will discuss the various constructs, variables, and values within a pre-established set of boundaries (Bacharach, 1989). Arriving at a point where the inquirer is either satisfied with the decision, or has maximized the search, it is time for the decision-maker to commit to a decision. Through this theoretical lens, the rationality of the decision-maker is limited by the amount of information they have (Simon, 1972, 1979). In almost all cases, participants expressed having to make a decision without having all of the desired information or having explored all of the available options due to limitations (i.e., time restraints). Participants described a conditional logic mindset for how they navigated complex decisions. For example, if the institution had the resources to allocate for such initiative, it was a financially responsible decision, it benefitted the stakeholders, and the college and/or the university president felt good about the option, then he or she would select that alternative as the best available choice. Because participants expressed not always having one hundred percent of the information prior to making decisions, Carfang's (2015) findings reveal that the participants were willing to adapt and adjust decisions after implementation and that the revisiting of a decision was expected.

The internationalization of higher education is a delicate, complicated, multifaceted endeavor. The decision to internationalize portends to complex decision-making approaches. An extensive literature review revealed quality factors such as, financial, reputational, environmental, and economic are crucial to making and managing decisions. Because there is not a single model of internationalization (Chan & Dimmock, 2008), decision-makers require a complex decision-making framework; one that employs strategic decision-making approaches, account for the multifarious variables that influence decisions, and avows for the development of more than one possible outcome.

This information may assist senior leaders both in higher education, as well as other fields, understand the interconnectivity of both complex and strategic decision-making processes as they endeavor to internationalize their organization. The findings may also assist practitioners in understanding how complex decisions are formulated when perfect or complete information is not available. In addition, this chapter provides an exploration of the decision-making process in order to understand the constructs that influence decisions, and the search and satisficing manner in which complicated choices are made.

This narrative gives credence to the complicated and versatile environment in which higher education is positioned and the findings offer perspicacity into the decision-making process for how institutional leaders navigate rational choice within the limitations of bounded rationality.

REFERENCES

Altbach, P. G., & Knight, J. (2007). The internationalization of higher education: Motivations and realities. *Journal of Studies in International Education, 11*, 290–305.
Association of International Educators (NAFSA). (2012). *Global citizenship-What are we talking about and why does it matter?* Washington, DC: Madeleine F. Green. Retrieved from http://nafsa.org/Explore_International_Education/Trends/
Bacharach, S. B. (1989). Organizational theories: Some criteria for evaluation. *Academy of Management Review, 14*(4), 496–515.
Bartell, M. (2003). Internationalization of universities: A university culture-based framework. *Higher Education, 45*, 43–70.
Brennan, M., & Dellow, D. A. (2013). International students as a resource for achieving comprehensive internationalization. *New Directions for Community Colleges, 161*, 27–37.

Butt, L., More, E., & Avery, G. C. (2011). Sustainable practice in universities-leading and championing change. *Proceedings of the 2011 European applied business research conference, Barcelona, Spain*, Clute Institute, Colorado. Retrieved from http://conferences. cluteonline.com/index.php/IAC/2011SP. Accessed on June 6–9, 2011.

Carfang, L. J. (2015). *Choices, decisions, and the call to take action: A phenomenological study utilizing bounded rationality to explore complex decision-making processes*. Doctoral Dissertation. Retrieved from ProQuest Dissertations and Theses.

Chan, W. W. Y., & Dimmock, C. (2008). The internationalization of universities: Globalist, internationalists, and translocalist models. *Journal of Research in International Education, 7*(2), 184–204.

Childress, L. K. (2009). Internationalization plans for higher education institutions. *Journal of Studies in International Education, 13*(3), 289–309.

Coryell, J. E., Durodoye, B. A., Wright, R. R., Pate, E., & Nguyen, S. (2012). Case studies of internationalization in adult and higher education: Inside the processes of four universities in the United States and the United Kingdom. *Journal of Studies in International Education, 16*(1), 75–98.

Creswell, J. (2012). *Educational research: Planning, conducting and evaluating quantitative and qualitative research* (4th ed.). Boston, MA: Pearson. ISMN: 978-0-13-1367395.

Creswell, J. W., & Miller, D. L. (2000). Determining validity in qualitative inquiry. *Theory into Practice, 39*(3), 124–130.

Deardorff, D. K. (2006). Identification and assessment of intercultural competence as a student outcome of internationalization. *Journal of Studies in International Education, 10*(3), 241–266.

DeWitt, H. (2009). *Internationalization of higher education in the United States of America and Europe*. Chesnuthill, MA: IAP.

Dooris, M. J., Kelley, J. M., & Trainer, J. F. (2004). Strategic planning in higher education. *New Directions for Institutional Research, 2004*(123), 5–11.

Edwards, J. (2007). Challenges and opportunities for the internationalization of higher education in the coming decade: Planned and opportunistic initiatives in American institutions. *Journal of Studies in International Education, 11*, 373–381.

Eisenhardt, K. M., & Zbaracki, M. J. (1992). Strategic decision making. *Strategic Management Journal, 1*(Winter), 17–37.

Finkelstein, M. J., Walker, E., & Chen, R. (2013). The American faculty in an age of globalization: Predictors of internationalization of research content and professional networks. *Higher Education, 66*, 325–340.

Friesen, R. (2013). Faculty member engagement in Canadian university internationalization: A consideration of understanding, motivations and rationales. *Journal of Studies in International Education, 17*(3), 209–227.

Gul, H., Gul, S. S., Kaya, E., & Alican, A. (2010). Main trends in the world of higher education, internationalization and institutional autonomy. *Social and Behavioral Sciences, 9*, 1878–1884.

Harris, S., & Wheeler, C. (2005). Entrepreneurs' relationship for internationalization: Functions, origins, and strategies. *International Business Review, 14*, 187–207.

Harrison, E. F. (1996). A process perspective on strategic decision making. *Management Decision, 34*(1), 46–53.

Kahneman, D. (2012). *Thinking, fast and slow*. London: Penguin Books.

Kehm, B. M. (2007). Research on internationalization in higher education. *Journal of Studies in International Education, 3*(3), 260–273.

Knight, J. (2001). Monitoring the quality and progress of internationalization. *Journal of Studies in International Education, 5*(3), 228–243.

Knight, J. (2004). Internationalization remodeled: Definition, approaches, and rationales. *Journal of Studies in International Education, 8*(1), 5–31.

Knight, J. (2015). Updated definition of internationalization. *International Higher Education, 33*, 2–3. Retrieved from http://ejournals.bc.edu/ojs/index.php/ihe/article/viewFile/7391/6588

Kotler, P., & Murphy, P. E. (1981). Strategic planning for higher education. *The Journal of Higher Education, 52*(5), 470–489.

Labib, A., Read, M., Gladstone-Millar, C., Tonge, R., & Smith, D. (2014). Formulations of higher education institutional strategy using operational research approaches. *Studies in Higher Education, 39*(5), 885–904.

Lee, J. (2014). Education hubs and talent development: Policymaking and implementation challenges. *Higher Education, 68*(6), 807–823.

Lien, D. (2007). The role of scholarships in study abroad programs. *Education Economics, 15*(2) 202–212.

Marginson, S. (2006). Dynamics of national and global competition in higher education. *Higher Education, 52*(1), 1–39.

Marginson, S., & Sawir, E. (2011). *Ideas for intercultural education*. New York, NY: Palgrave MacMillan.

Martinez, C. M., & Wolverton, M. (2009). *Innovative strategy making in higher education*. Charlotette, NC: Information Age Publishing, Inc.

Norris, E. M., & Gillespie, J. (2009). How study abroad shapes global careers: Evidence from the United States. *Journal of Studies in International Education, 13*, 382–395.

Ponterotto, J. G. (2005). Qualitative research in counseling psychology: A primer on research paradigms and philosophy of science. *Journal of Counseling Psychology, 52*(2), 126–136.

Qiang, Z. (2003). Internationalization of higher education: Towards a conceptual framework. *Policy Futures in Education, 1*(2), 248–270.

Raby, R. L. (2007). Internationalizing the curriculum: On- and off-campus strategies. *New Directions for Community Colleges, 2007*(138), 57–66.

Robson, S. (2011). Internationalization: A transformative agenda for higher education? *Teachers and Teaching: Theory and Practice, 17*(6), 619–630.

Rudzki, R. E. J. (1995). The application of a strategic management model to the internationalization of higher education institutions. *Higher Education, 29*(4), 421–441.

Scott, J. (2000). Rational choice theory. In G. B. Browning, A. Halcli, & F. Webster (Eds.), *Understanding contemporary society: Theories of the present* (p. 126). Thousand Oaks, CA: Sage.

Shirley, R. C. (1982). Limiting the scope of strategy: A decision based approach. *Academy of Management Review, 7*(2), 262–268.

Simon, H. A. (1972). Theories of bounded rationality. In C. B. McGuire & R. Rander (Eds.), *Decision and organizations* (pp. 161–173). Amsterdam: North-Holland Publishing Company.

Simon, H. A. (1979). Rational decision making in business organizations. *The American Economic Review, 69*(4), 493–513.

Stanovich, K. E., & West, R. F. (2002). Individual differences in reasoning: Implications for the rationality debate? In T. Gilovich, D. Griffin, & D. Kahneman (Eds.), *Heuristics and biases: The psychology of intuitive judgment* (pp. 678–686). Cambridge: Cambridge University Press.

Starks, H., & Trinidad, S. B. (2007). Choose your method: A comparison of phenomenology, discourse analysis, and grounded theory. *Qualitative Health Research, 17*(10), 1372–1380.

Stella, A., & Gnanam, A. (2004). Quality assurance in distance education: The challenges to be addressed. *Higher Education, 47*, 143–160.

Stohl, M. (2007). We have met the enemy and he is us: The role of the faculty in internationalization of higher education in the coming decade. *Journal of Studies in International Education, 11*, 359–372.

Stromquist, N. P. (2007). Internationalization as a response to globalization: Radical shifts in university environments. *Higher Education, 53*, 81–105.

Teichler, U. (2004). The changing debate on internationalization of higher education. *Higher Education, 48*(1), 5–26.

van Damme, D. (2001). Quality issues in the internationalization of higher education. *Journal of Higher Education, 41*, 415–441.

van der, W. (1999). An innovation perspective on internationalization of higher education institutionalization: The critical phase. *Journal of Studies in International Education, 3*, 3–14.

van der Wende, M. (2007). Internationalization of higher education in the OECD countries: Challenges and opportunities for the coming decade. *Journal of Studies in International Education, 11*, 274–289.

van der Wende, M., Beerkens, E., & Teichler, U. (1999). Internationalisation as a cause for innovation in higher education. In B. Jongbloed, P. Maassen, & G. Neave (Eds.), *From the eye of the storm: Higher education's changing institution* (pp. 65–93). Dordrecht: Kluwer.

Whitsed, C., & Green, W. (2014). What's in a name? A theoretical exploration of the proliferation of labels for international education across the higher education sector. *Journal of Studies in International Education, 18*(2), 105–119. Retrieved from http://jsi.sagepub.com. Accessed on June 14, 2013.

PART II
SUCCESSFUL PRACTICES

THE CENTRALITY OF THE FACULTY ROLE IN TRANSNATIONAL PARTNERSHIPS: A RESEARCH AGENDA

Rick J. Arrowood and Leslie Hitch

ABSTRACT

Much of the literature on higher education transnational, international and cross-border partnerships emphasize the partnerships' strategic importance to the institutions, the administrative complexities of negotiating in a different language or culture or both, and more often than not, financial gains. Other scholars discuss the importance of developing global citizens. Surprisingly, there seems to be a paucity of research on the role of faculty in cross-border and transnational partnerships. This chapter, through description of one transnational program and the literature, offers reflections that contribute to a much-needed research agenda that faculty are the keystone to forming sustainable, profitable, and strategic partnerships.

Keywords: Faculty; transnational; partnerships; university; international

University Partnerships for Academic Programs and Professional Development
Innovations in Higher Education Teaching and Learning, Volume 7, 39–54
Copyright © 2016 by Emerald Group Publishing Limited
All rights of reproduction in any form reserved
ISSN: 2055-3641/doi:10.1108/S2055-364120160000007010

The words international or global when used with the words higher education often trigger allied words such as student mobility, study abroad, foreign students, educational initiatives, research collaborations, and other strategic university alliances. Studies focused on the internationalization or globalization of higher education further expand this vocabulary. Sutton, Obst, Louime, Jones, and Jones (2011), editors of *Global Education Research Report* #6 present ways to sustain, build capacity, and design partnerships; Rumbley, Helms, Peterson, and Altbach (2014) reviews opportunities and challenges from collaborations with the United States (U.S.) community colleges to specialized engagements with institutions in the Indian sub-continent, South America, and, of course, China. In her compact compendium, Eddy (2010) shares case examples and even a game theory of partnerships. Sakamoto and Chapman (2011) offer a forecast of higher education's international and globalized future.

Largely, these publications and other literature on higher education cross-border partnerships emphasize a partnerships' strategic importance, the administrative complexities of negotiating in a different language or culture (or both), and more often than not, financial gains. Increasingly frequently, other scholars discuss the importance of developing global citizens (Leask, 2015). Surprisingly, however, there seems to be a paucity of research on the role of faculty in cross-border and transnational partnerships[1] (Cooper & Mitsunaga, 2010). The intent of this chapter is to offer examples from a partnership and from existing literature that contribute to this much-needed research agenda.

Here we target three foci on the premise that faculty are the keystone to forming sustainable, profitable, and strategic partnerships. We begin with an examination of a transnational Masters double degree partnership formed in 2007. This example highlights internal and external complexities and emphasizes the role of faculty. We consider common issues and dilemmas such as internationalization of the curriculum, teaching styles, financial expectations, cultural (both academic culture and that of the partnership countries), and the model itself. Based on this ongoing degree articulation, we turn to section "Section II: The Literature," a critical discourse vis-à-vis current literature of higher education partnerships and transnational degrees. These sections anchor section "Section III. Developing a Research Agenda," where we present a research agenda to examine the role of faculty in these partnerships. Our focus is to "shine a light where there is none" while simultaneously alerting and cautioning institutions to resolve these complexities when involved in or contemplating international partnerships. The light we use is the centrality of faculty in the delivery of transnational partnerships.

SECTION I: ANATOMY OF A PARTNERSHIP

The dual degree Master's program between a large U.S. research university and an Australian university similar in scope began in 2007. There was neither little indication at its genesis of its later significance to both institutions, nor was it seen as a model for creating anything other than a transnational partnership. Simply, it was a quiet and inauspicious beginning.

This particular model awards graduates two distinct and separate diplomas; one Australian and one from the U.S. One institution awards a Masters in Leadership and the other a Masters in either finance, marketing, accounting or international business. The Australian institution is the site of almost all the delivery of the entire curriculum, and conducts the program marketing. The American partner sends its faculty to the Australian institution. The time to complete both degrees is two years.

Top-Down Origin

The program's originating impetus is largely unknown, although most involved agree that the initiative was top-down, arranged by a senior administrator and an Australian senior chancellor as primary decision-makers. In higher education (and most organizational structures) this rarely predicts an omen for success (Skordoulis, n.d.). After almost a decade, most of the leaders have left the two universities. Program managers with academic or financial roles have also left, leaving little or no administrative information for successors. Moreover, the universities themselves have changed. Each is deeply absorbed in efforts to raise their international rankings while simultaneously seeking new revenue through online, satellite campuses or additional transnational activities. Both institutions have undertaken major building projects emphasizing their research commitment to science and technology.

External Pressures

These internal changes in administrative and support personnel can be easily attributed to routine personnel turnover. However, unexpected and significant external events in this past decade created additional unforeseen difficulties. Racial incidents in the host city resulted in a sharp decline in enrollment followed immediately by the 2007–2008 global financial crisis thereby exacerbating the enrollment decline. Then the near parity between the Australian and U.S. dollar caused the contribution margin to fluctuate wildly. Where previous enrollments allowed two U.S. faculty members at a time to travel to Australia, the combination of the declining enrollment, the financial crisis, plus the unfavorable exchange rates, reduced the number of visiting faculty to one.

Faculty Disconnections

Sustainable faculty-to-faculty connections often associated with such partnerships are only just emerging. Many partnerships begin with faculty connections (Cooper & Mitsunaga, 2010; Michael & Balraj, 2003) through research interests or previous affiliations with an international institution. In this particular situation, there was no initial faculty-to-faculty link. Almost 10 years on, it still remains difficult to establish such linkages. In Australia, faculty more and more need to be prepared at the doctoral level. Institutions are under government pressure to increase research output, while at the same time the government wants to restructure university funding, raising fees while reducing operational funds (Maslen, 2014). At the U.S. institution, most faculty who have taught in the program are, or have been, part-time instructors. These faculty have considerable teaching and work experience, but may not have a terminal degree or need for a research agenda. Further, many of the U.S. institution's faculty teach primarily online and have little or no substantial experience teaching in an international classroom. Finally, informal and anecdotal reports from students and administrative personnel indicate that some of the instructors, skilled in and used to online teaching, seem to be challenged by the intensive daily face-to-face time required of the assignment in Australia.

Inverted Calendars

Academic calendars are completely in reverse leaving the most convenient time for U.S. faculty to teach in Australia as their winter, the U.S. summer. Administrative systems are sometimes incompatible and often radically different. The grading system varies widely between the two institutions with a mark of 94–100 constituting an "A" for the U.S. institution and a range of 80–100 for an Australian High Distinction. Compounding this complexity is the Australian partner's requirement that faculty limit the number of high distinctions issued or awarded despite students' competency.

Curriculum Lost in Translation

The impediments are not just administrative. The majority of the enrolled students are neither Australian nor from the U.S., and English may be their second or even third language. The students represent panoply of nations, religions, and ideologies. Most have been schooled in a lecture format with rote learning the norm. In addition to the lengthy time it often takes such students to read texts and scholarly articles in English, students, often on limited budgets, are reluctant to purchase required texts. Printed books in Australia are expensive. E-textbooks might seem to be a logical substitution, but in Australia, as in the U.S., e-textbooks have been slow to be accepted by either faculty or students (Smith, Brand, & Kinash, 2013).

There is also concern regarding student motivation. For many students, the impetus to enroll stems, in part, from family pressure. Parents want to enable their child to gain proficiency in English. Sometimes students study abroad because they did not achieve sufficiently high entry test scores for admission to their nation's top institutions. Each of these factors severely diminishes students' desire to learn and therefore impacts both teaching and learning. Although, both the U.S. and Australia are English-speaking countries, the U.S. curriculum is highly Western-centric and oriented to leadership in corporations and in business. The students, however, are multicultural. They usually are recent undergraduates with little business or professional experience, and making assignments and readings relevant is challenging. The subject of leadership, unlike finance or accounting or even marketing, is subjective, culturally based, and situation-dependent.

Program Perseverance

Despite the incongruities mentioned above, through all of these vagaries and deviations, the partnership and program persevere. There are several reasons: the partnership serves both institutions' global ranking footprints – highly important in recruiting in the Asian market; it allows its graduates the opportunity to live and work in Australia for two years post-graduation, and, depending upon the rules of the Australian visa system and a student's ability to secure work, the prospect of gaining the coveted Australian Permanent Residency. From the institutional perspective, the partnership capitalizes on the benefit of offering a dual degree Master's curriculum that uses each institution's existing programs of study. These reasons are substantive. However, we argue that the centrality of faculty engagement focusing on student success is paramount, and this consistent influence has sustained the partnership.

The Role of Faculty

Examining the anatomy of the program alone, it would seem questionable that this partnership continues. What is the key to the partnership's sustainability, we maintain, is the tenacity of many faculty willing to transcend obstacles to use the partnership as an opportunity to develop a serious internationalized curriculum, prepare students for work and life goals in an increasingly interconnected world, and to satisfy their own personal and professional goals. While the origins of this partnership began top down, the program's continuing effectiveness is in the strength of the faculty's guiding classroom experience. Cooper and Mitsunaga (2010) call this "heart work" (p. 78) as promoted by an engaged faculty decidedly open to new experiences.

SECTION II: THE LITERATURE

The literature on international partnerships is heavily skewed to the administrative perspective primarily because cross-border collaborations have a lengthy history (Asgary & Robbert, 2010; Eddy, 2010; Hebert, 2013; Lane & Kinser, 2014). The Fulbright Program is one such example. In this second decade of the new millennium, financial realities, as well as global competition, continue to drive institutions to seek some type of international foothold (Foskett, 2010; Sakamoto & Chapman, 2011). That financial reality is palpably visible in the escalating number of international students being recruited to the United Kingdom (U.K.), Australia, U.S., and Canada (Peak, 2015). A by-product of this financial reality is that higher education institutions, formerly dominating discreet geographical areas, are now subject to global competition in much the same way as is the automotive and other worldwide industries. Through technology and global mobility, universities are and can no longer be the citadel of knowledge as practiced by their medieval counterparts (Hague, 1996). Beyond the bottom line, institutions are realizing that internationalization is not simply a strategic imperative: it is integral to the core tradition of the university – "interrogating and developing knowledge" (James, Cullinan, & Cruceru, 2013, p. 151).

To meet these challenges, higher education institutions have engaged in multiple forms and types of transnational (also known as cross-border) partnerships (Sakamoto & Chapman, 2011) for a variety of reasons including, but not limited to financial, organizational, strategic, individual and contextual (pp. 7–8) endeavors. Knight (2011) lists an array of program modalities from study abroad, franchising, development of branch campuses, and creation of wholly virtual or blended distance degree programs.

Michael and Balraj (2003) review the evolution of the most common of cross-border partnerships – a connection between two or more faculty members with similar research interests who may or may not extend their work into an offshore classroom. However, the authors state that in the past 10 years the growth of partnerships has been primarily through non-faculty-initiated programs:

> Recently, a new kind of institutional collaboration has been on the increase. This type of collaboration differs from the causal faculty-initiated form in that it requires full institutional approval and commitment .... (p. 132)

Currently, there is no single standard for how to deliver these programs or even a single strategy to create them. Most often, partnerships may begin in order to address changes in needed professional competencies or enrollment goals (Michael & Balraj, 2003), or enhance global branding efforts. To a greater or lesser extent, these types of programs may also take advantage of flexibility in delivery modalities through technology (Michael & Balraj, 2003), thus extending their reach and enrollment.

The specific definition of the U.S./Australian partnership described in section "Section I: Anatomy of a Partnership" is a "double degree" program (Lane & Kinser, 2014, p. 59) that is basically similar to the model described by (Michael & Balraj, 2003). In these programs the curriculum for each degree usually remains with each institution (p. 60). The impetus is often organizational rather than research-oriented or faculty-led because these types of programs require regulatory, accreditation and other administrative involvement (p. 61). The concept appeals to students because of the caché of receiving two separate degrees simultaneously.

Through the lens of a cost-benefit analysis, Asgary and Robbert (2010) argue the need for more international dual degree programs citing the requirement for students to spend extended periods of time in another culture. Culling from several reports, the authors advance the argument that these programs are emerging as a model through which students achieve different (and in some cases more substantive) international experience (p. 318). The benefits of such degrees, in these authors' estimation, are multifold including the opportunity to "enhance revenue, increase foreign student population and expand offerings" (p. 320). Benefits to faculty are referenced only as the potential to increase research collaborations.

Yet, in a competitive higher education environment, small isolated research collaborations may no longer carry enough academic gravitas. Leask (2015) maintains that globalization of the university goes hand in hand with the internationalization of the curriculum. Others, including the authors of this chapter, agree. Beyond status and revenue, partnerships need to be built on ethical standards, considering a world view that encompasses technology, individual responsibility, "knowledge socialism" (Hebert & Abdi, 2013), and willingness to include readings, assessments, ethical considerations, and teaching methodologies that may diverge from Western hegemony. All these factors are the domain and responsibility of faculty.

The academic literature on partnerships reveals another by-product of the globalization of higher education. We are an industry under increasing scrutiny to educate "global citizens" even as we struggle to define that amorphous, now trendy term. Global citizenship is sometimes used inter-changeably with intercultural competence (Ryan, 2013). We prefer, as a prelude to offering our research agenda, a definition coined by Killick (2013). He advocates that global citizenship as "self-in-the world" where "difference is recognized as legitimate, a characteristic of human beings in a globalizing world" (p. 186). Applying this definition to international part-nerships can have an immediate and profound impact, particularly on dual and double degree programs where, as stated earlier, an existing curriculum is indiscriminately "dropped into" the program with the partner institution because that is most expedient. In effective global partnerships, expediency is often not efficient. Nor may it be educationally sound.

The Institute of International Education, in its Survey of International Joint and Double Degree Programs (2011), reported that "two-thirds of respondents have launched these programs in the past decade." Some 84 percent of respondents, which represented universities from around the world, reported offering joint and double degrees. However, when viewed in the context of recruitment of students, 65 percent of U.S. institutions reported not prioritizing the recruitment of domestic students through a joint or double degree program. As the number and types of transnational partnerships increase, administrators and faculty alike need to understand how faculty contribute and why. Cooper and Mitsunaga (2010) state bluntly: "as institutions of higher education become more involved in inter-national collaborative efforts ... faculty who are able to build and sustain

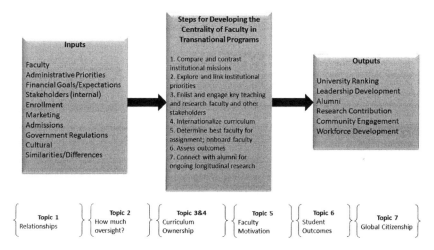

Fig. 1. Faculty Role in Establishing Transnational Programs.

long-term collaborations will play a key role" (p. 80). The minute faculty step into the classroom, they are the partnerships' face and program embodiment. This role can be seen in Fig. 1.

SECTION III. DEVELOPING A RESEARCH AGENDA

This section is framed by the work of Cooper and Mitusunaga (2010), Heffernan and Pool (2004), and our own experience as collaborators invested in the U.S./Australia partnership since its inception. What each of us reports is a substantial absence in the literature of transnational partnerships: the centrality of the role of faculty. To address this gap, we suggest seven areas warranting further research. There are undoubtedly more.

Research Agenda Topic 1: Relationships

In any global partnership, whether double-degree, dual degree, branch campus, or transnational program implementation, how important to the program's ongoing success is the relationship between the faculty, the program itself, and the partner institution?

Transnational partnerships continue to increase along with the continuing influx of students to and from their countries of origin. Tierney and
Lanford (2015) describe two successive "waves" of globalization in higher
education: ongoing student mobility is the first and academic staff, program and institutional mobility is the second (pp. 285−287). As evidenced
by issues that arose in the establishment of New York University's branch
campus in Abu-Dhabi, lack of or minimal faculty involvement in the
partnership process can delay and sometimes sabotage a partnership
(Tierney & Lanford, 2015).

According to Heffernan and Poole's (2004) amusingly titled article
"Catch Me I'm Falling" key factors in the deterioration of offshore education partnerships, is particularly relevant. Based at Australian universities,
the authors acknowledge the growth of academic partnerships in their
country with concerns for the quality and longevity of these partnerships
that often hinge on process. "In other words, one or both partners fail to
provide the resources, support, or commitment on which high quality academic, professional, and business oriented relationships must depend"
(p. 78). In an allusion to the role of faculty, they continue that "academic
and service qualities are linked to relationship quality" (p. 79). Most significantly, they found that a key point of deterioration "is a change of key personnel responsible for the development of the relationship at the early
interaction stage" (p. 88). In the description of the U.S./Australian partnership put forward in our article, we noted that almost all of the original
administrators at both institutions moved on to other positions. What has,
however, remained a constant has been several faculty returning to
Australia each year of the past eight years.

One of the unplanned factors of the U.S./Australian program is that it is
taught almost entirely on campus and U.S. faculties are housed within
walking distance. This proximity creates opportunities for informal conversations with students ordinarily not possible when teaching in the U.S. This
allows for forging deeper bonds with the students.

It has not, as stated earlier, been as easy to forge this same type of
bond with the Australian faculty who have ongoing, local work and
family commitments, and have not yet been involved with the U.S. part
of the double-degree program. "However, a joint degree initiative requires
collaborate curriculum development and greater interaction with faculty
members of other institutions" (Michael & Balraj, 2003). Cooper and
Mitsunaga (2010) concur and add that forging these relationships, as evidenced in the U.S./Australia program example, are not easy. We add
that relationships are particularly difficult if there is an imbalance in

some faculty goals, responsibilities, and status. These paradoxes warrant further examination.

Research Agenda Topic 2: How Much Oversight?

With many global partnerships originating from administrative objectives, the research question that looms is how much administrative versus academic oversight is optimal? Cooper and Mitsunaga (2010) quote a faculty director who complains that administrators who are not on site often make decisions that "are not in the interest of the students ... [or] the quality of the program" (p. 77). Heffernan and Poole (2004) also contend that the roles and responsibilities for each partner must be unambiguously defined. In the U.S./Australian partnership we described earlier, the absence of extensive administrative control as a result of personnel departures actually allowed faculty *more* latitude in adapting the U.S. (and Western-centric) curriculum to make it more relevant to the multinational, multilingual, multi-ethnic students. This ability to modify the curriculum from its Western-centric focus assisted faculty in continuing to use their own expertise, channel their creative energy, draw upon their own interests, and ensure that they could develop definable and meaningful student outcomes (Cooper & Mitsunaga, 2010)].

Research Agenda Topics 3 and 4: Curriculum Ownership and Teaching Methods

There are at least two research topics that are curricula-oriented: (1) should the curriculum remain exactly the same as it is taught in its home institution? The second topic, tied directly to the first and (2) how transferable are teaching methods?

The question of the curriculum itself is most surely at the core of faculty centrality. One of the benefits of transnational programming, and often the rationale for it, is that an existing program can be deposited in the country's institution. From an institutional standpoint, this is optimal. It eliminates the need to alter curriculum, and faculty who are familiar with the curriculum can then easily teach the same course thousands of miles away. However, is this ideal? If faculty cannot teach his or her course, are there concerns regarding intellectual property? To whom does the transnational curriculum belong, faculty or institution? This issue is often exacerbated by the varying requirements of some ministries of education, national entities, and international and regional accrediting agencies, to review curriculum and to require that the offerings be identical. [This question is germane to many areas of higher education beyond global partnerships.]

Leask (2015) builds a case for internationalizing the curriculum. She advocates, however, that for curricular change to occur, leaders within the institution need to be identified and they must then work with small groups of others to create "critical spaces where dynamic and transformational curriculum internationalization conversations can occur" (p. 114). Internationalization of the curriculum may be difficult if a program is simply placed in the partner institution.

Teaching styles, too, may affect outcomes. A continuing dilemma is where the emphasis should be in the content or in adaptation of the content? Ryan (2013) advocates for group work common to the U.S. classroom. However, students who have been previously taught by lecture and assessed by rote learning may not adapt easily to this more fluid and subjective format. For example, students may take less or even more time on task time in unfamiliar subject formats. Cultural and linguistic difference may also impede effective group work.

Research Agenda Topic 5: Faculty Motivation

Research is needed to understand the attributes of faculty who are successful in delivering transnational programming both at their home and partner institution. Are faculty preparation programs needed? What changes in pedagogy or understanding of globalization do faculty bring back to the institution from their time teaching abroad?

In examining the anatomy of the U.S./Australia partnership we found a strong connection between faculty motivation and student engagement and satisfaction. Not all faculty who taught in the U.S./Australian partnership wanted to or were asked to return. Not everyone can or should teach in unfamiliar, foreign environments. Yet others excel in this experience and "can't wait to return." There seem to be several reasons why some faculty thrive and others do not. Cooper and Mitsunaga (2010) advise that "... staying flexible is central to the success of these international endeavors. Faculty must be open to other pedagogical goals and strategies. Rigid control of events with an attitude that it is "my course" is a barrier to successful collaborations" (p. 80).

Tierney and Langford (2015) speculate that institutional culture may be a factor, especially if the primary reason for the partnership is financial or to increase institutional visibility. We speculate that intercultural competency along with flexibility of both personal style and ability to circumvent "rigid course requirements" (Cooper & Mitsunaga, 2010, p. 80) is critical to faculty, and as a consequence, student satisfaction. The lure of a teaching assignment outside of one's country may at first be (wrongly) seen as a professional and personal opportunity for travel and tourism. The reality is quite different. The faculty member may be far away from home, family, and routine. The fact that Australia is both an English-speaking country and highly Westernized does not mean it is culturally identical. For some this is surprising. Cooper and Mitsunaga (2010) approach this aspect of faculty experience. Adding to the "culture shock" is the new reality of teaching in a classroom that may often have an array of heavily accented English, representing many nationalities, including Australians.

Research Agenda Topic 6: Student Outcomes

How should a transnational, cross-border, globalized program be assessed? Higher education institutions worldwide are increasingly coming under scrutiny to quantify and codify student outcomes (Tremblay, Lalancette, & Roseveare, 2012). Missing from much of the literature is the potential or realized impact on students enrolled in double or dual degree programs. In programs such as where the curriculum is primarily Western-centric but the students are multicultural, a static "same as we teach back home" curriculum may impede student outcomes. What do we know or understand of student outcomes from these types of programs? Michael and Balraj (2003) suggest that there needs to be regular communication with program graduates for two reasons. The first is to learn where they are employed and the nature of their work. The second is for continuous improvement in the program itself. We strongly recommend that examination of employability is not enough. Research should be designed to understand the *components* of the program, specifically content and pedagogy, leading to employment or success in other pursuits and passions.

Research Agenda Topic 7: Global Citizens

Do students and faculty actually become more inter-culturally aware as a result of the experience? If so, how? Do these programs actually promote global citizenship? The final suggested research topic is undoubtedly dependent upon faculty's role in the formulation and delivery of these types of programs. We also understand this final topic can be seen as a foil for the age-old debate of whether higher education is a public or private good. That is not our intent. Rather, we propose an examination of the attributes of global citizenry using a definition put forward by Killick (2013) – *"self-in-the world* as a sense of self-dwelling ... where difference is recognized as legitimate, a characteristic of human being in a globalizing world" (p. 186) and further codified by Matilla (2009) who states that "... we need to focus perhaps less on quantitative indicators of student mobility and more on creation of communities of learning that involve diverse inhabitants of varies localities and multiple scales of globality" (p. 101).

Transnational partnerships, as outlined in this chapter are frequently designed for financial or strategic reasons. Global citizenry, however, is the welcome unintended consequence (Culver, Puri, Spinelli, DePauw, & Dooley, 2012):

> ... the benefits of a dual degree perceived by all of the stakeholder groups related more to personal growth, communication skills, and cross-cultural skills and less to subject matter or professional knowledge growth. The added value comes directly from experiencing a degree program in two cultures. For example, students particularly feel that they become more self-reliant and confident having had to immerse themselves in a foreign culture. Alumni of several institutions who completed a degree program also reported that they learned that people of different cultures approach problem solving differently and that understanding this perspective added value to their educational program. ... students, alumni, and faculty appreciate that the faculties at different institutions may also have differing approaches to solving problems. (p. 57–8)

CONCLUSION

Yes, higher education will continue to reap the financial and strategic benefits from transnational, cross-border, and international partnerships. That is a given. The need and rationale of this proposed research agenda is deeper. It is to foster learning from success in transnational programs from the faculty perspective. The "light we shine where there has been no light" is in the centrality of the faculty to the greatest good that should come from these partnerships – from future development of transnational double degree programs to global citizenry.

NOTE

1. For the purposes of this chapter, we use transnational, cross-border and international partnerships interchangeably as we consider the issues outlined in the proposed research agenda transcend semantic differences.

REFERENCES

Asgary, N., & Robbert, M. (2010). A cost-benefit analysis of an international dual degree programme. *Journal of Higher Education Policy and Management, 32*(3), 317–325. doi:10.1080/13600801003743513

Cooper, J., & Mitsunaga, R. (2010). Faculty perspectives on international education. The nested realities of faculty collaborations. In P. Eddy (Ed.), *International collaborations: Opportunities, strategies, challenges* (pp. 69–82). San Francisco: Jossey-Bass.

Culver, S., Puri, I., Spinelli, G., DePauw, K., & Dooley, J. (2012). Collaborative dual-degree programs and value added for students: Lessons learned through the evaluate-E project. *Journal of Studies in International Education, 16*(1), 40–61.

Eddy, P. (Ed.). (2010). *International collaborations: Opportunities, strategies, challenges*. San Francisco: Jossey-Bass.

Foskett, N. (2010). Global markets, national challenges, local strategies: The strategic challenge of global markets. In F. Maringe & N. Foskett (Eds.), *Globalization and internationalization in higher education*. London: Continuum.

Hague, D. (1996). *Beyond universities: A new republic of the intellect*. London: Institute of Economic Affairs.

Hebert, Y., & Abdi, A. (Eds.). (2013). *Critical perspectives on international education* (pp. 43–60). Taipei: Sense Publishing.

Heffernan, T., & Poole, D. (2004). "Catch me I'm falling": Key factors in the deterioration of offshore education partnerships. *Journal of Higher Education Policy and Management, 26*(1), 75–90. doi:10.1080/1360080042000182546.

Institute of International Education. (2011). *Survey on international joint and double degree programs*. Retrieved from http://www.iie.org/en/Research-and-Publications/Publications-%20and-Reports/IIE-Bookstore/Joint-Degree-Survey-Report-2011

James, C., Cullinan, C., & Cruceru, A. (2013). Internationalizing post-secondary education: Opportunities, possibilities and challenges. In Y. Hebert & A. Abdi (Eds.), *Critical perspectives on international education* (pp. 149–164). Rotterdam and Taipei: Sense Publishing.

Killick, D. (2013). Global citizenship and campus community: Lessons from learning theory and the lived-experience of mobile students. In J. Ryan (Ed.), *Cross-cultural teaching and learning for home and international students* (pp. 182–195). New York: Routledge.

Knight, J. (2011). "Doubts and dilemmas with double degree programs". In "Globalisation
    and internationalisation of higher education" [online monograph]. Revista de
    Universidad y Sociedad del Conocimiento (RUSC), 8(2), 297–312. Uoc. Retrieved
    from http://rusc.uoc.edu/ojs/index.php/rusc/article/view/v8n2-knight/v8n2-knight-eng
Lane, J., & Kinser, K. (2014). International joint and double-degree programs. In L. Rumbley,
    R. Helms, P. Peterson, & P. Altbach (Eds.), Global opportunities and challenges for
    higher education leaders: Briefs on key themes. Taipei: Sense Publishing.
Leask, B. (2015). Internationalizing the curriculum. Oxford: Routledge.
Maslen, G. (2014). Issue No: 337. Future of Australia's Universities at risk. University world
    news online. Retrieved from http://www.universityworldnews.com/article.php?story=
    20141002071402429
Matilla, A. (2009). Internationalizing curriculum: A new kind of education? In C. Kreber
    (Ed.), Internationalizing the curriculum in higher education (pp. 95–104). San Francisco:
    Jossey-Bass.
Michael, S., & Balraj, L. (2003). Higher education institutional collaborations: An analysis of
    models of joint degree programs. Journal of Higher Education Policy and Management,
    25(2), 131–145. doi:10.1080/1360080032000122615.
Peak, M. (2015). UK is top host of international students, but for how long? Retrieved from
    http://www.britishcouncil.org/blog/uk-top-host-international-students-how-long
Rumbley, L. E., Helms, R. M., Peterson, P. M., & Altbach, P. G. (Eds.). (2014). Global oppor-
    tunities and challenges for higher education leaders: Briefs on key themes. Rotterdam:
    Sense Publishers.
Ryan, J. (2013). Cross-cultural teaching and learning for home and international students.
    London: Routledge.
Sakamoto, R., & Chapman, D. (2011). Cross-border partnerships in higher education.
    New York: Routledge.
Skordoulis, R. (n.d.). Change management in higher education: Top-down or bottom-up?
    International Journal of Applied Management Education and Development, 1(3), 1–19.
Smith, D., Brand, J., & Kinash, S. (2013). Turn on the book: Using affordance theory to
    understand the adoption of digital textbooks by university lecturers. In Electronic
    Dreams 30th ascilite Conference, Macquire University. Sydney. Retrieved from http://
    www.ascilite.org/conferences/sydney13/program/papers/Smith,%20Debborah.pdf.
Sutton, S., Obst, D., Louime, C., Jones, J., & Jones, T. (2011). Developing strategic interna-
    tional partnerships: Models for initiating and sustaining innovative institutional
    linkages. In Sociology & anthropology faculty book and media gallery. Book 21. New
    York: AIFS Foundation, Institute of International Education.
Tierney, W., & Lanford, M. (2015). An investigation of the impact of international branch
    campuses on organizational culture. Higher Education, 70, 283–298. doi 10.1007/
    s10734-014-9845-7.
Tremblay, K., Lalancette, D., & Roseveare, D. (2012). Assessment of higher education learning
    outcomes, AHELO (Vol. 1). OECD. Retrieved from www.oecd.org/edu/ahelo

INTER-INSTITUTIONAL COLLABORATION THROUGH NON-POSITIONAL LEADERSHIP: A STEM HIGHER EDUCATION INITIATIVE

Sherri Cianca

ABSTRACT

This chapter traces how non-positional faculty led an inter-institutional STEM initiative. Starting with one faculty member's seed idea, the chapter traces how that idea grew into a vision and that vision into an agenda and that agenda into a joint, sustainable STEM concentration. The initiative was organized around Bolman and Deal's (2008) framework for making sense of an institution and for leading organizational change through an awareness of multiple lenses. The faculty member who initiated the vision analyzed the institution and her place in that institution. Building from her strengths, she sought to enhance her intellectual, emotional and communication skills. Understanding organizational complexities, Dr. C became involved across campus to build relationships and trust, which then led to the formation of a committed STEM team. The STEM team set a clear agenda and pursued cross-campus ownership and collaboration, all the

University Partnerships for Academic Programs and Professional Development
Innovations in Higher Education Teaching and Learning, Volume 7, 55–75
Copyright © 2016 by Emerald Group Publishing Limited
All rights of reproduction in any form reserved
ISSN: 2055-3641/doi:10.1108/S2055-364120160000007013

while maintaining respect for diverse opinions, political interests and concerns. Challenges, pitfalls and setbacks, though initially painful, confusing, and disheartening, led to reflection, and most often, became opportunities for realignment and clarity. Though non-positional faculty led the effort, it was cross-campus collaboration that made it possible, and the final approval of the administration made it a reality.

Keywords: Leadership; partnerships; faculty; university; STEM

Higher education is changing. With the challenges of changing student demographics, decreased budgets, increased expectations from federal and state governments, and pressure from accrediting bodies and the public, institutions continue to look to faculty leaders to respond to these challenges (Kezar & Lester, 2011). Historically, university and college faculty who lack formal authority have assumed strategic roles in directing the future of higher education. The term *non-positional leadership* is used for those who lead through other than title, rank, or formal position. Faculty without governance or administrative posts have, for example, been instrumental in designing freshman learning programs, retention initiatives, faculty learning communities, and collaborative endeavors with local schools and businesses. So too, it is appropriate that higher education faculty lead STEM (science, technology, engineering, and mathematics) initiatives in their institutions. Faculty unaccustomed to assuming a leadership role may ask, "What do I do?" "Where do I start?"

This chapter addresses those questions by exploring how one non-positional faculty team led an inter-institutional initiative through various stages of collaboration leading to a joint, sustainable academic program. The chapter organizes the initiative around Bolman and Deal's (2008) four perspectives: symbolic, structural, human resources, and political. Within this multi-frame model, the chapter covers such topics as forming a vision, building social and emotional intelligence for the journey, selecting and empowering a core leadership team, developing and employing personal and collaborative leadership strengths, supporting change through common values, viewing barriers and setbacks as opportunities, and keeping the focus on the vision. As readers follow the steps of a particular STEM higher education project, they will find enough details and universally applicable situations to make generalizations to their own contexts.

Though the most obvious readers are non-positional faculty in institutions of higher learning, the principles found here will be of interest to anyone involved in directing higher education collaborations and partnerships.

BEGINNINGS

From a Seed Idea to a Vision

As with all change, STEM initiatives start with a seed idea that must then grow into a vision. Someone needs to be that fertile ground into which the idea is planted. At Niagara University the faculty member with the seed idea was a newly tenured, non-positional faculty member in the College of Education (COE), hereafter referred to as Dr. C.[1]

The state designated the district surrounding the university as a "special needs" district. To increase at-risk students' early exposure to STEM fields, the district had recently passed a referendum for the construction of a STEM lab in each of the area schools. Having visited one such STEM lab, Dr. C considered the following questions: (1) How might the university equip future teachers for STEM education? (2) How might the university attract, keep, and educate future STEM teachers from the area's non-dominant cultures? (3) What might she do to further this cause?

To better acquaint herself with this emerging environment, Dr. C visited area schools set in low-income neighborhoods. She listened to stories of children who came to school dirty, sick, and hungry, children who lived in condemned buildings and who cried when snow days sent them home before receiving a free school lunch. Looking into the eyes of children who lined up to hold her hand, the seed was planted for a STEM initiative. Dr. C contemplated how her university might contribute to educating future generations out of the cycle of poverty.

Without a top-down directive from her department or the college, from the institution or from the state, Dr. C formulated a vision for the university:

Develop a STEM concentration for future teachers by collaborating across colleges and departments. And for that concentration, attract and support future teacher candidates from non-dominant cultures.

ANALYZE ASSETS AND BARRIERS

Initiating and leading a university-wide STEM initiative felt daunting. Bolman and Deal's (2008) four-quadrant model gave Dr. C a place to start,

which was to make sense of the university by viewing it from various perspectives. She also noted that a vision needs a strategy, and, "A strategy has
to recognize major forces working for and against the agenda" (Bolman &
Deal, 2008, p. 215). Table 1 delineates, within Bolman and Deal's four-frame
model, what Dr. C considered the university's assets and barriers. Table 1
also contains what she considered her own assets and barriers.

Table 1.   University and Personal Assets and Barriers.

University Assets	Symbolic frame	• Vincentian tradition of service to the poor and the community, • Commitment to issues of diversity and social justice.
	Structural frame	• Liberal arts university with strong science, technology, and mathematics departments, • Goals, roles, polices, and responsibilities clearly delineated, • Long-term goals embedded in strategic plans, • Highest administrative personal (provost, president) accessible to faculty, • COE departments organized by teacher certification grade level, narrowing departmental faculty focus to areas of greatest impact and concern, • Faculty Learning Community in place to improve across campus communication and collaboration, • Grant opportunities for students, especially minorities, • Courses on cultural diversity – graduation requirement: at least one cultural diversity course.
	Political frame	• Some decision making at the departmental level (subject to administrative approval), • Empower faculty to invest in their own and the university's development, • Pressure from the top to increase student enrollment, especially of minorities, • Articulation agreements with community colleges where many minorities begin their education, • Excellent reputation in the community built on expertise and community mindedness, • Close proximity to low employment, high poverty neighborhoods, • Networking with area schools (e.g., student teachers, after school programs, summer camps).
	Human resource frame	• Friendly and supportive staff, • Commitment to the Vincentian mission, • Middle management support and investment in faculty self-actualization, • Energetic and talented individuals across campus.

Table 1. (*Continued*)

University Barriers	• Attracts only a few minority students, resulting in a weak core for STEM minority students to relate to and share support, • Small pool; colleges and departments competing for the same prospective students, • No engineering courses (the "E" in STEM), • A large population of science majors (a waiting list of students), making science departments reticent to educate even greater numbers of teacher candidates who may, conceivably, take the seats of potential science majors, • Science and mathematics faculty feel overworked and may be resistant to dedicating time and effort to revamping courses to meet Common Core State Standards for preparing STEM teachers, • Lack of undergraduate STEM education course/s for teachers in training, • Decisions in the COE are tightly controlled, with centralized authority within a rigid chain of command, • Due to extensive responsibilities COE dean is not readily accessible to COE faculty, • COE and the science departments in the College of Arts and Sciences have a weak history of positive collaboration, • Individual colleges somewhat isolated and territorial with a lack of communication between and among colleges, • Little faculty collaboration across colleges and among departments within colleges. [As is mentioned in "strengths" there is a growing Faculty Learning Community established to address these last two obstacles.]
Dr. C's Personal Assets	• Understands STEM education and the Common Core State Standards • Strong background in STEM disciplines, • Member of the Faculty Learning Community, • Experienced working with ethnically and culturally diverse cultures, both in North American and Africa, • Experience developing and teaching methods courses to teacher candidates, • High energy and stamina.
Dr. C's Personal Barriers	• Inexperienced in collaborating and networking with personnel, either in the COE or across campus, • No positional power, • Non-assertive, an introvert with little history of exercising personal power, • No experience having led or having been part of a university initiative, • Few direct connections or contacts with principals or faculty in area schools, • Little experience recruiting students, minority or otherwise, • Heavy teaching, service, research and writing responsibilities.

Build on Assets and Overcome Barriers

Dr. C started with things she had personal power to change: design a STEM methods course and improve her own negotiation and collaboration skills. Building from her background in STEM disciplines and her expertise in designing curriculum and courses, Dr. C readily developed a STEM methods course. She brought a proposal for the newly developed course to the early childhood department (ECE), of which she was a part. The chair of that department resisted including the STEM methods course on the roster of course offerings. The ECE chair gave the argument that our accrediting body does not require a methods course for STEM. Dr. C was flooded with negative feelings: a crushed spirit, a replacement of creativity and innovation with compliance, and eroding trust. The passion for her vision, however, proved stronger. As she considered what she could control, Dr. C determined to work on her under-developed negotiation skills.

Cultivate Social and Emotional Skills

To better equip herself for working within the human relations frame, Dr. C began a personal study to cultivate skills for the task. One of the first and most powerful insights came from Rath and Conchie (2008) who express that imitating others and striving to be good at everything makes an *in*effective leader. To determine her own leadership strengths, Dr. C completed the StrengthsFinder survey, an extension of Rath & Conchie's book. The survey suggested strengths she might build on and then call on at opportune times.

From Monarth (2010), Dr. C became more aware of emotional and social intelligence skills and of living a life centered in awareness, honesty, and empathy. She increased her knowledge of strategies for dealing with reactions and feelings, skills for living with authenticity and presence, and skills for gaining a keen sense of perspectives and values, her own and others. She saw the worth of removing her image-promoting masks, and in their place, began to focus on real relationships based on respect and caring. She was reminded of the importance of building genuine affiliations and forming powerful, deep, and empathetic connections with persons who share a desire to contribute to the greater whole (Fullan, 2001). Brown's (2012, 2010) books helped Dr. C put aside feelings of helplessness, of needing to be right to feel validated, and of letting go of the idea that refusing the proposed course was evidence of not being respected or not being

heard. It also helped Dr. C accept her imperfections and live with vulner-
ability and, rather than beating herself up over failures and shortcomings,
she began to view criticism and setbacks as opportunities for growth.

Cultivate Communication Skills

In addition to emotional and social intelligence, operating from the human
relations frame requires clear and precise communication. Re-reading
Kotter (1998) pressed Dr. C to analyze her failure to persuade the ECE
chair. She asked: "Did I clearly identify the need for a STEM concentration
and the opportunities it would afford the COE?" "Did I lucidly communicate the vision and how it firmly rests in the institutions' core values?"
"Did I communicate urgency?" "Did I communicate a direction and how
we might address obstacles that may stand in the way?" Dr. C surmised
that having skipped these steps she had been ill equipped to build trust or
inspire the cooperation of the ECE chair.

Reframe the Vision

Dr. C re-framed "her" vision into "our" vision, both in her own mind and
in reframing her approach. The next time she brought the course proposal
to ECE faculty, she would ask for departmental input and then listen and
act on, or at least, seriously consider their suggestions. In place of frustration and impatience, she would practice optimism, decisiveness, and
strengthened resolve. To further prepare, she reflected on the characteristics
of effective negotiation and conflict resolution skills and was impressed
with the importance of communicating with candor and respect (Patterson,
Grenny, McMillan, & Switzler, 2012). With the above in mind, Dr. C
brought the proposal for a STEM methods course to the next semester's
ECE meeting. At this meeting, the ECE interim-chair and ECE faculty
were more open to change and more willing to engage in discussion around
the topic. The STEM methods course was approved, unanimously.

Cultivate Political Skills

The role of a non-positional leader is complex. To better understand the
political complexity, Dr. C interviewed (audiotaped) a positional leader she
respected, one who was approachable, well informed, and connected across
the university. This person (Dr. F) stressed the importance of aligning the

STEM vision with the university's bigger vision. Dr. F advised Dr. C to compare her vision to what is already being done across campus, to determine and be able to articulate the uniqueness of her vision, and to gain awareness of university level requirements for bringing the plan all the way to fruition. Dr. F emphasized analyzing possible problems and potential solutions to those problems, not expecting anyone else to solve those problems for you, and of shepherding the vision while taking advantage of the structures in place, empowering others to do what needs to be done. The final advice was to realize that being a leader and promoting a vision is difficult these days, especially in light of changes taking place across higher education. Money is tight, enrollment is down, and everyone is expected to do more, often with fewer people and fewer resources. Dr. F cautioned Dr. C that there are likely parts of the job she may not want to do, parts she may feel unqualified to do − like recruitment − and yet, that is what must take place for the vision to move forward. Dr. C asked Dr. F what skills she thought were important for Dr. C to cultivate. The response was, "get involved". Break through the isolation of the various colleges by forming relationships across campus. Serve on committees with faculty from the science, math, and technology departments, go to lunch with faculty, serve on the research committee to become aware of others' interests, study the organizational chart and interact socially to find out what people do − a person's title does not always tell what that person actually does. Dr. F's candidness strengthened the focus, informing and affirming Dr. C's commitment to the task.

Dr. C joined a faculty writing group, became active in the faculty learning community, went to social functions across campus, and, rather than seeking out familiar faces, she made a point of talking to people she did not know. As she interacted with others, Dr. C listened, and she talked about STEM to seek out individuals who might be interested in the vision and who had strengths and circles of influence other than her own. She read faculty biographical sketches on the university webpage and listened to the recommendations of trusted peers.

BUILD RELATIONSHIPS

To get a pulse for the science departments, Dr. C scheduled meetings with science chairs and faculty. The initial response was negative. Past attempts at collaboration had resulted in long-standing tension between the COE and science departments. Dr. C focused on rebuilding trust.

Build Trust

At this juncture, it was essential to listen to science faculty's complaints without judgment or defensiveness, and to introduce the STEM initiative with care and sensitivity. Speaking from a science perspective rather than a COE perspective, Dr. C appealed to logic by citing research studies and governmental actions related to STEM. She appealed to their humanity by being an empathetic listener and by sharing stories of what she observed in area classrooms. She asked science faculty to share childhood experiences that drew them to the field of science, and she asked faculty with children what they thought of the science teaching their children were receiving in school. The motive was always to be authentic, open, and trustworthy. Dr. C was careful to not take criticism and resistance personally. She viewed the scientists' frustration as real and painful. Using empathy, intuition, and optimism, she saw these meetings as opportunities to build a united resolve for a STEM initiative, and that the united resolve would, in the process, strengthen relations between colleges. Dr. C realized more than ever the importance of having a science faculty member on the core STEM team.

Build Teams

According to Rath and Conchie (2008), strong teams are composed of individuals with diverse leadership strengths and diverse ways of acting and thinking. Dr. C set out to form inter-institutional teams. She viewed those teams as a set of concentric circles: (1) a team of three or four individuals to form the inner circle, (2) faculty from the ECE department, the next circle out, (3) science, mathematics, and technology departments, the third circle, (4) and recruitment and promotion, grants office, director of external affairs, university administration, and diversity support personnel the fourth circle. Especially critical was a strong and empowered inner circle that would establish domain-specific objectives and function as a part of and a resource for all other teams.

Build the Core Team
When interviewing science faculty, one science professor in particular stood out. That professor, Dr. S, asked to be involved in the STEM initiative. Dr. S had prior experiences working in at-risk schools, was highly respected by her science peers, and was involved in committees and informal groups across campus. Dr. S joined Dr. C as the second member of the core STEM team.

For a third team member, Dr. C recruited another COE faculty member, Dr. G. Dr. G's talents, disposition, and experiences added to the strength of the team. He had expertise in technology and design, training and experience working in special education, and during his tenure at a different university had been instrumental in procuring and overseeing the implementation of a STEM grant. The three members of the team differed greatly in personality, leadership style, experiences, and perspectives, which combined, made for a well-rounded team.

Dr. C came to the team's first meeting with rough plans. By the end of that meeting, the team had developed a clear understanding of each member's leadership strengths (Rath & Conchie, 2008), and the team culture had become one of trust, candidness, and commitment.

Set an Agenda

During the first meeting, the members openly brainstormed and debated various options, each expressed areas of greatest interest. By the meeting's end, implementation plans had been made and each member had assumed specific roles and timelines in relation to those plans (Table 2).

Phase 1
Dr. C had developed the vision, designed and gained approval for the STEM methods course, and she had begun the ongoing work of building knowledge and skills for the project. Core team members contributed to the vision, and now, the building of greater understanding and skills rested with those individuals, as they saw fit.

Inter-Institutional Buy-In

Phase 2
Dr. C interviewed science chairs and faculty and formed the core team. Though Dr. C would support and encourage all efforts, the greatest challenge of gaining support from science faculty lay with Dr. S.

Table 2. Undergraduate Elementary Education STEM Concentration.

Phase 1	*Develop Vision and Background Knowledge for Project*
	Meet with COE Middle Management – Secure Support, Direction & Possible Barriers Conduct Research on Institutional Change Theory and Practice Issues Review State Requirements for STEM Concentration for Teacher Education Develop STEM Methods Course Build Emotional and Social Skills and Strategies for the Task Gain ECE Departmental Approval for STEM Methods Course
Phase 2	*Gain Support and Insight; Set Course of Action*
	Interview Science Department Chairs and Faculty Form Core STEM Leadership Team Set Agenda for the STEM Initiative & Delineate Responsibilities for Each Core Team Member Research & Unpack Next Generation Science Standards (NGSS) Collaborate with Key Science Faculty to Align Science Courses with NGSS Research & Decode Common Core State Standards for Mathematics (CCSSM) Collaborate with Key Mathematics Faculty to Align Mathematics Courses with CCSSM Interview Key Technology Faculty to Align Technology Expectations with Technology Standards Meet with Third-Circle Team Members (Grants Office, Recruitment, Student Teaching, etc.) Meet with Provost

Phase 3 — *Curriculum Mapping*

COE Curriculum Mapping. ←——→ Align with state approved Liberal Arts concentration, literacy minor, ECE certifications & internships	Science Departments Curriculum Mapping Align with NGSS and science course offerings Collaborate between COE and science departments Mathematics Department Curriculum Mapping Align with CCSSM and mathematics course offerings

Phase 4 — *STEM Concentration Approval*

Prepare Documents →	COE Dean →	ECE →	COE →
○ Curriculum cards ○ Program Sheets ○ Alignment Matrix with accrediting bodies NCATE, ACEI, NAEYC, ALST, edTPA	○ Present STEM concentration for COE Dean's approval	○ Present concentration for ECE department approval	○ COE Curriculum Committee ○ COE faculty vote (NU Senate approval.) →

Table 2.   (Continued)

Recruitment			

Phase 5

Grants	Community Colleges & High Schools	Flier	Recruitment Visits
○ Grants Office ○ STEM teacher prep grants for underrepresented minorities & poverty	○ Dual Enrollment Agreements & Curriculum Mapping	○ Design and print	○ Community Colleges and High Schools

Mentor for Success & Sustainability			

Phase 6

STEM Support Team	Grants	NU Support Groups	Summer STEM employment opportunities
	○ To support STEM student leaders	○ Learn from and work with campus support groups	

Evaluation			

Phase 7

Enrollment	State Tests	Student Teaching Reports	Results
• Minimum of 15 students enrolled in STEM concentration by 2017	• edTPA: Disaggregate data • ALST: Disaggregate data compare STEM & non-STEM candidate scores; areas of greatest weaknesses • Survey graduating teacher candidates (Survey Monkey)	• STEM-related items • Disaggregate results for all items to compare STEM and non-STEM concentration	• Disseminate results to consider revisions to recruitment, mentoring, and STEM course content and pedagogy

Science Faculty Buy-in
Using leadership strengths of deliberation, self-assurance, and strategic thought, Dr. S guided her fellow scientists into seeing the big picture and into seeing how their science courses might fit into and benefit from the STEM initiative. She collaborated with small groups of faculty to align individual courses with the *Next Generation Science Standards* (NGSS). Her work with the physics faculty was especially commendable: they designed a new physics course to meet all NGSS engineering expectations, thus laying a foundation for the "E" in STEM. Within weeks, Dr. S completed this challenging body of work.

Overcoming Obstacles
Juxtaposed to the list of science courses, Dr. S expressed science faculty's unresolved fears and frustrations. In response, Dr. C composed a roster of science courses analogous to those on the list, suggesting that when necessary, STEM teacher candidates might complete commensurate courses online or at community colleges as a temporary solution. The future goal being to add science courses designed exclusively for teacher candidates once the STEM program grew to where numbers merited additional sections of science courses and hiring of additional science faculty. The solution eased science faculty's angst over STEM education students taking seats from science majors. The team had, thus, approached the problem from a political perspective, working from Fisher and Ury's (2011) stance that the search for a win-win solution is essential for attaining buy-in, and for creating openness and trust for long-term affiliation.

Math and Technology Faculty Buy-in
As Dr. S collaborated with science faculty, Dr. C met with the mathematics department chair and faculty. Two existing courses aligned with most expectations found in the *Common Core State Standards for Mathematics* (CCSSM). Mathematics faculty discussed possibilities, and they decided to add the missing expectations to a third course. During this time, COE faculty worked with the technology department, making revisions to an existing course entitled *Introduction to Computers and Programming for Teachers.* In concert with science, mathematics, and technology departments, the core team now had the information needed to compose STEM curriculum cards and program sheets.

Fourth Circle Buy-in
The next step involved building relationships with personnel in the fourth leadership circle: grants office, director of external affairs, COE director of

student teaching, recruitment and promotion, director of freshman support, and university administration.

Grants Office. First, the core team met with personnel from the Grants'
Office. The director printed a list of specific agencies and organizations to
which STEM teacher candidates – especially minority students – might
appeal to secure assistance with tuition, books, and housing costs.
Personnel in the Grants' Office directed and supported the core team's
completion of a grant application to finance the STEM initiative.
Unfortunately, upon submission, the agency emailed the director that the
grant was for work to be completed that coming summer, a timeframe later
than the goal set for completion of the STEM inter-institutional collaboration. Nonetheless, a working relationship had been established between the
Grants Office and the STEM core team.

Director of External Affairs. The core team met with the Director of
External Affairs to discuss common interests in underrepresented minorities and girls in STEM. The team became aware of the university's summer
STEM camp for girls. The director and the core team brainstormed ideas
for involving STEM teacher candidates in the summer STEM camp.
Students might, for example, serve some of their freshman or sophomore
field experiences in the camp, or camp work might be integrated into education courses and/or science courses. Dr. S shared specifics on how she
might integrate teacher candidates' inquiry-based research in the summer
camp with her summer chemistry course.

Director of Student Teaching. Teacher candidates fulfill three types of
internships: five semesters learn and serve, two semesters teaching assistant
(TA), and one semester student teaching. In the meeting with the core
team, the Director of Student Teaching, and the Student Teaching
Placement Officer, the group discussed the learn and serve placements and
the option of freshmen fulfilling one learn and serve placement in the university's summer STEM camp. The core team requested one TA internship
and one student teaching placement be completed in schools with STEM
labs. The director was open to suggestions, but she cautioned that area
schools might feel overburdened if asked to accept teacher candidates for
both classroom placements and STEM lab placements. In response to this
possible hurdle, Dr. S emailed a colleague from another university who
works with STEM charter schools. This colleague then contacted a number

of out-of-area schools with STEM labs. These schools expressed interest in having STEM teacher candidates fulfill either their teaching assistantship or their student teaching at their schools. At a second meeting with the Director of Student Teaching, Dr. S shared the list of charter schools and contact information, and the director welcomed the opportunity to place teacher candidates in these schools, provided candidates had their own transportation. The team agreed to work with the student teaching office on transportation options once the STEM student population justified it.

Recruitment and Promotion. Core team members met with a COE recruitment representative. The representative was underwhelmed with the proposal. She expressed concern that STEM students would be drawn from the same pool of prospective students and, as a result, the number of education students would remain constant with fewer students enrolled in each program. The team, who had already considered alternative sources for STEM students, suggested pitching the STEM concentration to students already enrolled in one or more of the STEM disciplines at a community college and students in area high schools interested in science, technology, engineering, or mathematics. These students may not have considered a profession in both a STEM discipline and teaching, or these may be students who, after taking a few science or mathematics courses, were reconsidering their major. The director's fears were assuaged. She asked to see the proposed STEM curriculum cards and program sheets and, upon examination, said that once the concentration was approved, she wanted an outline for a flier. She would send the outline to the university recruitment office to create a flier to promote the program. The core team expressed interest in accompanying the recruitment team on recruitment visits, and the director agreed that it would be essential for her team to work with faculty from both COE and science departments.

Director of Freshman Support. The core team met with the Director of Freshman Support. He gave the team pointers and resources on mentoring and agreed to work with the team on setting up a STEM mentoring group, though he felt the Freshman Support Department needed to be an instrumental part of any campus mentoring group. The details of the collaboration will be worked out once a handful of STEM concentration students enroll in the program. In the meantime, the team had identified the principle agent of influence, and channels of communication with this support group had been opened.

University Provost. The last phase 2 visit was with the university Provost. The team presented the proposal from Bolman and Deal's (2008) symbolic and political perspectives, basing the *why* of the proposal on the national call for STEM education and appealing to the university's Vincentian mission. The team shared the vision, prospective plans, and inter-institutional collaboration engaged in thus far. They shared their desire to keep administration abreast of the proposal and sought administrative support and advocacy. They asked for clarification of the politics involved and for feedback and advice from an administrative perspective. The Provost leaned forward in his chair and encouraged the team with the words, "Get it done!" He suggested forging a district buy-in: survey principals and teachers, and from the survey results, form focus groups from different schools, especially schools with STEM labs. STEM teams would meet and consult with these external groups; thus, extending inter-institutional collaboration to include collaboration with the greater, external community. The team embraced the idea, and Dr. G volunteered to write and administrate the survey after the team met again with the Director of External Affairs, this time to collaborate on the Provost's suggestion.

FORMALLY STRUCTURED PROPOSAL

The team felt ready for phase 3: revisit curriculum mapping for the STEM concentration, this time to write a formally structured proposal that adhered to State Education Department requirements for a teacher education concentration. The following are highlights from the proposal:

What does the Proponent Hope to Teach Students in the Concentration?

The STEM concentration seeks to prepare STEM elementary teachers to address the national call for qualified STEM teachers (US Department of Education) by equipping teacher candidates with the subject matter knowledge and pedagogical (teaching) expertise to effectively teach STEM subject area content to elementary grade students. The goal includes candidates' scientific and mathematical literate and functional knowledge of science, mathematics, engineering, and technology required to teach the rigorous expectations found in the CCSSM and NGSS. To accomplish this goal, the STEM concentration includes the following. Content area 1, chemistry/physics/earth science: five 3-hour courses, plus lab. Content area 2, biology:

three 3-hour courses, plus lab. Content area 3, mathematics: three 3-hour courses. STEM courses within the liberal arts requirement but outside of the three-content area concentration are as follows: introduction to computers and programming for teachers, classroom assessment (STEM focus), two to four additional science or mathematics courses and one capstone STEM senior seminar course. Within the teacher education courses, teacher candidates take one STEM methods course. All but two general education electives are required. Three program sheets were developed: one a straight STEM concentration, a second with a literacy minor, and a third with a special education minor. All program sheets matched semester and yearly course rotations found in science and mathematics departments.

What Should Students be Capable of Doing Under Successful Completion of the Concentration?

Teacher candidates should be capable of unpacking concepts and skills inherent in knowing and teaching the various scientific, mathematical, engineering, and technology expectations for children in Kindergarten through Grade 6 classrooms, as those expectations are delineated in CCSSM and NGSS documents. Candidates should be capable of integrating across disciplines and of adhering to teaching practices associated with STEM education (e.g., inquiry-based learning, exploration, problem solving, collaboration, critical thinking, models of continuous improvement, and societal connections).

How will Outcomes Assessment be Accomplished?

Outcome assessment will be accomplished through course work and field experience assessments. Course work will build a solid base for teaching K-6 mathematics, technology, biology, environmental science, chemistry, earth science, physics, engineering (embedded in physics courses and STEM methods course). Assessment of this knowledge base will be in the form of course assignments, projects, and exams. Internships include 100 hours of learn and serve in birth to grade 6 classrooms; one 20-hour and two 30-hour teachers' assistant placements, one in a K-6 classroom with a STEM lab; and one semester of student teaching in two different K-6 schools and grade level classrooms, at least one placement in an elementary school with a STEM lab. Associate teachers will assess STEM teacher candidates' knowledge and application of STEM content and pedagogy using field placement assessment forms, each with items specific to STEM education criteria.

The Bachelors of Arts with a STEM concentration will provide the graduate with the knowledge, understanding and skills to assume the role of a full-time teacher in a K-6 classroom, public or private, in schools with or without a STEM lab. To assess STEM candidates' pedagogical and content knowledge for teaching, state certification data will be disaggregated, most especially Pearson's edTPA performance-based assessment and New York's Academic Literacy Skills Test (ALST). The STEM concentration will prepare graduates to further their education in STEM education through Master's level schooling. A record will be kept to discern the number of STEM graduates accepted in a graduate degree program.

The need for STEM elementary teachers is expected to expand throughout the nation as the federal government increases funding for institutions preparing teachers for the STEM workforce (Bureau of Labor Statistics, 2013–2014). With a STEM concentration, elementary teacher candidates can gain expertise for existing and emerging roles as STEM teachers. The COE will maintain a record of the number of teacher candidates enrolled in the program from inception to graduation and on to employment. The results of all assessments will be disseminated to the appropriate personnel to consider revisions to recruitment, mentoring, and STEM-related course content and pedagogy.

Dean Approval
For six months the team had been planning and sharing the vision, had worked to overcoming challenges, suspicion and resistance, and had experienced approving nods across campus. The team contacted the COE dean ... and ... the momentum stopped. The team hit the wall of delayed and cancelled meetings. None of the well-thought-out plans could be initiated without the dean's approval. After weeks of trying, the team secured an appointment, only to be cancelled when a snowstorm closed the campus. A date was set for three weeks later, then cancelled when another, more urgent matter demanded the dean's attention. University break. Holidays. Weeks of inactivity became months. Time was slipping away. After two and a half months of waiting, Dr. C went to Dr. F to ask if she could give consent rather than the dean. The next day, the team was granted a meeting – during Christmas vacation. Dr. C alone was available. She met with the dean and gained the necessary approval. The dean clarified that only one more approval was necessary: ECE departmental approval (no need for COE or university or state approval) as the concentration fit within the previously approved teacher education concentration.

ECE Department Approval
The first meeting of the spring semester, the team brought the proposal to the ECE department for their final approval. Some debate ensued, but Dr. C and Dr. G were prepared with answers to all questions and solutions to all proposed problems. Convinced of its value and feasibility, ECE faculty approved the STEM concentration. The process from inception to approval had taken a little over a year.

Team Reflection
The team reflected on the extended delay in procuring this essential meeting. They mulled over strategies they might have implemented, or might implement in the future. Again looking to Bolman and Deal (2008) they considered how they, as non-positional faculty, might reframe their actions to deal with the structural gap between faculty and administration, and how they might strengthen overall communication between these structure levels. The team brainstormed options and concluded that a combined human resource frame and political/social frame might be appropriate. From the political lens, the team might have sent an email or left a voice mail, using Cialdini's (2007) "because" strategy – "We request a meeting this coming week because our plan is to increase the number of teacher education students"; Kotter's (1998) sense of urgency strategy – "The number of teacher candidates in the COE has decreased. We request a meeting this week to discuss a way to increase that number"; or Cialdini's (2007) social proof strategy combined with Bolman and Deals (2008) symbolic frame – "You will be happy to know the provost expressed interest in advancing a STEM initiative, especially as it aligns with the university's Vincentian mission. We are eager to discuss the project with you as soon as possible". Though the team had little opportunity for direct contact with the dean, they might have appealed to the human resources frame by establishing an interpersonal relationship with the dean's secretary, and from that foundation asked the secretary for weekly cancelation updates. They might then have slotted into the schedule when others cancelled, even if it meant only one team member would be available to represent the team, and even if it meant all core team members would need to be prepared to meet instantaneously.

SUMMARY

This chapter began with the questions, "What do I do?" and "Where do I start?" Though answers to these questions are unique to individuals and to particular institutions of higher learning, the STEM initiative presented in this chapter suggests how organizing inter-institutional collaboration around Bolman and Deal's (2008) four perspectives may serve as a framework for answering these questions.

Through the four perspectives, Dr. C better understood the university as a complex matrix of human resources, structures, symbols, and politics. From a human resources perspective, she more keenly viewed people as the center of the organization and saw her non-positional leadership role as based in social and emotional intelligence with an emphasis on inclusion, trust, and empowerment. The structural perspective demanded that the core team explicate relationships across campus by clarifying the overall STEM vision and goals and by specifying the roles individuals play in that overall vision. Lacking formal authority, the team's structural frame relied on clearly delineated tasks, facts, and expectations, and on recommendations for overcoming obstacles. They were sensitive to the university's symbolic perspective, viewing the STEM initiative as deeply representative of the Vincentian mission. Most often team members began presentations with a clear articulation of how the STEM concentration would promote the university's core Vincentian values (to help the underprivileged and impact the community). According to Bolman and Deal (2008), the political perspective is the most essential frame for non-positional leadership, the success of which rests on recognizing various interest groups and agendas, on knowing how to deal with conflict, and on developing strategies for working within institutional policies and within college and departmental guidelines. The team gained insight into feelings, fears, experiences, and needs of those involved in developing a joint academic program, and they used that insight to frame strategic approaches for collaboration. Struggles and obstacles are inevitable, and they grew from each encounter, managing conflict as productively as possible, negotiating differences, and compromising where reasonable with the ultimate goal of reaching win-win outcomes. They committed to ongoing skill development, and their implementation of a four-frame analysis of situations and strategies ultimately led to inter-institutional collaboration and the realization of a STEM concentration.

NOTE

1. List of Abbreviations:
   STEM—*science, technology, engineering, and mathematics*
   COE—College of Education
   ECE stands for Early Childhood Department (K-8 teacher education)
   CCSSM—*Common Core State Standards for Mathematics* (CCSSI, 2010)

NGSS—*Next Generation Science Standards* (NGSS Lead States, 2013)
Dr. C—COE faculty member who initiated the plan.
Dr. F—middle-management member of the COE
Dr. S—science faculty; one of the three-member STEM core team.
Dr. G—COE faculty member; one of the three-member STEM core team.

REFERENCES

Bolman, L., & Deal, T. (2008). *Reframing organizations: Artistry, choice and leadership* (4th ed.). San Francisco: Jossey-Bass.

Brown, B. (2010). *The gifts of imperfection: Let go of who you think you're supposed to be and embrace who you are.* Center City, MN: Hazelden.

Brown, B. (2012). *Daring greatly: How the courage to be vulnerable transforms the way we live, love, parent, and lead.* New York: Gotham Books, Penguin Group, Inc.

Bureau of Labor Statistics. (2013–2014). *Labor force statistics from the current population survey.* Retrieved from http://www.bls.gov/cps/demographics.htm

Cialdini, R. (2007). *Influence: The psychology of persuasion.* New York: Harper Collins: Collins Business.

Common Core State Standards Initiative (CCSSI). (2010). *Common Core State Standards for Mathematics (CCSSM).* National Governors Association Center for Best Practices and the Council of Chief State School Officers. Washington, DC: authors.

Fisher, R., & Ury, W. (2011). *Getting to yes: Negotiating agreement without giving in.* London, UK: Penguin Books.

Fullan, M. (2001). *Leading in a culture of change.* San Francisco: Jossey-Bass.

Kezar, A., & Lester, J. (2011). *Enhancing campus capacity for leadership: An examination of grassroots leaders in higher education.* Redwood City, CA: Stanford University Press.

Kotter, J. (1998). Leading change: Why transformations efforts fail. In *Harvard business review on change.* Brighten, MA: Harvard Business School Press.

Monarth, H. (2010). *Executive presence: The art of commanding respect like a CEO.* New York: McGraw Hill.

NGSS Lead States. (2013). *Next generation science standards: For states, by states.* Washington, DC: National Academies Press.

Patterson, K., Grenny, J., McMillan, R., & Switzler, A. (2012). *Crucial conversations: Tools for talking when the stakes are high.* New York: McGraw Hill.

Rath, T., & Conchie, B. (2008). *Strengths-based leadership: Great leaders, teams, and why people follow.* Washington, DC: Gallop Press.

INTERINSTITUTIONAL COLLABORATION IN DUTCH PROFESSIONAL HIGHER EDUCATION

Rutger Kappe, Domien Wijsbroek,
Marjon Molenkamp, Olof Wiegert, Gerwin Hendriks,
Zuke van Ingen and Jaap van Zandwijk

ABSTRACT

This chapter describes the emergence and functioning of an interinstitutional research group. The topic of this research group, which was started by five large universities of applied sciences (UAS) in the western metropolitan area of the Netherlands, is the study success of ethnic minority groups. With only minor funding by the Dutch Ministry of Education, Culture and Science a dedicated research team, representing each of the UAS involved, set out to address several unresolved research questions and issues. The Dutch Ministry of Education, Culture did also provided access to an essential national research data which is normally not accessible for individual institutions. Besides working together on study success research, regular consultation started at the corporate/ board level and at the strategic level (directors of education policies) on

University Partnerships for Academic Programs and Professional Development
Innovations in Higher Education Teaching and Learning, Volume 7, 77–91
Copyright © 2016 by Emerald Group Publishing Limited
All rights of reproduction in any form reserved
ISSN: 2055-3641/doi:10.1108/S2055-364120160000007014

various study success-related topics, such as new legislation and diversity issues. What differentiates this cooperation from other networks is its multilayered structure and the sharing of detailed data about sensitive strategic issues, policymaking and institutional research by competing UAS. This chapter provides insights on effective working methods, dilemmas and first year achievements of this intensive interinstitutional collaboration. The chapter concludes with ten factors for success in the context described.

Keywords: Database-driven research; ethnic minority; research team; study success; Universities of applied sciences or UAS

THE DUTCH HIGHER EDUCATION SYSTEM IN A NUTSHELL: A SHORT INTRODUCTION

The Dutch education system consists of eight years of primary education, 4, 5 or 6 years of secondary education (depending on the type of school) and 2–6 years of higher education (depending on the type of education and the specialization). Like many Continental European countries, Dutch higher education has a binary system, which means that a distinction is made between research-oriented education and higher professional education. Research-oriented education takes place primarily at research universities. Higher professional education takes place at UAS. As well as having different objectives, each of the two types of education has its own admission requirements, program duration and titles. Students who graduate from a research university are supposed to be equipped with enough knowledge about research designs and statistics to start a career in research-oriented jobs, enter a PhD-program or create knowledge in other ways. In the workplace they are considered to be rather analytical. Graduates from UAS are supposed to be smart users of (applied) science in their professions. The language of education in universities of applied science is Dutch, but under the influence of the Bologna process more and more study programs are being offered in English.

Research-oriented education is provided by 14 research universities in the Netherlands (253,482 students). Higher professional education is primarily provided by UAS. The 37 Dutch UAS have over 440,000 students. The UAS have seven educational sectors: economics, health care, agriculture, teacher training, social work, arts and engineering. Within these sectors, students can choose from various educational profiles. Almost all types of study programs can be followed at UAS, located all over the Netherlands. Some UAS specialize in certain fields, such as agriculture, teacher training or art, but most offer a broad range of study programs.

The *Netherlands Association of Universities of Applied Sciences* looks after the interests of its members in the public arena, in discussions with the ministry and in central wage bargaining agreements with unions. Although this association could function as a platform for collaboration, intensive interinstitutional collaboration is usually arranged by the UAS themselves. This article is an example of research-intensive collaboration between six large UAS in the western part of the Netherlands on the topic of student success. These UAS have approximately 40% of the market share of UAS students in the Netherlands.

HOW DID WE SET OUT?

Before We Started as a Research Team

The study success of all kinds of student groups is monitored annually at the national level. For every institution, academic program and student groups, three study success criteria are reported: (a) dropout rate (retention rate); (b) switch rate (dropped out but started another program); (c) graduation rate. Groups are made up on the basis of variables such as gender, type of pre-entry diploma, ethnic background and socioeconomic background. For example, in the Netherlands native, female students with a secondary theoretical background have an 83% retention rate in the health-care educational sector, as opposed to a 72% retention rate for male students in the same sector.

The insights that are gained from this monitoring process are used to analyze which groups need attention on a national level or within (certain) UAS. In 2009, research universities and UAS in the metropolitan region in the western part of the country received funds to improve the retention and completion rates of ethnic minority students at the higher education institutions (HEIs). The UAS were asked to develop policies that fit their systems and students.

Role of the Dutch Ministry of Education, Culture and Science

Funding of initiatives to improve the study success of ethnic minorities by the Dutch Ministry of Education started in 2009 and ended in 2011. Although at the end of this three-year project the HEIs gained a lot of knowledge, the difference in the study success between native students (the student and their parents were born in the Netherlands) and ethnic minority students (the student or at least one parent was born abroad) still existed. Nevertheless, the funding stopped and the people involved feared that, as is often the case, the knowledge base and the intercollegiate network would dissolve. By that time several networks between the five UAS had emerged. Board members had half-yearly meetings, policy advisors met each other every quarter and in addition lecturers met peers from other institutions to share knowledge and experiences. To retain cooperation the university boards of five of the largest UAS in the suburban western part of the Netherlands decided to structurally continue working together on study success research. This initiative, our research team, was named the G5 research team (G5RT), meaning the five largest ("G") UAS in the metropolitan region. The Ministry of Education agreed to support this research cooperation for the first year with a small start-up grant. In the following paragraphs we will describe our cooperation, goals, working methods, our lessons learned and our achievements.

Common Goals and Mission of the G5 Research Team

The goal was to jointly develop and share knowledge on the success of various student groups in higher education in a metropolitan context. This knowledge should focus on improving the study success of these students. There were some clear reasons for a directed effort by the five UAS.

- Since diversity and city dynamics are concentrated in the larger cities, our UAS share a special position and challenges as metropolitan UAS and have a common interest in finding effective ways to deal with these challenges.
- A common interest in the pooling of scarce expertise in the area of policy research and in pooling data from the different UAS.
- As a team we can gain access to data and files that are not normally available for individual UAS.

- Joint analysis on the effects of interventions in the various UAS contributes to finding more generic intervention strategies.
- A joint approach can create a good platform that can be used to connect and interact with similar research or research groups.

The UAS further realize that policy issues concerning the study success of ethnic minorities in the metropolitan context will always be a challenging task. Through demographic factors and developments in education and society, these issues will develop over the years in an unpredictable way. Therefore, a focus on longitudinal research designs is expected to be necessary in this particular context.

Members of the Research Team

The following UAS participate in the research cooperation: UAS Inholland; UAS Utrecht; UAS the Hague; UAS Rotterdam; UAS of Amsterdam. UAS Leiden jointed a year later. All these UAS are situated in the western, metropolitan part of the Netherlands. Each UAS selected one researcher to participate as a dedicated member of the research group. If necessary, the researcher involves other members of their institute for specific tasks or analyses. The selected researchers share a common interest in the topic of the research group – study success – and generally have many years of research (and policy) experience.

Requirements for Success

In this particular venture, commitment from the participating UAS management and board turned out to be essential for success. The decision that each G5 UAS dedicates 0.4 full-time units to the research team (two days per week) and the decision to allow the sharing of sensitive performance data in our research team, contributed strongly to a good basis for joint research. An additional government grant made it possible to hire additional expertise.

HOW WE WORK

Our Research Agenda, Different Projects, Frequency Meetings

The basis for our cooperation is a joint research agenda. In the process of creating a viable research agenda, the input and reflection of strategists and boards is essential for aligning research topics and (longer-term) policy issues and agendas of the UAS. As a team, we create a concept research agenda, based on a mixture of emergent and long-term topics provided by strategists and UAS board members. Therefore, we first contact strategists and boards to find out about their focus. On the other hand, as researchers we also have themes or trends that we consider to be important. We aim to formulate an agenda that is balanced and relevant for all our stakeholders. The research agenda contains a short description of the research project, its aim, the research questions and methods. Strategists and board members decide on the final agenda. When projects are agreed upon, we make a more elaborate project plan, including a timeline that is used during the following year. Usually, two researchers from different UAS work together on a research project. Annually, the research agenda consists of three research projects.

It has become evident that our research team has quite an autonomous position in choosing and designing the research agenda, as long as it fits the framework set by the authorities of the institutions. We also find inspiration in analyses that have already been done (by us or by other researchers) and question whether further elaboration on a topic brings relevant knowledge for policy decisions. Whatever we do, we want to be sensitive to the interests of each individual member. This is probably one of the advantages of working with a group with positive chemistry and group members that like each other and enjoy working together, despite individual differences.

Responsibilities and Deadlines

During the first year of collaboration the research team partially relied on the expertise of Risbo, a renowned Dutch research institute, for data-preparation, research analysis and reporting. In the second year, Risbo only prepared the database and performed some analyses. As previously mentioned, each research project was assigned to a team of two researchers. Based on the research questions their responsibility was to formulate a research plan, perform the research, report the analysis and write a research report. In other words, be responsible for the whole research cycle. In a democratic meeting each research project was assigned to a duo. Some chose to take on a research project in their field of expertise, while others chose a topic that was quite challenging for them. In the latter case an additional researcher was asked to participate in the research project, without ultimate responsibility.

Frequency of Meetings

During every monthly meeting the team as a whole discusses the progress of each (joint) research project; members present their results and provided feedback on draft versions of research reports. The location of the face-to-face meetings is rotated so that every UAS hosts two to three research team meetings each year. Sometimes deadlines are not met, making the meetings less efficient. Despite the democratic nature of the group, we do have a chair who prepares and chairs the meetings, addresses issues like underperformance by team members, and handles the communication with the stakeholder like the strategists.

From Best Practice to Evidence-Based and Experimental Designs

Study success has always been an elusive topic in educational research in higher education. Evidence of factors influencing study success that can easily be changed by institutions is often weak and the search for more powerful interventions is ongoing (Tinto, 2012; Van den Bogaard, 2015; Van der Westen & Wijsbroek, 2014). The monitoring of the effects of study success interventions also remains a weak spot in educational research and often lacks a proper research design (Knol, 2013; Slavin, 2008). Our research team studied the current methodologies used in evaluation and effect-studies in our UAS and wrote a thematic paper on the current status and which other methodologies (like random controlled trails) could and should be used in evaluation and effect-studies of interventions. We observed that quite often effect-studies within our UAS focused on the satisfaction of students and lecturers with the interventions, a conclusion already drawn by Knol (2013) within the research university context. When intervention groups were compared to other groups, almost as a rule the group comparison could not be used to assess the effects of interventions because the intervention was not the only thing that differed between these groups (in other words, there were no proper control groups). "Control groups" often consisted of students that chose not to participate in the intervention. The conclusion touches a common phenomenon by stating that the G5 UAS had no examples of rigid monitoring of interventions with a strong research design. As we stated earlier, also outside of the G5 effect-research on intervention on study success in higher education often lacks rigid research design (Knol, 2013). An inquiry into the reasons for this phenomenon by our research team showed that quite often policies are implemented for all students because everyone should be able to benefit. From this perspective a control group is considered unethical. On a micro scale it turned out to be difficult for lecturers to withhold an intervention, that they believe in, from a (randomly chosen) group of students for the sake of research.

Another reason for the lack of rigid designs might be that evaluation is only considered at the last moment rather than beforehand. An important outcome of last year's agenda of our team was a strong plea for enriching effect-studies with controlled experimental designs.

ACHIEVEMENT IN THE FIRST YEAR

We focused on three things during the first year: setting up a research infrastructure, creating a research agenda and working on our first research reports. Besides a grant for one year, the Ministry of Education was willing to share the national database of all students in the Dutch system of higher education (both research universities and universities of applied science). This database contains the records of the educational careers of all students who have entered higher education in the Netherlands. We decided to only monitor data dating not further back than the year 2009 in order to make it possible to merge databases of our UAS with the national database. The ministerial grant was used to hire the Risbo institute to modify the information in the national database, which was CSV formatted, into a research format, in our case into a SPSS file.

As an illustration a few interesting first year research outcomes are shown in the box.

We presented our first report in winter 2013. In the national student statistics we created groups on the basis of variables like prior education and analyzed their success rates. In this way it was possible to identify groups at risk of dropping out or of switching internally in their first year, and to identify groups that were less likely to graduate within the nominal timeframe. We then compared the success rates of these groups within the collaborating G5 UAS with the success rates within other big UAS in other parts of the country. It turned out that groups that are prone to institutional dropout in their first year were overrepresented at the G5 UAS. This overrepresentation was increasing over time. Even if the G5 cluster was compared with the most similar UAS outside the collaboration, overall dropout rates were still 10% higher in the G5 cluster, while internal switch rates were about 7% lower in the G5 cluster. We assumed this effect might be partially caused by the fact that all the G5 UAS are within one hour's traveling distance by public transport (free of charge for students). Switching from on program to the other usually means dropping out of your institution and continuing at another UAS rather than making a switch to another program within the same institute. The second quantitative study in the spring of 2014 showed that G5 students did indeed tend to switch to other institutions instead of switching within their institution.

An example of a study performed in our second year of collaboration regards a study on the role of socioeconomic factors and study success at UAS. The national student statistics database and the national database on the socioeconomic status (SES) of postal/zip codes were combined to estimate the SES of every student in the Dutch UAS. Contrary to our expectations, it transpired that students from our G5 UAS in the larger cities generally come from more affluent backgrounds. Students from the poorest families are very often ethnic minority students. When it comes to study success, it emerged that students from the poorest and the richest families did less well. Students from middle-income families performed best on a wide range of indicators of study success. Some of the differences in performance between the G5 UAS and the other large UAS in the Netherlands could be explained by SES (Kappe et al., 2015).

The first research project was inspired by the fact that in 2012 the Minister and the UAS agreed on targets regarding study success for the year 2015. These targets were for (a) first year dropout (retention rate); (b) switch rate in the first year (change of study program within the same UAS); (c) graduation rate. Our first research reports, amongst the one in which we reported the longitudinal trend in dropout, switch and graduation rates, were well received by our strategists and university boards. They also gained the attention of the National Association of UAS and we were provided with the opportunity to collate and publish our first reports in a book titled: *Study success in the G5* (Kappe et al., 2014), which was distributed to our stakeholders. The book gained even wider attention than the individual research reports. We started to present our work at several symposia on study success and now do so on a regular basis. Recently, a session was organized with researchers and G5 strategists in order to assess the policy implications of the research outcomes. From time to time the Ministry shows interest in our work and also the Association of (Research) Universities in the Netherlands is interested in the way the G5 UAS cooperate in the field of research on study success. Our latest research efforts have recently been published in a second book for which there is a lot of interest.

One of the major advantages of our G5 research collaboration is that we can share and use data that individual institutions do not have access to. Another is the pooling of resources, which makes it possible to perform large scale studies that cannot be performed by the smaller institutional research units of the individual UAS. The collaboration also secures a certain level of quality, but also a growth of expertise of the researchers involved. Another important advantage is the opportunity to share and compare. Sharing provides a much broader base for assessing the effects of interventions on study success, despite the lack of a rigid research design. An attempt to assess the effects of interventions with compromised designs did, however, yield an unexpected result. Lecturers and policymakers have become much more interested in data and the effects of interventions. Lecturers seem to feel that they should reflect on their actions and evaluate the results they achieve with their students more often.

WHAT HAVE WE LEARNED

The members of the research team got to know each other in 2011 during the evaluation of the program to enhance the position of ethnic minority students in the UAS, which are situated in the western metropolitan region of the Netherlands. We did not yet know that we would be working together in the future. We simply shared information and research outcomes together with the group that evaluated the national study success program. Mutual interest in each other's research grew rapidly and formed a basis for organic knowledge exchanges. Given the possibility to work together, we immediately focused on content. Driven by our shared research interest, we initially did not spend much time on team building of underlying group processes. Tensions started to emerge after some time, most often when we approached deadlines. Some members made it clear that they could not remain motivated and stay connected in this way. A focal point of tension turned out to be around the role of the chairman. He was freer in making important decisions than some members of the team had expected. In retrospect this was logical, since we never took the time to discuss our expectations. By the time that a process evaluation was scheduled much wisdom and insight had already emerged. We agreed on a set of principles and roles and clarified which decisions team members and the chair can make on their own and which decisions require team consultation. This strengthened the group to a large extent and made us much more aware of and sensitive to our own group process.

Working for a UAS and the Team at the Same Time

We all work for different UAS with, on the one hand different cultures, strengths and weaknesses, and at the same time similarities and similar processes on many levels. It seems that the culture and values that come with being a researcher are very strong. The cultural differences between our UAS that we also carry with us are rather weak compared to the values that bind us together (culture of profession vs. culture of organization). We manage to easily respect and capitalize on the differences between our UAS. Maybe because we, as researchers, look at our organizations with a certain detachment, which enables us to see both the positive and negative themes that come with our cultures. Organizational differences are always a source of humor in our team. So we have to conclude that the issue(s) we had in our team did not have to do with cultural differences between our organizations. It seems the struggle in our group was an archetypal struggle, the type you will find in many (traditional) books about group dynamics. Tuckman (1965) talks about forming, storming (power struggle), norming, performing. Theorists like Schutz (1958) also see stages in group development, but considered these processes as circular, so we should expect more struggles in the future. Other theories focus on group roles (Forsyth, 2009). For us, the level of inclusion in the group is also important, since we can playfully choose between being a dedicated member of the G5 research team or primarily being an employee of our UAS. In retrospect, it seems our struggle was primarily about who could decide what.

About which issues need team consultation and which decisions can be decided by individual team members and/or the chairman. It seems we have currently found a good balance and can be productive as a team. As mentioned previously, last year our team expanded with the entry of an additional UAS, namely UAS Leiden. The new team member has a much more action-oriented and qualitative research background. It then became clear that we had developed our own team culture, but eventually a focus on action research and qualitative research turned out to be a welcome contribution.

We have learned to be patient as well. Working for a UAS and a team means juggling with priorities. For this reason and because of the sometimes unpredictable nature of the research we do, deadlines are not always met. Eventually, however, we succeed in getting the work done, helped by the fact that we also really like what we are doing and are committed to results. Sometimes we help each other in all kinds of ways. If a structural problem with workload emerges in the work life of one of the team members, the chair sometimes flags this up to the strategist of the UAS involved.

Communication and Dissemination, Transparency and Politics

In the process of creating a research agenda it is very important to be in contact with strategists and boards to know what their focus is. Our first report was received well by the G5 strategists and boards and generated a lot of questions that were addressed in the next research agenda. We did not only report about the differences between our UAS as a cluster and other large UAS as a cluster, but we also gave more specific insights into the individual G5 UAS. Some strategists/board members became rather reluctant to publish this kind of information. They felt it was better not to distribute research outcomes on a bigger scale before more research was done. We decided to create internal and external versions (without in-depth information about specific UAS) of our reports. We also decided to present our reports to our strategists and boards before dissemination to a larger audience than G5 research professionals. This procedure seemed to work rather well. Trust increased between the G5 research team and the boards and strategists who became less reserved over time. As was indicated in the previous section, the steady dissemination of research outcomes means that we are seen as an example of successful cooperation and gives us the opportunity to discuss our results with many parties. These discussions provide

us with new input and ideas. We tend to think that our research input deepens cooperation on a strategic level. The themes we work on are compared
and discussed by the strategists and the boards. This shows even more that
we have common issues, like study success, and that cooperation is the way
forward. Our successful cooperation might have inspired the boards to create another "thematic" G5 team around a new Dutch phenomenon called
"matching." Matching allows students to reflect on their study choice after
they have submitted their application to a UAS. Every UAS developed its
own matching procedure so they vary between institutions in content and
intensity. The G5 research team monitors what happens to students that
participate in matching. Policy reasons mean it is not possible to evaluate
here the effects with an experimental research design, but sharing data
makes it possible to compare the effect on dropout and retention rates
between different matching procedures.

We seem to be linked into the strategy process rather well, but we
strongly feel the need to contribute to education itself. We should translate
our results in such a way that they are of increasing interest to faculties, lecturers and, preferably, students. An example of an effort in this direction is
the interactive Internet tool we developed that shows student movements
on a study program level between our G5 institutions, to other UAS, to
research universities or to a life outside higher education.

THE NEXT STEP

Softer and Harder Research at the Same Time

We have now gained insight into the success rates of a variety of groups
and in the movements of students between institutions of higher education.
We will continue to monitor developments and trends in this field and
remain committed to this database-driven research, but it seems we are in a
transitional phase. It is time for us to move to other kinds of research.

We want to deeper understand how we can improve student success. We
are now exploring differences in study success at similar programs (e.g.,
business & management studies, pedagogy) between the G5 UAS. The
question is whether we can, after adjusting for the composition of the student population, find reasons for any of the differences? This kind of
research is qualitative (some would say "softer") in nature and, we think,
complementary to searching for correlations in large data files. This

approach needs insight into educational processes and discussions with lecturers and management of study programs. If we find variables that seem to be relevant to study success, it might be possible that we could transfer these into generic factors that could fuel effective interventions. During a phase of action research, exploring the effect of interventions brings us back to a well-known theme: the need to measure the effects of interventions. We still need to embrace experimental (some would say "harder") designs when we want to make a proper assessment of the effects of interventions or the changes at stake.

CONCLUSION: SUCCESS FACTORS FOR INTERINSTITUTIONAL COLLABORATION

The purpose of this chapter was to share the journey of the emergence, development and continuation of our joint research effort between six UAS, including some results of our joint research. Upon reflection we conclude that our successful cooperation was realized because certain factors were in place. We think that, depending on the kind of cooperation and the situation at hand, it is worth considering whether the factors we found are relevant to other situations. Important factors for cooperation in our team were:

• Access to data and information (in our case a national database)
• Continuing interest for a common topic (in our case study success)
• Opportunity to benchmark and compare with peer institutions
• Top-level commitment and connection to developments at board level
• Pooling and availability of dedicated research time of 0.4 fte at each UAS
• Combining data, ideas, and policy processes delivers value
• Ability to do things that single parties are not able to do; useful results for all stakeholders
• Personal growth of the people involved at all levels
• Awareness of group dynamics and, preferably, chemistry
• Collaborative action in third-party/governmental issues

REFERENCES

Forsyth, D. R. (2009). *Group dynamics*. New York, NY: Wadsworth.

Kappe, F. R., Molenkamp, M. J. D., Wijsbroek, D. H. J., Wiegert, O., Hendriks, G., & van Ingen, J. A. (2014). *Studiesucces in de G5. [Study success in the G5 metropole]*. Haarlem: Inholland Press.
Kappe, F. R., Molenkamp, M. J. D., Wijsbroek, D. H. J., Wiegert, O., Hendriks, G., Van Ingen, J. A., & Van Zandwijk, J. (2015). Studiesucces in de G5. Opbrengsten studiesuccesonderzoek door zes Randstadhogescholen. Haarlem: Inholland Press.
Knol, M. (2013). *Improving university lectures with feedback and consultation.* Amsterdam: Ipskamp.
Schutz, W. (1958). *FIRO: A three-dimensional theory of interpersonal behavior.* New York, NY: Rinehart.
Slavin, R. E. (2008). Perspectives on evidence-based research in education (what works). *Educational Researcher, 37*(1), 5–14.
Tinto, V. (2012). *Completing college: Rethinking institutional actions.* Chicago, IL: University of Chicago Press.
Tuckman, B. W. (1965). Developmental sequence in small groups. *Psychological Bulletin, 63*, 384–399.
Van den Bogaard, M. E. D. (2015). *Towards an action-oriented model for first year engineering student success. A mixed methods approach.* Delft: Delft University of Technology. doi:10.4233/uuid:7e3ea63e-3f28-4f9d-a340-95acc8828763
Van der Westen, W., & Wijsbroek, D. H. J. (2014). Taalbeheersing een garantie voor studiesucces? In *Dynamic Dialogue, duurzame professionalisering in het hbo.* Den Haag: De Haagse Hogeschool.

More information about the Dutch system of higher education:

Nuffic. *The education system in the Netherlands.* Retrieved from https://www.nuffic.nl/en/library/education-system-the-netherlands.pdf
Website of the Association of Universities in the Netherlands (VSNU) with a list of the research universities in the Netherlands. Retrieved from www.vsnu.nl
Website of the Vereniging Hogescholen, the Netherlands Association of Universities of Applied Sciences (former HBO-Raad) with a list of all universities of applied sciences. Retrieved from www.vereninghogescholen.nl

THE EVOLUTION OF A FOUNDATION PROGRAM: REFLECTIONS ON THE FIVE YEAR PARTNERSHIP BETWEEN UNIVERSITY COLLEGE LONDON AND NAZARBAYEV UNIVERSITY

Dominic Mahon and Rachel Niklas

ABSTRACT

The purpose of this chapter is to investigate and explore the five year partnership between University College London (UCL) and Nazarbayev University (NU) in Astana, Kazakhstan. Now that the partnership has ended, there are many valuable lessons that have been learned. This chapter will report on interviews with key members of staff from both UCL and NU revealing their reflections about what went well, the most important lessons that have been learned. The goal of the study is to explore the expertise and experiences of those involved in the UCL/NU partnership in order to provide a record and contribute to the scholarly body of work on Higher Education partnerships. Critical case sampling

University Partnerships for Academic Programs and Professional Development
Innovations in Higher Education Teaching and Learning, Volume 7, 93–109
Copyright © 2016 by Emerald Group Publishing Limited
All rights of reproduction in any form reserved
ISSN: 2055-3641/doi:10.1108/S2055-364120160000007016

(purposeful sampling) was employed to select staff members from UCL and NU who were involved in key roles in the establishment and running of the foundation program. It was necessary to include only those staff who had both a key role, and were involved throughout the entirety of the project. Subsequently a small sample of four participants representing both UCL and NU were involved in semi structured interviews. In order to ensure confidentiality, the initials of these individuals have been changed. The interviews revealed a series of key recommendations when entering into transnational higher education partnerships. These are the importance of cultural understanding, patience and flexibility.

Keywords: Partnerships; collaboration; academic; interinstitutional; university

INTRODUCTION

The following chapter focuses on the five year partnership between University College London (UCL) and Nazarbayev University (NU) in Astana, Kazakhstan.

From its inception, the development model for Nazarbayev University was based on partnerships with top ranking universities from around the world. The aim was to develop a world-class university and research institute which, by 2020, would 'appear in the upper third of various international university ranking league tables' (Nazarbayev University, 2013, p. 24). The standards upon which the university would operate were to be recognised and accepted internationally. Such an institution was considered to be vital to the growth, development and economy of the society of Kazakhstan.

Each of the University's schools was developed in cooperation with a world-renowned university. Those institutions were as follows:

- University College London (UK) – partner in the Centre for Preparatory Studies and School of Engineering
- University Wisconsin-Madison (USA) – partner in the School of Humanities and Social Sciences
- University of Pittsburgh (USA) – partner in the School of Medicine
- Duke University, Fuqua School of Business (USA) – partner in the Graduate School of Business

- National University of Singapore, Lee Kuan Yew School of Public Policy (Singapore) – partner in the Graduate School of Public Policy
- University of Pennsylvania (USA) – partner in the Graduate School of Education
- University of Cambridge (UK) – partner in the Graduate School of Education

In September 2010 the first cohort of students arrived at the university and entered UCL's foundation program. A foundation year was deemed necessary for all students because the secondary education system of Kazakhstan at that time ended a year earlier than that of most western secondary education systems. Students entering the foundation all studied English for Academic Purposes (EAP) but had the choice of also studying Biology and Chemistry, Mathematics and Physics or International Relations and Economics. Having successfully completed the foundation year, students would then choose the faculty they wanted to enter into as full undergraduate students. Approximately 2,500 students, all beneficiaries of full scholarships for their education, have passed through the foundation program in the last five years.

Now that the partnership has come to an end, many valuable lessons have been learned. This chapter will report on interviews with key members of staff from both UCL and NU, revealing their reflections about what went well, the most important lessons that have been learned and what they would do differently if they were starting over again.

The goal of the study is to explore the expertise and experiences of those involved in the UCL/NU partnership in order to provide a record and contribute to the scholarly body of work on Higher Education partnerships. Critical case sampling (purposeful sampling) was used to select staff members from UCL and NU who were involved in key roles in the establishment of the foundation program and who were involved throughout the lifespan of the partnership. Subsequently a small sample of four participants representing both UCL and NU were interviewed in order to obtain their personal reflections on the project. In order to ensure confidentiality, the initials of these individuals have been changed.

CONTEXT

After the fall of the Soviet Union and Kazakhstan's independence in 1991, the country underwent dramatic change in the education sector. According to UNICEF (n.d.) the Kazakhstani education system has seen reforms in the form of increased expenditure, modified education laws, new schools and state-wide standards for education. In addition to these changes, Heyneman (2011) explains that after the collapse of the Soviet Union, Central Asia has experienced transformations in structure, curriculum, educational opportunity and exposure to international information. With these reforms in mind, Nazarbayev University is a remarkable example of such development. This university is uniquely structured and, unlike any other in Kazakhstan, is based on a partnership system with American and British Universities that aims towards the development of an elite university high up in international rankings.

The current climate in Kazakhstan of growth and progression has fostered the development of Nazarbayev University. This is largely owing to wealth coming from oil which has promoted financial growth and a thriving environment for investments (Sharman, 2012). Nursultan Nazarbayev has been the president of the country since 1991. His government strives to achieve modern development in the nation. Aitzhanova, Katsu, Linn, and Yezhov (2014) describe the government's 'Kazakhstan 2050' plan which is aimed towards economic, social and institutional development and sets a goal for Kazakhstan to become one of the top 30 developed nations by 2050. This plan is an illustration of the emphasis the nation's leaders are currently putting on education.

The word Bolashak is the Kazakh word for 'future' and the name of the scholarship that was developed by the Kazakh government in order to equip students with the knowledge and skills necessary for a competitive international economic environment. This study abroad programme was a common path for the elite students of Kazakhstan and an excellent opportunity for these students to get a Western education in countries such as the U.S. and England funded by the government. Abazov (2011) explains the rationale of the programme is to send students abroad to study progressive fields such as energy production and engineering. Since 1993, 11,126 students have benefitted from the programme (Bolashak, 2015). However, along with elements of success, the programme has experienced some problems with returning students adjusting to the work environment once back home, limited jobs available for graduates and the loss of strong students (brain drain) in local universities. Tolymbek (2006) wrote that a solution to address these issues would be to advance university standards within Kazakhstan which ultimately was implemented as a focused aim with the opening of

Nazarbayev University in 2010. In 2011, grants for bachelors programs were discontinued (Bolashak, 2015).

In addition to the need to accommodate the nation's best students within the country, there were two other areas that required consideration with regard to the higher education system in Kazakhstan. The two areas highlighted as issues were language and the legacy of Soviet organisation and corruption.

LANGUAGE FACTORS

The English language appears to be a key element of the internationalisation of HE and as a result it was important to develop English in the Kazakhstani higher education system. There is pressure among many states to incorporate English into their education systems. One implication of not doing so is that research findings not published in English are easily overlooked. This can be illustrated by publications in Russian, as Kirchik, Gingras, and Larivière (2012) point out, 'In 2011 the Russian electronic scientific library (e-library.ru) comprised no less than 6,834 scientific journals produced in Russia, 6,426 of which are published in the Russian language, virtually invisible to colleagues from other countries' (p. 1412). This lack of recognition was observed with regard to research on the disposal of nuclear waste carried out in Kazakhstan after the fall of the Soviet Union. As TG observed:

> New scientists will transform themselves into nuclear waste experts. So actually you kept the momentum going in terms of the advances in nuclear research, but what they were doing was they were publishing in Russian, so the world didn't know a lot about this.

The language issue for Kazakhstan has been a particularly complicated one because Russian was the lingua franca of the Soviet Union and a successfully implemented one. Kazakhstan has multiple ethnicities, with the 2009 estimated breakdown being Kazakh 63.1%, Russian 23.7%, Uzbek 2.9%, Ukrainian 2.1%, Uighur 1.4%, Tatar 1.3%, German 1.1%, other 4.4% (Central Intelligence Agency, 2015). Russian is known as the language of interethnic communication and many Kazakhstanis use Russian as their first language. In 2001 the estimate was that 95% were Russian speakers with 64.4% being Kazakh speakers (Central Intelligence

Agency, 2015). Subsequently, introducing an additional lingua franca was not an easy thing to do.

LEGACY OF SOVIET ORGANISATION AND CORRUPTION

The second issue facing HE in Kazakhstan was the legacy of Soviet administration. Higher education was under the control of a very centralised system which resulted in a lack of autonomy for institutions. Universities had limited scope to make curriculum or organisational choices and as Medeuov (2004) notes, such a system is 'not one consistent with the demands of democracy, a market economy, or the new information age' (p. 363). Furthermore, during the Soviet Union, universities were controlled by sectors and curriculum was often very straightforward because the employers, for instance factories, ran the university and the students would go straight from school to their work assignment (Heyneman, 2011). When the Soviet Union fell, this all changed rapidly and it is understandable that universities have struggled to keep up with the necessary modifications needed in order to internationalise.

As a result the new university would have a different governance structure. This is reflected in the university's core governance principles which stress independence in management and decision-making and which provide a 'guarantee of academic freedom of teachers and researchers within their research, educational, and clinical activities' (Nazarbayev University, 2013, p. 10).

This legacy also fed into the further problem of corruption in higher education. During the Soviet Union, the position of university professor offered high pay and status in society. However, with the upheaval in the years following the dispersal of the USSR, this all changed. Niyozov (2004) states that civil service salaries were reduced to a fraction of their previous worth after the fall of the Soviet Union. The decline in pay and quality of conditions resulted in supplementing income with gifts becoming a relatively common occurrence (McLendon, 2004). Many teachers reacted to this dire situation by resorting to corrupt measures. As McLendon notes, 'It is not uncommon to hear accounts, both first and second hand, about faculty and staff accepting material gifts from students in exchange for favourable grading, academic assessments, and selection or admission to university' (2004, p. 285). It was clear then that a degree of reform and a new approach was needed when facing the establishment of the new university.

THE ORIGINS OF THE PARTNERSHIP MODEL

The Bolashak program of scholarships for Kazakhstani students to study overseas started in 1993, right at the beginning of independence for Kazakhstan. However, as was noted earlier, it was clear that this was not a sustainable long term project to achieve the country's ambitious aims for higher education. As a result, it was decided that a world class university would be established in the capital, Astana. The question at this point, was what the university would look like. However, the goal from the point of view of both sides of the partnership seemed to be the same. As PH commented, 'we wanted to help Kazakhstan develop a modern western style education which would help develop the students and country'. A well-established route for emerging economies to tap into the world of elite university institutions was through the establishment of a branch campus. This model has been used with varying degrees of success in Vietnam, China, Malaysia, Dubai and several other nations. However, the development team in Kazakhstan did not want a branch campus. 'We didn't want to get dwarfed and did not want to be a branch campus. We didn't want to be a branch of say Georgetown, in the shadow of one big name' (VC).

One of the driving principles behind the establishment of the university was sustainability. It was felt that the branch campus model would not offer a guarantee of sustainability into the future. Furthermore, it was felt that a new institution needed to be built rather than adapting an existing university. As Salmi (2013) observes 'it may be easier to reach world-class status by establishing a new institution than by attempting to upgrade an existing one' (p. 9).This concept was the foundation for the idea of developing partnerships with multiple universities, one university for each department. The idea for this was formed quite unconventionally:

> After talking and talking, I said, jokingly, 'what if we invited a top university for each unit?'. My colleague looked and me and said 'it's a good idea'. That's how we started working. (VC)

Another difference with a multiple partnership model was that partners risked their reputation and name in ways that would not be the case with a branch campus. This initially made finding partners difficult. However, it was here that the Bolashak program proved to have great benefits. To begin with, it had facilitated the establishment of relationships with over 200 universities. In addition, the reputation of Kazakhstani students was very high. As VC stated, 'they (the partners) know us because of the quality of our students'. A sentiment backed up from the London side of the partnership.

> Kazakh students came to London to study and this proved very successful. It provided a foundation for the interest in UCL for the foundation program. (PH)

Also, experiences of visiting Kazakhstani universities reflected well on the students. As TG noted when recounting an anecdote about being questioned on the topic of corruption in the United Kingdom by students during a lecture in Almaty. After the lecture, a 10 minute scheduled question period turned into an hour and a quarter during which time TG had commented that corruption was not a feature of the UK HE system.

> I got back to Britain and two days later the Daily Telegraph started publishing details of the MPs expenses scandal. These young people got hold of my email address and individually sent me emails saying 'you said there was no corruption' and I thought, 'well, that is pretty good of them, I'm impressed'. So I wrote back to them. (TG)

From the first discussions in 2008 to signing the agreement took a year. LM expressed the interest some parties in London had from the start:

> When the scheme was advanced under the World Bank's auspices I thought that was very exciting and potentially transformational here. I'd always thought we'd missed out on these kinds of really sort of high level, national projects. ... I thought this was a pleasant climate with the potential for us to do something quite radically different in both its scale and scope.

In effect, a very short amount of time was allocated to find partners and begin running the university. In early 2009 there was a meeting of the potential partners in Kazakhstan. TG described the process by stating:

> It was something like a beauty competition. A best of breed ... I was the only person, we were the only university, arguing that we would be very interested in helping them to build a Kazakh university but that we didn't want to have a campus here ... what we felt was right for Kazakhstan was for it to have its own world leading research university. The other universities wanted satellite campuses.

The development team spent six weeks travelling around the various partner institutions they had connected with through the Bolashak program. UCL was the final stop on that tour. At that meeting, the foundation program was presented to the development team and they liked what they saw. LM recalled, 'they didn't see anything else that matched what we were offering – it was their last visit'.

UCL made an agreement with Nazarbayev University to run the foundation year program for the school for a period of five years. This foundation year would make up for the one year of high school that Kazakhstani schools lacked in comparison to their British and American counterparts. The course that was to be taught at NU was an exact replica of the undergraduate preparatory certificate that is taught at UCL's centre for languages and international education. As a part of this agreement UCL would also run the entrance exams that would divide students into three subject areas: maths and physics, biology and chemistry and international relations and economics. The entrance exam was important as it would ensure transparency in the admission procedures and provide the university with a credible foundation. At the end of the foundation year the students would be awarded a certificate from UCL and would move on to their faculty programs in the university. The importance of this foundation year was not underestimated:

> The skills, and actually the basic things were really formed, shaped and moulded in the foundation year ... It was not only bridging but it was really changing the mentality of the young people who came from totally different cultural and academic backgrounds. (VC)

This partnership was quite different than the others at the university because a solid, internationally recognised foundation with an independently overseen admissions process was felt to be essential to the establishment of the reputation of the university. UCL was much more in control of the programme than the other partners involved with Nazarbayev University. Teaching staff in the programme was employed by UCL, which was not the case for the faculty in the other programs who were employed by NU. UCL's programme was the first to start running at NU and it began in September of 2010. The contract would last until 2015 when Nazarbayev University planned to take over the foundation year program. By this time the reputation of the university would have been established.

THE OBSTACLES

A Non-existent, Unknown University

We started from scratch. From zero. (VC)

At the beginning one of the most significant obstacles was that there physically was no university. Prior to that, the first obstacle to be overcome was the law. Under that previous system, Universities were governed by the central government/ministries. A new law was brought in to guarantee autonomy, academic freedom and a new governing structure.

However, even after the law had changed, the lack of a physical university caused problems. As VC observed, 'other universities didn't want to work with a non existent, unknown university'. But the fact that UCL was the first to sign, the first to commit publically meant that the case had in effect been made and after that, other universities signed onto partnerships with the various schools at NU.

The scale of the construction project was enormous. Not only did a brand new campus need to be built from scratch, but time was limited and the building specifications coming from the partner universities were a change from what the country was accustomed to handling. Right from the start there were problems:

> Construction was a disaster at the beginning. We had to redesign and all the labs were redesigned ... The construction began in 2006. In September 2009, we had less than 9 months and there was nothing. Only walls, no roofs nothing. At that time we took everything into our hands. And we started redesigning. (VC)

UCL thought that Nazarbayev University would be able to progress with the construction without much involvement, but this was not the case. In London, assumptions were made that lists of materials requested were turning into orders and that those orders were materialising in Astana. However, this too was not the case. PH explained:

> It was not planned that I would visit as frequently as I did. I did visit at the beginning to talk about the laboratories, the plans and things, and then there was effectively a late spring and summer and even early autumn when people from NU came over to talk to us and there was list building. And what emerged when we started in autumn 2010 was that the laboratories had not been constructed ... I think that was an error. There was no particular reason why the laboratories couldn't be ready on time but I think NU and UCL underestimated the length of time that it takes.

The laboratories needed to match their counterparts in London and this was a huge undertaking complicated by the procurement of supplies from abroad. When the facilities were eventually installed there had been another lack of communication which resulted in them having to be stripped and installed a second time. However, although the delays were challenging, they were not fatal. The Kazakhstani teaching assistants helped with the setup of labs which worked well. Practicals started late in January and were not done in the correct order because there were only materials for later practicals rather than the earlier ones. However, as PH noted, 'out of this came the physics project which doesn't exist in London, but which is a positive thing'. Overall the campus construction was a massive undertaking and some factors were side-lined that should not have been. This aspect of the project has proved to be a valuable learning experience for both parties.

Bureaucracy

As noted earlier, one of the most significant issues facing the development of higher education in Kazakhstan has been dealing with a legacy of corruption. One of the methods established to overcome this problem was lengthy bureaucracy, which at times caused problems for the developing partnership. Procurement, for example, was one such issue:

> There was one time where people were getting very very upset about how difficult it was to get a box of pencils. You can't just go out and buy a box of pencils. You have procurement issues. Umpteen forms ... but you have to understand that this is a country which is struggling to defeat corruption and that is why they put in place all these terribly cumbersome things to try to put a stop to corruption ... So in a sense it's a real bore, but it's for a good purpose and you have got to see beyond the day to day irritation of it and see the wider aim of trying to eradicate corruption. (TG)

At a more strategic level, there were implications on the time it took to make decisions and how decisions were made. LM emphasised the implications of this by stating:

> Procurement and monitoring. Very important, but the overhead associated with them is crippling. The overhead in terms of time. If you have to get 12 people to sign a document then you need to have time.

From the point of view of NU, it was understood that bureaucracy could be a frustrating issue for partners coming from other countries. Instead of ignoring the matter, it was approached with care by ensuring that some steps were simplified and also by carefully explaining the reasons behind such bureaucratic steps. Although frustrating at times, these systems are in place to guarantee that government funding is being spent appropriately. VC explained how these situations were handled:

> Sometimes people get frustrated because of our bureaucracy, regulations and laws. For example, procurement procedures. It is not a private university and we are one hundred percent funded by the government and need to be held accountable for the money we are using ... We handled bureaucratic issues by trying to explain, wherever possible we tried to simplify the process by working together in 2011 with an American lawyer and

our chief lawyer on our strategy and laws and simplifying our procurement procedures.
In this way we have also influenced and changed the system in Kazakhstan.

Cultural Perceptions

In many ways one of the most difficult aspects from the Kazakhstani
perspective was to deal with the quite different UK and US cultures. As
VC noted, 'we learned a lot about how you operate in different cultures'.
One experience that stood out was the initial negotiations, which were
complicated due to cultural differences in how negotiations take place. The
team from London had certain cultural preferences, as TG remarked:

> I really don't like getting into game playing negotiation. I believe very strongly I will
> play straight. I will give you prices. This is it and we are not going to discuss it.

However, the Kazakhstani contingent were used to a different style of
negotiation. It was important culturally for them to reach a price based on
negotiation. The solution to this was to limit the number of people involved
in the negotiations, but this then had the knock on effect of upsetting the
side-lined members of the team from London. Ultimately an agreement
was reached because, as TG notes, both sides actually wanted the same
thing and both sides got what they thought was fair.

THE SUCCESS

Five years on, the university is up and running. After UCL signed, other
partners joined and now NU has close relationships with 12 top international universities. LM reflected on the experience by stating:

> We can be proud of the fact that we did it. I think this was a pretty ambitious, well
> very ambitious project. ... but the team really stepped up and did it. When you think
> about it, we signed on around the 19th of February and we opened in September that
> year. We recruited 50 or 60 staff. Involved with the testing of 4,000 students around the
> country. Recruited 500 students ... the spirit of working as a team was pretty remark-
> able really.

Perhaps the most obvious signal of the success of the partnership is the
first graduating class from Nazarbayev University. In June 2015, 446
undergraduate and graduate students graduated. Of those, 115 students
went on to pursue graduate degrees at elite international institutions,

indicating that the success enjoyed by Kazakhstani students under the Bolashak program is being continued.

> I was surprised by the quality of the students. In hindsight, perhaps I shouldn't have been. This is a national project and people wanted to get involved. Whereas in the UK, a start up operation like this would be more difficult to get people interested in. Of course people want to be part of a national project, but they were still putting their futures on the line, so you have got to admire their bravery. That exceeded my expectations really. (LM)

Conceivably less apparent is the change that the success of NU has made to the educational structure in the wider country. The influence has expanded beyond the institution. The secondary education system is moving to 12 years from 11. The 20 new Nazarbayev Intellectual Schools (NIS) have at the centre of their vision that students will be fluent in English (Nazarbayev Intellectual Schools, 2013) as these institutions are seen as preparatory for entry to NU. Anecdotal evidence suggests an improvement in English language proficiency across the country. Ten established universities are adopting elements of the NU model with the aim of becoming research led institutions specialising in the needs of the region in which they are located.

Additionally, in a further move to ensure academic integrity, the admissions process had to be transparent. This was another aspect of the partnership that proved a success:

> Especially with the help of UCL we were able to establish a transparent system of selecting students, the admissions process; that helped to gain a good reputation for us, that promoted Nazarbayev University as an internationally recognized university. (VC)

As discussed earlier, the establishment of a transparent and fair admissions system was very important to the success of Nazarbayev University. Having this in place from the beginning has shown their partners and the HE community around the world that they are committed to meeting international standards in higher education.

There were also benefits for UCL. In general the programme created opportunities for people to travel, acquire knowledge and skills and bring this back to UCL. Also a number of developments which started in Astana were implemented elsewhere. TG noted:

> The program created organic growth. It was the basis for other programs such as in Qatar. It helped to create innovative programs. The 6 months diploma in applied research methods for example, was based on work done here at UCL NU.

LESSONS LEARNED

The experiences of the five year partnership offer some lessons for those considering entry into similar partnerships in the future. Oelke (2014) states that the most important lesson in partnerships is learning from each other on a variety of levels and the challenges presented during the UCL/NU partnership provided both institutions with the opportunity for mutually beneficial learning experiences. Given the growing trend in the internationalisation of Higher Education coupled with the seeming decline of the branch campus model, different models of institutional partnerships are bound to emerge. There seems to be general consensus that the five year partnership was a success. However, the value of the insight here is in considering lessons for future university partnerships.

Firstly, an understanding of and tolerance towards culture is essential on both sides of any partnership. Etling and McGirr (2005) highlight the areas of language, non-verbal communication and stereotypes as potential problematic areas in terms of cultural misunderstanding when partaking in an international partnership. In order to overcome such potential issues it was found that individual relationships can be of great significance in building more robust subsequent relationships. Koehn (2014) presents the notion of symmetry in collaboration, emphasising the necessity of open and supportive relationships while planning and designing as well as identifying problems. This approach to relationship building can aid in breaking down cultural misunderstandings that could be potentially damaging to programme development. Furthermore, an understanding of all the cultural factors impacting the relationships can make initial negotiations and subsequent interactions far smoother. Often the issues that seem insurmountable, can come down to a simple misunderstanding of how the other party operates. When the goals are aligned, as was the case with the UCL/NU partnership and cultures understood, successful interactions are far more likely. VC expressed this by observing:

> Of course like in every project, in everything we are doing, everyday life, we have some tensions when people work together which are unavoidable. But the main thing is understanding, tolerance and patience. And we really appreciate this understanding, tolerance, patience and friendship of our partner institutions.

In addition, it seems worth noting that universities are not single minded institutions but rather represent multiple and often conflicting viewpoints. As LM pointed out, 'it would have been better to get more institutional buy in back home'. Support from both sides plays an enormous role and

TG explained how much time was spent selling the endeavour to UCL in London where they were sceptical of the project. Koehn and Obamba (2014) further discuss the importance of symmetry and trust building during the beginning stages of the partnership along with ensuring that stakeholders aim to meet on a regular basis with an aim towards equal communication and decision-making (pp. 192–193). This could be applied to the case of UCL in that more support from London could have been achieved by clearer communication of the aims of the project and a better understanding of the situation and context in Kazakhstan.

Finally, and perhaps one of the most significant lessons, is the importance of flexibility. For reasons related to the nature of the contract mentioned earlier, NU wanted the UCL program as it was delivered in London. However, this was perhaps not the best fit:

> They wanted it to be totally the same as the program in London. I would say it can't be totally the same in that some of the things, especially things like History, there needs to be more of an understanding of what is Kazakhstan ... you need to look at the local environment and be sensitive to that .... It could be exactly the same standard, but not exactly the same content. (TG)

It was not the case that the exact same course was necessary. A result of the agreement was the course delivered needed to be the same and this did not provide room for changes. Throughout the progression of the programme, it became obvious that room for adaptation is necessary when working in a different context.

Finally, while recruiting the best fitting staff was an obvious requirement, it was also the case that recognising the contributions those staff made was noted as being important. The teaching staff working for UCL in Astana came from many different parts of the world and were thrown into quite a challenging, although rewarding project. As TG reflected:

> We weren't telling the colleagues here early enough, often enough and strongly enough what a transformational job they are doing here for Kazakhstan. And I think that the whole issue about the critical thinking in the schools and the fact that they are moving towards a 12 year school curriculum instead of 11and the fact that they are now strengthening the regional universities are all things that we have argued for. But I think it is the practice of our staff that really has been the main thing and we need to celebrate that because the teachers really have been extraordinary here and have really have been transforming and you are kind of pedagogical missionaries. It is changing people's lives. I think that we perhaps as an institution should have been celebrating that with our staff out here and saying 'this is why we admire you'. (TG)

This insight and the others noted in this chapter can be useful lessons not only for UCL, but also for university partnerships around the world.

The five year duration of UCL and NU's partnership was not accomplished without challenges but the overall feeling at the end of the project is one of achievement. These lessons will undoubtedly help NU as they enter a new phase of the foundation program as well as other higher education institutions interested in participating in similar partnerships.

REFERENCES

Abazov, R. (2011). *Kazakhstan takes universities global. The Central Asia-Caucasus Analyst*, April 13. Retrieved from http://www.cacianalyst.org/publications/analytical-articles/item/12262-analytical-articles-caci-analyst-2011-4-13-art-12262.html. Accessed on June 10.

Aitzhanova, A., Katsu, S., Linn, J. F., & Yezhov, V. (2014). *Kazakhstan 2050: Toward a modern society for all.* Retrieved from http://econpapers.repec.org/bookchap/oxpoxbooks/9780199450602.htm. Accessed on June 10.

Bolashak. (2015). *History of the program.* Retrieved from http://www.bolashak.gov.kz/en/o-stipendii/istoriya-razvitiya.html

Central Intelligence Agency. (2015). *Kazakhstan. In The World Factbook.* Retrieved from https://www.cia.gov/library/publications/the-world-factbook/geos/kz.html

Etling, A., & McGirr, M. (2005). Issues and procedures in forging international university partnerships. *Journal of International Agricultural and Extension Education, 12*(2), 15–21.

Heyneman, S. P. (2011). A Comment on the changes in higher education in the post-Soviet Union. In I. Silova (Ed.), *Globalization on the margins* (pp. 27–39). Charlotte, NC: Information Age Publishing.

Kirchik, O., Gingras, Y., & Larivière, V. (2012). Changes in publication languages and citation practices and their effect on the scientific impact of Russian science (1993–2010). *Journal of the American Society for Information Science and Technology, 63*(7), 1411–1419. doi:10.1002/asi.22642

Koehn, P. H. (2014). Developments in transnational research linkages: Evidence from US higher-education activity. *Journal of New Approaches in Educational Research, 3*(2), 52–58. doi:10.7821/naer.3.2.52-58

Koehn, P. H., & Obamba, M. O. (2014). *The transnationally partnered university: Insights from research and sustainable development collaborations in Africa* (pp. 192–193). New York, NY: Palgrave Macmillan.

McLendon, M. K. (2004). Straddling market and state: Higher education governance and finance reform in Kazakhstan. In S. P. Heyneman & A. J. DeYoung (Eds.), *The challenge of education in Central Asia* (pp. 275–294). Greenwich: Information Age Publishing.

Medeuov, Z. K. (2004). The reform of Kazakhstan's education system: The problems of state monopoly on higher education quality. In S. P. Heyneman & A. J. DeYoung (Eds.), *The challenge of education in Central Asia* (pp. 357–364). Greenwich: Information Age Publishing.

Nazarbayev Intellectual Schools. (2013). *Autonomous educational organization Nazarbayev Intellectual Schools – 2020 development strategy.* Retrieved from http://www.nis.edu.kz/en/about/str-doc/

Nazarbayev University. (2013). *Nazarbayev University strategy.* Retrieved from http://nu.edu. kz/cs/groups/public/documents/document/mdaw/mdmy/~edisp/apkecm.nu.edu.032561. pdf

Niyozov, S. (2004). The effects of the collapse of the USSR on teachers' lives and work in Tajikistan. In S. P. Heyneman & A. J. DeYoung (Eds.), *The challenge of education in Central Asia* (pp. 357–364). Greenwich: Information Age.

Oelke, N. D. (2014). The benefits of international university partnerships: The perspectives of a Canadian faculty member. *Revista Gaúcha de Enfermagem, 35*(1), 12–13.

Salmi, J. (2013). Can young universities achieve world-class status? *International Higher Education, 70,* 2–3. Retrieved from http://ejournals.bc.edu/ojs/index.php/ihe/article/view/8701

Sharman, A. (2012). Modernization and growth in Kazakhstan. *Central Asia Journal of Global Health, 1*(1). Retrieved from http://cajgh.pitt.edu/ojs/index.php/cajgh/article/view/11

Tolymbek, A. (2006). Public policies in the higher education of Kazakhstan. *Social Sciences Research Network.* Retrieved from http://papers.ssrn.com/sol3/papers.cfm?abstract_id=1928311

UNICEF. (n.d.). *Country profile: Education in Kazakhstan.* Retrieved from http://www.unicef.org/ceecis/Kazakhstan.pdf

CROSS-COUNTRY FACULTY LEARNING COMMUNITY: AN OPPORTUNITY FOR COLLABORATION AROUND THE SCHOLARSHIP OF TEACHING AND LEARNING

Anabella Martinez, Cathy Bishop-Clark
and Beth Dietz

ABSTRACT

In 2013−2014 academic year, the authors led a Faculty Learning Community (FLC) on the Scholarship of Teaching and Learning (SoTL). The goal of the FLC was to increase participants' knowledge of and experience with SoTL. The facilitators resided and worked in United States; the co-facilitator and the participants worked at Universidad Del Norte in Colombia South America. The facilitators in the United States spoke English; the participants spoke Spanish. While the technology was sometimes problematic, the translation difficult, and the distance inhibiting, overall the learning community was very

University Partnerships for Academic Programs and Professional Development
Innovations in Higher Education Teaching and Learning, Volume 7, 111−139
Copyright © 2016 by Emerald Group Publishing Limited
All rights of reproduction in any form reserved
ISSN: 2055-3641/doi:10.1108/S2055-364120160000007017

successful in meeting its goals. We conclude with the lessons learned from this cross-cultural FLC experience.

Keywords: Partnerships; faculty; university; community; international; SOTL

INTRODUCTION

Knowledge of how people learn has expanded tremendously in recent years. For example, cognitive approaches to the study of learning suggest that deep processing of information leads to better recall of the material (Chew, 2010). Similarly, the contributions of neuroscience have led to changes in education that focus on how information is processed by the brain (Doyle & Zakrajsek, 2013; Medina, 2008). Advances and innovations in our understanding of learning ultimately require application of the methods that faculty use to teach, as well as tests of whether or not those methods are effective. There are, of course, many ways for faculty to educate themselves about these innovations in learning, but doing so inevitably requires time and manipulation of ever-increasing demands (Flaherty, 2014). To help ease those burdens, it is helpful to have faculty development opportunities (Kuijpers, Houtveen, & Wubbels, 2010). One faculty development approach is participation in Faculty Learning Communities (FLCs). FLCs provide a supportive structure for faculty to learn about new approaches to learning, as well as the methods necessary to test the effectiveness of those approaches.

In this chapter, we will report on an exploratory study that assessed the effectiveness of a cross-country FLC focused on testing new approaches to teaching and learning. The name of the FLC was *Cambio Magistral 2 (the name of the course transformation initiative at Universidad del Norte)*, and we will refer to it in the rest of the text as the SOTL FLC. We will first provide a brief overview of FLCs, including the definitions and effectiveness of FLCs. We will focus on alternative FLC formats before describing the structure and format of our cross-country FLC. Finally, we will report on our analysis of the effectiveness of the cross-country FLC with regard to faculty learning.

FACULTY LEARNING COMMUNITIES

Generally speaking, FLCs are defined as a group of people who actively engage in a collaborative program around a topic, which might be general or specific (Cox, 2004). As Cox (2004) notes, some FLCs are organized topically, such as "use of technology in teaching and learning" or "writing across the curriculum." Others might be cohort based, such as a group of pre-tenured faculty. Regardless of the type of FLC, there is a strong emphasis on "community," which is demonstrated by a sense of interdependence, concern for one another, and a commitment to the goals of the FLC. Although there are differences in FLCs, they tend to share a number of characteristics, including shared values and vision, collective responsibility, reflective professional inquiry of educational issues, collaboration, and the promotion of group and individual goals (Stoll, Bolam, McMahon, Wallace, & Thomas, 2006). Clearly, to the extent that these characteristics are displayed, the stronger the sense of community.

One potential goal of a FLC is to aid in professional development. Because education is an ever-changing landscape, faculty and staff need to constantly attend to professional development. FLCs can clearly serve that goal and meet the needs of faculty in this regard. But there are other goals that participation in FLCs can meet. While most of these goals are related to teaching and learning, such as increasing interest in teaching and learning, creating awareness of the complexity of teaching and learning, and encouraging reflection about teaching and learning, others focus on career-oriented aspects, such as getting to know faculty in other disciplines and aiding in promotion and tenure (Cox, 2004).

Overall, FLCs are effective in meeting their goals of improvement of instruction. For example, Brydges et al. (2013) report a number of positive benefits of participating in a yearlong FLC about issues in student learning, including increased knowledge of educational research, increased awareness of student learning in large classes, and greater awareness of the benefits of teaching assistants. Similarly, in a review of the literature on FLCs, Stoll et al. (2006) report that they are generally effective in improving instruction. Daly (2011) linked the enhancement of faculty learning and growth with specific characteristics of the FLC. Specifically, when FLCs allowed for autonomy in activities, provided opportunities to build areas of competence, and built relationships across departments, faculty learning was strengthened. Of course, when faculty learning is strengthened, pedagogical improvements abound. As an example, Hershberger et al. (2009) report on the ripple effect for faculty: "identifying ways to teach more *efficiently* not only strengthened their research agendas, but also led simultaneously to more *effective* teaching" (p. 147). More comprehensively, Vescio, Ross, and Adams (2008) found in their review of the research that participation in FLCs impacts teaching practice and benefits students as well (as evidenced by improved achievement scores).

It seems clear, then, that FLCs tend to be effective in meeting their goals, whether those goals involve faculty improvement, improved teaching, or enhanced student learning. Likewise, there is a need to provide evidence attesting to the effectiveness of pedagogical innovations in improving student learning. In the next section, we provide a brief overview of the tools that faculty can use to assess the effectiveness of innovative teaching and learning ideas – the Scholarship of Teaching and Learning.

In a study of those interested in SoTL, Healey (2003) found that 90% of participants agree that SoTL "involves studying, reflecting on, and communicating about teaching and learning, especially within the context of one's discipline" (p. 14). Shulman (1999) defines SoTL with similar attributes. These are: "It becomes public; it becomes an object of critical review and evaluation by members of one's community; and members of one's community begin to use, build upon, and develop those acts of mind and creation" (p. 15). There is clearly a role for SoTL in the evidence-based culture that has permeated education. Faculty and institutions are being called upon to articulate student learning outcomes, and then to provide evidence that these outcomes have been achieved. Therefore, it is no surprise that institutions are encouraging faculty to become more scholarly in their approach to teaching and to student learning. At some institutions, there are FLCs devoted to SoTL. Richlin and Cox (2004), for example, report on the effectiveness of a SoTL FLC. Likewise, Maurer, Sturges, Shankar, Allen, and Akbarova (2010) provide a case study of a FLC that focused on SoTL, showing how the FLC was productive and rewarding for all of the participants. Both of these cases included institutions that housed SoTL experts, making the conduct of the FLC more efficient. If an institution does not have these expertise, there may be a need to extend beyond the institution and make use of an alternative FLC format.

ALTERNATIVE FLC FORMATS

A review of the literature reveals a number of FLCs that make use of online technology. This type of format is worthy of exploration if an institution does not have local expertise on a particular topic of interest. One type of format is completely online, whereby all communication is conducted virtually (either synchronous, asynchronous, or a combination).

Chen, Chen, and Tsai (2009) report on the effectiveness of an online FLC focused on assessment for math teachers that communicated primarily with online synchronous discussions. Interviews with FLC members revealed that the online discussions were not viewed as effective and helpful. Similarly, Macdonald and Poniatowska (2011) describe a learning community about the use of online tools for supporting students. Their participants report that although the discussions stimulated creative thinking, there was a need for more community building and interaction. In a more positive experience with online FLCs, Tsai, Laffey, and Hanuscin (2010) indicate that members reported developing a sense of community and gained additional knowledge and confidence in their teaching.

There are also FLCs that make use of hybrid formats, combining face-to-face and virtual interactions. In two separate studies, Matzat (2010, 2013) reports on the benefits of having a blended FLC. For example, in mixed communities (a blend of virtual and real-life) there is more trust and less free riding, but membership stability is compromised. The increase in trust is likely due to "embeddedness," which Matzat defines as the extent to which FLC members share activities and interests in common. Not only does embeddedness reduce the issue of free riding that is so often evident in virtual groups (Matzat, 2010), but it is also shown to improve teaching skills, improve teacher knowledge of the subject, and greater receptivity to information (Matzat, 2013). Overall, there are mixed results about alternative (to the traditional face to face) formats for learning communities. These are challenges that any online community faces, but there appear to be advantages to having a hybrid or mixed format. On the face of it, a hybrid format appears to offer the advantages of online features with those of face to face.

None of these studies or cases address the issue of crossing cultural or geographic boundaries. Nor they do they explore the possibility of an online component within an FLC with professors in the same location. What if an institution encouraged faculty to engage in a particular topic, but the local expertise did not support that topic? And what if the experts were in a different country and spoke a different language? One solution is to develop a cross-country FLC, where the participants and a facilitator are in one country, and the other facilitators are in another. To date, we can find no evidence for the existence or effectiveness of a cross-country FLC. When the need for a SoTL FLC in one country with little SoTL expertise arose, a cross-country FLC, which used hybrid elements, was formed. The possibility of developing a new form of FLC that included a cross-cultural component led to the following considerations at the planning stage: (1) communicating with language differences; (2) creating community at a distance; and (3) FLC curriculum pertinence. In regards to the first aspect, when planning we were not sure how much this would impact the FLC participants given that they reported being able to understand English; experience showed us differently, which led to adjustments. For the second aspect, we initially planned for a site visit midway through the FLC in order to provide an opportunity for face-to-face interaction. For the final aspect, we planned to explore FLC needs and interests in regards to SOTL; we did have information from the on-site co-facilitator that these professors had none or limited prior experience in undertaking SOTL projects. In addition, there was also the question of the pertinence of the curriculum on SOTL given the cultural differences.

A CROSS COUNTRY SOTL FACULTY LEARNING COMMUNITY

Content and Organization

The SoTL Faculty Learning community described in this paper was one in which the facilitators of the learning community were in the United States (English speaking) and the participants were in Colombia South America (Spanish speaking). The learning community started in July of 2013 and was completed in May of 2014. The community met every three to four weeks. Initially, both facilitators were in the United States; however, a facilitator in Colombia was added in the first month. The two US facilitators had experience leading SoTL Faculty Learning communities at their home institution; the Colombia facilitator led the Center for Teaching Excellence at Universidad del Norte. The Colombia facilitator also spoke fluent Spanish and English. An online learning-management system (Blackboard) was used to post resources and facilitate conversation. E-mail, webex, and conference calls were used for communication.

The content of the community was organized around the structure of the book, Engaging in the Scholarship of Teaching and Learning: A Guide to the Process, and How to Develop a Project from Start to Finish (Bishop-Clark & Dietz-Uhler, 2012). All participants had copies of this book. This practical book leads participants through a process of designing and implementing their own SoTL projects in a hands-on fashion. There were three types of interactions in the learning community: lectures, a site visit and remote consulting sessions with individuals or small groups. The lectures included presentations and conversation around the various stages of creating a SoTL project. The facilitators created lectures to include activities, conversation with one another as well as conversation with the facilitators. About half way through the learning community, the US facilitators visited the participating faculty at Universidad del Norte. For several days the facilitators worked face to face with participants both in small groups, and in larger groups. After the site visit, the facilitators began consulting with the SoTL teams. Each team (or individual) worked on their own SoTL project and therefore had unique questions and issues. The consulting sessions allowed the facilitators to advise on the individual issues each group experienced.

FLC Participants and Projects

The SOTL FLC participants were seven full time faculty members at Universidad del Norte from STEM. Six professors were male and one was a female; five had Ph.Ds and two had masters' degrees. All taught in the STEM discipline and each worked on a SoTL project. Table 1 provides further information on the nature of the projects of the FLC participants.

Table 1. SOTL FLC Projects and Participants.

Proposal Title	Course Involved	Number of Faculty Involved	Number of Sections Involved	Number of Students Involved
Teaching and assimilation of physics concepts, principles and laws applying TFEAM theory	Heat-wave physics	2	1	120
Educational strategies for a differential equations course	Differential equations	2	4	257
Significant learning in physics through the project-based learning and home experiments	Heat-wave Physics	2	1	120
Student engagement techniques in a large lecture physics class	Heat-wave Physics	1	1	120

The Lectures

There were six two-hour lectures, each sequentially organized around steps in the SoTL research process. Lectures initially included conversation and questions. Skype or WebEx was used as the technology to connect the participants with the two facilitators in the US. Each of the chapters and corresponding lectures had two primary goals. The first goal was to provide enough background information and resources so that participants could successfully complete the steps in the research process. The background information included a review of the literature and knowledge particular to each of the five steps. Also the facilitators gave practical examples and illustrations of SoTL studies to highlight particular aspects of the step. Often those examples included studies that the facilitators had implemented in their own classrooms. The second and primary goal of each lecture and corresponding chapter was to provide participants with a step-by-step guide to help them work through all of the steps of their SoTL project. Each of these lectures ended with a worksheet assignment which corresponded to the topic. For instance when the topic was "Generating the Research Idea" participants were asked to identify general topics, create more specific topics, identify literature related to that topic, read their research questions to at least two other colleagues, and create a refined research question. The facilitators asked participants to post their worksheets on a shared Blackboard site. The five lectures are: introduction and overview of SoTL, generating the research question, designing the study, collecting and analyzing data, and reporting results.

The Site Visit

In December 2013, the facilitators in the United States visited the Universidad Del Norte in Colombia, South America. The US facilitators had worked with the participants through e-mail, Blackboard, WebEx and/ or Skype, but had not yet met face to face. The formal two-day visit included sessions with individual team members as well as sessions oriented with the larger groups. The informal part of the visit allowed the US facilitators to learn more about the people, the culture, the University and the country. Getting to know several of the members prior to the formal and more structured visit created a friendly and open atmosphere.

We began the site visit by meeting with each of the four teams to talk about the individual projects. Each team was at a different stage in the development of their SoTL project. Although we were several months into the learning community, some of the groups were struggling to clearly define their research questions. Other groups not only had a well-defined research question but also had piloted their project. Working individually with each team allowed the facilitators to meet the groups where they were and move forward. These one-on-one sessions proved to be quite valuable. Because the facilitators had been working with participants on their projects throughout the learning community it was possible to make substantial progress in that hour. Each team was left with an "assignment" for the following day. Some teams were asked to reconsider their research question while others were asked to incorporate some qualitative methods into the design of the project. The following day we met with each team and made additional progress.

While some of the participants could understand and speak English quite well, others could speak only Spanish. Nonetheless, some of the SoTL sessions were translated. Both the facilitators and the participants wore earphones and microphones. When the facilitators spoke, a translator in a separate room translated the English to Spanish. The participants could then hear the lecture or conversation in Spanish. Similarly, when the participants spoke, the translator spoke in English so the facilitators could hear questions and comments in English. This allowed the conversation to occur in real time. While the conversation was awkward in the beginning, everyone adjusted quickly and the conversation flowed naturally.

*Remote Consulting Sessions with Individuals or
Small Groups*

After the site visit, it became clear that additional one-on-one time with each group would be very beneficial. While it was not initially planned the facilitators added two separate individual sessions with each of the groups in the Spring of 2014. These consulting sessions allowed the facilitators to address issues specific to a project. For instance, due to some mix up with technology, in one case the treatment group did not get the intended treatment. The group had to create an alternate design. One group had a particularly difficult time identifying a clear, unambiguous research questions. The facilitators worked to identify an appropriate question. In sum, these sessions helped to clarify questions about the specific projects that came up during their implementation.

ASSESSMENT OF THE SOTL FLC

In this section, we describe the process used to assess the FLC. We drew on information regarding participants' satisfaction with the activities conducted in the FLC, as well as their views on how participating in such activities contributed to what they learned about SOTL. We used both quantitative and qualitative techniques. We present our assessment organized around the FLC constructs that were studied. These include views on FLC goals, satisfaction with SOTL FLC experience, effect of SOTL FLC on attainment of participants' learning outcomes, and effect of SOTL FLC on participant's views of teaching and learning. Table 2 illustrates the alignment of each of the phases of the assessment process with the instruments used and the constructs explored.

Assessment Results

Views on FLC goals
In order to explore participants' views on the goals of the SOTL FLC, they completed the Faculty Learning Community Goals Inventory (Sandell, Wigley, & Kovalchick, 2004) (see Appendix A). Participants completed this

Table 2. Alignment of Assessment, Instruments and Constructs.

Phase	Instrument	Construct
Phase 1 August 2013	Faculty Learning Community goals inventory	Views on FLC goals
	Semi-structured interviews with FLC participants	
Phase 2 December 2013	Focus group with FLC participants	Satisfaction with SOTL FLC experience Effect of SOTL FLC on participants' views of teaching and learning
Phase 3 June 2014	Application of Assessment of Program Components and Faculty Development Outcomes	Effect of SOTL FLC on attainment of participants' learning outcomes Effect of FLC Components on SOTL FLC learning experience
	Focus group with FLC participants	Effect of SOTL FLC on participants' views of teaching and learning Effect of SOTL FLC on participants' feelings toward teaching Satisfaction with SOTL FLC experience

questionnaire in the first SOTL FLC meeting in August of 2013. The results indicate that the majority of participants perceived that the goal of the FLC was to develop increased ability and capacity for teaching. At the midpoint focus group, participants expressed that after their first semester they considered that the FLC experience was conducive to attaining the goals set out in the teaching innovation project. At the focus group conducted at the end of the process, participants agreed that their FLC experience allowed them to learn from the implementation of new pedagogical strategies in their teaching. Furthermore, the focus of the FLC on SOTL allowed them to garner evidence on the effect of those innovations on student learning. A Physics professor explained "... and you don't know if it works, you believe that what you do, you do it well, nevertheless now it has quantitative and qualitative elements that allow you to say more or less you are doing this well or it's working." In this statement, the professor is comparing the kinds of evidence on the impact of his teaching on student learning available to him prior to his participation in the FLC, and the kinds he has after his FLC participation. He expresses shifting from believing he was doing something well, to basing such assumptions on evidence provided by the results of his SOTL project.

Satisfaction with SOTL FLC experience
In order to gauge participant's level of satisfaction with the FLC experience, we included an item on our adaptation of the Assessment of Program Components and Faculty Development Outcomes survey developed by Cox (2007) (see Appendix C) asking participants to rate on a 5 point scale their overall satisfaction with the FLC experience. Participants were asked this question twice: at the end of the first semester (Fall, 2013) and at the end of the second semester (Spring, 2014). Participants rated their overall satisfaction with the FLC highly; they reported being either totally satisfied or satisfied with the experience at both points in time.

Effect of SOTL FLC on Attainment of Participants' Learning Outcomes
The primary purpose of the FLC was for participants to learn the process and at the same time create their own SOTL project. This construct measured the degree to which faculty participants considered that the overall FLC experience contributed to their attainment of the learning outcomes. Through their FLC experience we expected that participants would be able to: (1) Create a well-defined research question for a SOTL project; (2) Identify an appropriate research design for a SOTL project; (3) Understand the data collection techniques and processes involved in a

SOTL project; (4) Analyze the data resulting from their SOTL project; and (5) Present and publish their SOTL project. To assess this, we used an adaptation of the Assessment of Program Components and Faculty Development Outcomes survey (Cox, 2007). We asked participants to rate on a scale of 1–10 how much they considered that the overall FLC experience contributed to their learning of each step. The average of participants rating for components (1) and (2) was 9.3; for components (3) and (4), 8.3 and for component (5) 8.2.

Effect of FLC Components on SOTL FLC Learning Experience
We were also interested in assessing participants perceptions of the impact of the different FLC components on the attainment of the goals. For this we used a subset of items (general components of all FLCs such as curriculum, sense of community and teaching project, and specific ones related to the nature of this specific FLC) on the Assessment of Program Components and Faculty Development Outcomes survey developed by Cox (2007), where participants had the opportunity to rate on a 1 (weak impact) to 10 (strong impact) scale.

Overall, faculty participants agreed that the FLC components were conducive to the attainment of the FLC goals. All participants considered that the following FLC components had a strong impact on the effectiveness of the FLC experience: (1) the whole group virtual sessions in fall of 2013, (2) the use of a book to develop the FLC curriculum: *Engaging in the Scholarship of Teaching and Learning*, (3) the on-site visit by the co-facilitators in December of 2013 and (4) the individual per project virtual sessions in spring of 2014. Regarding the overall feeling of camaraderie and community, as well as their views on how other FLC participants contributed to the attainment of the FLC goals and learning outcomes related to SOTL, 67% considered these FLC components had a high impact and 33%, a median impact. The following excerpt from the final focus group exemplifies participants' views on the value of participating in experiences that allow them to interact with colleagues around teaching: *Well, let's say that at first it has allowed to interact with other colleagues, to have contact with other colleagues teaching the same subject matter, to try to agree to work together .... I think it's a little about sharing with colleagues and focusing that conversation about the types of activities that one can develop in teaching, then I think there is positive feedback regarding in that interaction, in relation to conversation, to comments that can come up that can help you to improve a little the pedagogical task.*

In this excerpt the faculty member highlights what he values related to teaching and learning: the possibility of exploring ideas that as a teacher he may not be sure about, but that with the feedback and perspective provided by his colleagues he can gain insight, and a different perspective as to what may work in his teaching. The possibility of sharing with a group of peers ideas about teaching was valued positively by these FLC participants.

Effect of SOTL FLC on Participants' Views and Feelings on
Teaching and Learning
Faculty learning communities have the potential to positively impact participants' views and attitudes on teaching and learning. To assess this in the SOTL FLC, we used a subscale of the Assessment of Program Components and Faculty Development Outcomes survey (Cox, 2007) (see Appendix C) at both the middle and end of their FLC experience. In regards to faculty development outcomes, this instrument contains 24 items that collectively explore conceptions, attitudes and feelings toward teaching and learning. Fig. 1 summarizes these findings, contrasting results for fall of 2013 (at the middle of the FLC experience) and spring of 2014 (at the end of the FLC experience).

Overall the results indicate that participating in the FLC contributed positively to enhancing views on teaching and learning. Results indicate that throughout the FLC experience participants enhanced their view of teaching as a source of knowledge through the implementation of the phases of a SOTL project. These results confirm that the FLC accomplished its purpose in regards to supporting faculty learning about how to undertake a SOTL project, and how engaging in SOTL contributes to enhance teaching.

The significance of the FLC experience in contributing to professors' views of teaching as an intellectual pursuit and legitimate source of knowledge that can serve to support its practice is also evident in the qualitative data collected through the focus groups. During a focus group a physics professor emphasized the importance he views as a teacher on being able to assess the impact of a teaching innovation on student learning. He emphasizes that data related to the effect of what he does in his teaching on student learning allows to respond to what he views as key when innovating in teaching: being able to assess and reflect on the results with the ultimate goal of improving student learning.

The Assessment of Program Components and Faculty Development Outcomes survey (Cox, 2007) also explores how the FLC experience

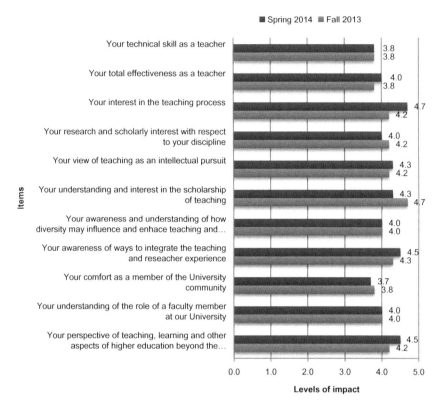

Fig. 1. Effect of SOTL FLC on Participant's Views of Teaching and Learning.

contributes to changes in feelings and attitudes on teaching and learning as a whole (Fig. 2).

Overall the results indicate a slight decrease in participants' feelings of comfort and ease in their role as teachers, when we compare their perspectives at the middle and end of their FLC experience. We interpret this uneasiness as a natural outcome of faculty gaining insight and learning that what they thought was best or worked in their teaching was not necessarily conducive to the student learning they aspired. Even though faculty engaged in SOTL projects, their results could indicate that the intervention they implemented was not prompting student satisfaction and/or learning. Such was the case for one of the projects where the faculty participants did not notice significant changes in student learning as a result of their innovation. These "negative" results could contribute to moving faculty out of

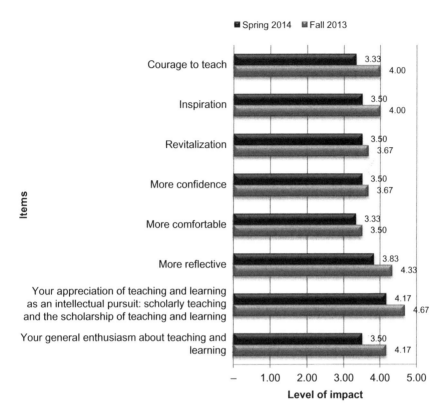

Fig. 2. Effect of SOTL FLC on Participants' Feelings toward Teaching.

their comfort zone and feeling the need to learn, and ultimately make changes in their teaching.

LESSONS LEARNED

Overall, we regard the experience of this cross-country FLC as one of value for the facilitators, as well as the faculty. The results of the assessment demonstrated attainment of the FLC goals. Still, there were valuable lessons to be learned from this maiden cross-cultural FLC experience. These lessons revolve around the following issues: language barrier, benefits of an on-site visit, use of common reading material, adaptability, technology issues, cultural differences, and sense of community. We will elaborate on each of these below.

1. The learning community facilitators learned quickly that when both facilitators were in a different country, it was difficult to create the camaraderie that is part of learning communities. The language barrier made it even more difficult. By the second session the facilitators agreed that it was critical to have someone on-site at the University. This on-site facilitator was perhaps the most important ingredient to the success of the learning community. She worked with the teams and acted as a resource when the teams needed immediate advice (in their own language). She organized appropriate dates and times to meet. She was able to moderate discussions during periods of interaction. Finally, she often served as the translator between the facilitators and the participants.

2. Including a site visit proved to be an important factor in the success of the learning community. The United States SoTL facilitators physically visited the University midway through the learning community. That face-to-face meeting provided the facilitators and participants an opportunity to get to know one another. It allowed for extended conversations in which the facilitators were able to make quick progress with the individual teams. That site visit and the team meetings actually changed the direction of future distance meetings. Prior to the face-to-face meeting, the facilitators delivered their lectures in English. After the site visit, the facilitators realized that the new topic, combined with the language barrier made comprehension difficult.

3. Using the textbook provided structure for faculty as they engaged in research in a new area, especially when the spoken language was sometimes difficult to understand because of the language. The book provided the participants with a complete source on the different steps, challenges and opportunities inherent in undertaking SOTL projects. The group of faculty participating in the SOTL FLC described the book as beneficial, especially given that for 90% of them, this was the first time they engaged in a SOTL project. Having the book as a guide and the authors as co-facilitators of the FLC provided participants with a certain sense of security that they would be able to undertake the new task.

4. Flexibility in the way sessions are planned to take into consideration unexpected outcomes. Initially the facilitators in the US created interactive two-hour lectures. It became clear quickly that both the technology

and the language barrier made the interaction an inefficient use of time. Much of the two-hour lecture was spent simply trying to understand one another. After the first lecture, the facilitators modified the lectures so that if questions and discussions were incorporated, they were incorporated toward the end.

5. The technological tools that were available were both an advantage and a disadvantage. Of course, tools such as Skype, Webex, Blackboard, etc. allowed us to communicate and share ideas across both countries. Depending on the type of technology, it also allowed for synchronous and asynchronous communication, which made for less dependence on time and place. But, there were also technological challenges as not everyone was technologically proficient. We soon learned that it was helpful to have IT technicians in both countries during our synchronous sessions. And there are limits to technology – virtual communication is indeed different than being in a room together, which allows for richer communication. Still, we found that making use of the available communication technologies were required in order to achieve the success that we did.

6. Differences in culture matter when working collaboratively. Part of the experience of working with facilitators on one continent and participants on another was understanding differences in culture, and being prepared to understand how these differences can influence both intentions and outcomes. An example of this influence is the sense of timeliness in starting meetings. In the experience of this FLC, the two facilitators tended to be very timely in starting meetings, and in their interventions, get to the point quickly. The Colombian culture emphasized social conversation at the start of the meeting prior to jumping into business. It was important for the US facilitators to adapt to these slight delays in the start of the session.

7. It is necessary to build in meeting time for the FLC to come together as a group and bond as a community around teaching. Building community is an essential component of a FLC experience. Given the characteristics of the FLC described (facilitators in two different countries, language barriers, technology challenges), fostering camaraderie among participants was more of a challenge. The focused agenda and the need to reduce interaction did not allow for participants to interact with each other as we would have envisioned they would. For future experiences of this sort, we would recommend that aside from the sessions with the facilitators, the FLC schedule include sessions where participants can come together to share their experiences on their projects.

In sum, FLC constitute an effective strategy to engage faculty in projects and initiatives related to the development of teaching and learning on college campuses. The experience shared in this chapter shows that FLC can take on a different format involving collaborative work among faculty that crosses national boundaries. A new format for FLCs like the one discussed presents both challenges and opportunities for faculty learning: technology setbacks, language barriers, cultural differences, shared interests in teaching, common goals for student learning, among others identified. These challenges and opportunities represent genuine contexts for faculty development, and may continue to do as long as universities and their faculty are willing to take the steps necessary to foster international collaboration around teaching and learning.

REFERENCES

Bishop-Clark, C., & Dietz-Uhler, B. (2012). *Engaging in the scholarship of teaching and learning: A guide to the process, and how to develop a project from start to finish*. Sterling, VA: Stylus Publishing, LLC.

Brydges, S., Chilukuri, L., Cook, G., Feeley, M., Herbst, M., Tour, E., & Van Den Einde, L. (2013). Building a faculty learning community at a research university. *Currents in Teaching & Learning, 5*(1−2), 17−35.

Chen, Y., Chen, N., & Tsai, C. (2009). The use of online synchronous discussion for web-based professional development for teachers. *Computers & Education, 53*, (Learning with ICT: New perspectives on help seeking and information searching), 1155−1166. doi:10.1016/j.compedu.2009.05.026

Chew, S. L. (2010). Improving classroom performance by challenging student misconceptions about learning. *APS Observer, 23*, 51−54. Retrieved from http://goo.gl/zEc2Pf. Accessed August 25, 2014.

Cox, M. D. (2004). Introduction to faculty learning communities. *New Directions for Teaching and Learning, 97*, 5−23.

Cox, M. D. (2007). *Faculty learning community program director's handbook and facilitator's handbook*. Oxford, OH: Miami University.

Daly, C. J. (2011). Faculty learning communities: Addressing the professional development needs of faculty and the learning needs of students. *Currents in Teaching & Learning, 4*(1), 3−16.

Doyle, T., & Zakrajsek, T. (2013). *The new science of learning: How to learn in harmony with your brain*. Sterling, VA: Stylus.

Flaherty, C. (2014). So much to do, so little time. *Inside Higher Education*. Retrieved from https://www.insidehighered.com/news/2014/04/09/research-shows-professors-work-long -hours-and-spend-much-day-meetings. Accessed on June 21, 2015.

Healey, M. (2003). The scholarship of teaching: Issues around an evolving concept. *Journal on Excellence in College Teaching, 14*(2−3), 5−26.

Hershberger, A., Spence, M., Cesarini, P., Mara, A., Jorissen, K. T., Albrecht, D., & Lin, C. (2009). The ripple effect: Lessons from a research and teaching faculty learning community. *Journal on Excellence in College Teaching, 20*(3), 145–173.

Kuijpers, J. M., Houtveen, A. M., & Wubbels, T. (2010). An integrated professional development model for effective teaching. *Teaching and Teacher Education: An International Journal of Research and Studies, 26*(8), 1687–1694.

Macdonald, J., & Poniatowska, B. (2011). Designing the professional development of staff for teaching online: An OU (UK) case study. *Distance Education, 32*(1), 119–134.

Matzat, U. (2010). Reducing problems of sociability in online communities: Integrating online communication with offline interaction. *American Behavioral Scientist, 53*(8), 1170–1193. doi:10.1177/0002764209356249

Matzat, U. (2013). Do blended virtual learning communities enhance teachers' professional development more than purely virtual ones? A large scale empirical comparison. *Computers & Education, 60*, 40–51. doi:10.1016/j.compedu.2012.08.006

Maurer, T., Sturges, D., Shankar, P., Allen, D., & Akbarova, S. (2010). A faculty learning community on the scholarship of teaching & learning: A case study. *International Journal for the Scholarship of Teaching & Learning, 4*(2), 1–7.

Medina, J. (2008). *Brain rules: 12 Principles for surviving and thriving at work, home, and school.* Seattle, WA: Pear Press.

Richlin, L., & Cox, M. D. (2004). Developing scholarly teaching and the scholarship of teaching and learning through faculty learning communities. *New Directions for Teaching and Learning, 97*, 127–135.

Sandell, K. L., Wigley, K., & Kovalchick, A. (2004). Developing facilitators for faculty learning communities. *New Directions for Teaching and Learning, 2004*(97), 51–62.

Shulman, L. S. (1999). Taking learning seriously. *Change, 31*(4), 10–17.

Stoll, L., Bolam, R., McMahon, A., Wallace, M., & Thomas, S. (2006). Professional learning communities: A review of the literature. *Journal of Educational Change, 7*(4), 221–258. doi:10.1007/s10833-006-0001-8

Tsai, I. C., Laffey, J. M., & Hanuscin, D. (2010). Effectiveness of an online community of practice for learning to teach elementary science. *Journal of Educational Computing Research, 43*(2), 225–258.

Vescio, V., Ross, D., & Adams, A. (2008). A review of research on the impact of professional learning communities on teaching practice and student learning. *Teaching and Teacher Education, 24*, 80–91. doi:10.1016/j.tate.2007.01.004

APPENDIX A

Faculty Learning Community Goals Inventory (FLCGI)

Adapted from Appendix A, Developing Facilitators for Faculty Learning Communities, in *Building Faculty Learning Communities* (Sandell et al., 2004, pp. 59−61).

Instructions: Read through each statement and circle the number that best corresponds to the degree of importance in relation to the outcomes you would like to achieve − for yourself and the other participants − through your faculty learning community next year.

For these items:

1	2	3	4	5
Very Unimportant	Not important	Neither important Nor unimportant	Important	Very Important

Scale	Item	Item #
1 2 3 4 5	Develop a perspective on teaching, learning and other aspects of higher education beyond the perspective of your individual discipline	1
1 2 3 4 5	Heighten appreciation of scholarly teaching and the scholarship of teaching	2
1 2 3 4 5	Increase reflection on and about teaching	3
1 2 3 4 5	Increase inspiration about teaching and scholarship	4
1 2 3 4 5	Broaden view of teaching as an intellectual pursuit	5
1 2 3 4 5	Learn more about the specific topic around which your learning community will be built	6
1 2 3 4 5	Increase understanding and awareness on campus about the specific topic of your learning community	7
1 2 3 4 5	Develop new course modules about the specific content of your learning community	8
1 2 3 4 5	Increase student achievement in relation to the specific focus of your learning community	9
1 2 3 4 5	Learn more about how your specific topic may influence and enhance teaching and learning	10
1 2 3 4 5	Increase comfort in your role as a member of the faculty	11
1 2 3 4 5	Heighten awareness and understanding of the role of a faculty member at your institution	12

(Continued)

Scale	Item	Item #
1 2 3 4 5	Develop a community of colleagues who continue as an informal support system after this FLC project ends	13
1 2 3 4 5	Develop a sense of community with colleagues around specific teaching projects that you carry out	14
1 2 3 4 5	Experience revitalization as a faculty member at my institution	15
1 2 3 4 5	Successfully develop new/more learning objectives for your course	16
1 2 3 4 5	Increase your general enthusiasm about teaching and learning	17
1 2 3 4 5	Increase total effectiveness as a faculty member	18
1 2 3 4 5	Increase technical skill as a teacher	19
1 2 3 4 5	Increase comfort with and confidence in your teaching	20
1 2 3 4 5	Increase understanding of and interest in the scholarship of teaching	21
1 2 3 4 5	Heighten awareness of ways to integrate the teaching and research experiences	22
1 2 3 4 5	Develop research and scholarly interests with respect to your discipline	23
1 2 3 4 5	Produce a scholarly article or paper on teaching through your work in the community	24
1 2 3 4 5	Learn more about student achievement through scholarly research on teaching and learning	25

Instructions: Rank-order the following five foci for your learning community in order of importance, where 1 = least important and 5 = most important (be sure to rank all 5!)

_____Thinking about teaching beyond the classroom—in its broadest implications

_____Learning more about a specific pedagogical tool or strategy

_____Colleagueship and learning from others

_____Developing increased individual teaching skill and ability

_____Carrying out a teaching project and sharing it with the scholarly community

Once you have completed the inventory, please proceed to the next page to tally and interpret the results.

APPENDIX B

Midpoint Focus Group Protocol
SOTL Faculty Learning Community

About the proposed goals:

During the first FLC meeting, you completed the Faculty Learning Community Goals Inventory. The following goal was found as the most frequently reported among the FLC participants:

_____ Thinking teaching beyond the classroom.
_____ Learning more about an specific pedagogical tool or strategy.
_____ Companionship and learning from others.

_X_ Developing greater teaching skill and capacity.

_____ Carry out a shared teaching project in the teaching community.

To what extent do you believe that progress has been made toward achieving this goal?
What factors have contributed to the achieving this goal?
What factors have challenged progress toward this goal?

About the proposed goals:

What has been the proposed goal to achieve by the FLC during the first semester?
To what extent do you consider to have achieved this goal?
What factors have contributed to achieving this goal?
What factors have challenged the achievement of this goal?

About the knowledge generated during this period:

Do you consider that your participation in the FLC thus far has changed your teaching, your conception of teaching and your perception of yourself as a professor? (*If yes, probe about the way in which these changes have occurred and if no, probe why they consider that their participation in the FLC has favored their current conceptions on teaching and practices.*)

So far, has this experience changed your view/conception of the large lecture class? In which way? (*If the professor answers no, investigate why he/she considers that their conception haven't changed*)

Thinking a bit about your students and their learning processes, do you consider that participation in the FLC has changed your conception about your students? (*If yes, investigate about the way the professor considers it has changed, if no, probe about why he/she considers that the experience hasn't changed his/her teaching conception.*)

So far, how has this experience changed your conception about SOTL (scholarship of teaching and learning)?

The fact of working together with other professors on similar interests around teaching has impacted somehow the way in which you understand or address those interests? What factors influence? How?

Suggestions:

What aspects of this FLC could be changed in order to improve this experience for future opportunities? And for future participants? Do you have any suggestions (add, delete, replace, restructuring, etc.) in terms of content or form of the FLC program? (for the group, for the coordination and management of the FLC program).

APPENDIX C: ASSESSMENT OF PROGRAM COMPONENTS AND FACULTY DEVELOPMENT OUTCOMES: LIKERT AND OPEN-ENDED SURVEY

Institution's Name:_____

Faculty Learning Community Name: _____

Participant Assessment Survey

200x–200x

Please complete and return to _____, _____, by _____

Please complete as an individual and return this report by e-mail as a word document or print out and mail. Before you begin, you may wish to review your application to this community and its goals. Your community facilitator may also review this report or an excerpt or summary as he or she plans for the future. Thank you.

A. Estimate the impact of this Faculty Learning Community on you with respect to each of the following program components. Place an "X" right beside the number on the scale below that reflects your judgment. "NA" means "does not apply." "1" indicates a very weak impact and "10" a very strong impact. Also, if you have brief comments to make about any of the items, use the space provided. Open-ended questions occur at the end of the survey.

Core Questions 1–7 about program components:

1. Retreats and conferences (An Opening Retreat if you had one, national, regional, or local conferences the community attended, etc.).
   1 2 3 4 5 6 7 8 9 10 n/a
   weak impact   strong impact

2. Seminars (Which topics/sessions were most helpful and/or interesting?)
   1 2 3 4 5 6 7 8 9 10 n/a
   weak impact   strong impact

3. Your FLC individual project (your FLC-related initiative)
1 2 3 4 5 6 7 8 9 10 n/a
weak impact   strong impact

4. Professional expenses you received for teaching and learning support
1 2 3 4 5 6 7 8 9 10 n/a
weak impact   strong impact

5. The colleagueship and learning from the other community participants
1 2 3 4 5 6 7 8 9 10 n/a
weak impact   strong impact

6. Student associates (students you may have worked with in connection with FLC goals and activities)
1 2 3 4 5 6 7 8 9 10 n/a
weak impact   strong impact

7. One-to-one partnerships related to the program
1 2 3 4 5 6 7 8 9 10 n/a
weak impact   strong impact

B. In a similar manner, estimate the impact of this faculty learning community on you with respect to each of the following development outcomes. "1" indicates a very weak impact and "10" a very strong impact.

Questions specific to this FLC's goals (to be supplied by your FLC Facilitator):

Core Questions about development outcomes in any FLC:

8. Your technical skill as a teacher
1 2 3 4 5 6 7 8 9 10 n/a
weak impact   strong impact

9. Your total effectiveness as a teacher
1 2 3 4 5 6 7 8 9 10 n/a
weak impact   strong impact

10. Your interest in the teaching process
    1 2 3 4 5 6 7 8 9 10 n/a
    weak impact   strong impact

11. Your research and scholarly interest with respect to your discipline
    1 2 3 4 5 6 7 8 9 10 n/a
    weak impact   strong impact

12. Your view of teaching as an intellectual pursuit
    1 2 3 4 5 6 7 8 9 10 n/a
    weak impact   strong impact

13. Your understanding of and interest in the scholarship of teaching.
    1 2 3 4 5 6 7 8 9 10 n/a
    weak impact   strong impact

14. Your awareness and understanding of how diversity may influence and
    enhance teaching and learning
    1 2 3 4 5 6 7 8 9 10 n/a
    weak impact   strong impact

15. Your awareness of ways to integrate the teaching and research experience
    1 2 3 4 5 6 7 8 9 10 n/a
    weak impact   strong impact

16. Your comfort as a member of the University community
    1 2 3 4 5 6 7 8 9 10 n/a
    weak impact   strong impact

17. Your understanding of the role of a faculty member at our University
    1 2 3 4 5 6 7 8 9 10 n/a
    weak impact   strong impact

18. Your perspective of teaching, learning, and other aspects of higher edu-
    cation beyond the perspective of your discipline
    1 2 3 4 5 6 7 8 9 10 n/a
    weak impact   strong impact

C. If not covered by the above questions, what have you valued most from your participation in this faculty learning community?

D. What aspect(s) of this faculty learning community could be changed to make it more valuable for future participants? Do you have any suggestions for modification (additions, deletions, substitutions, restructuring, etc.) of the content or form of the Program?

E. In what ways have you used your professional expense account and how has/will this affect(ed) your teaching and your students learning?

F. If you have developed a project related to this faculty learning community, please report your progress and indicate your plans for next year. Do you have presentations or publications planned?

G. If you involved a student associate in your work, report the ways in which, and the frequency with which, you have interacted with your student associate(s). Which activities and outcomes were helpful? Which were not helpful? What suggestions do you have for future involvement?

H. In what ways have you investigated and tried teaching differently as a result of participating in this FLC? Please be as specific as possible, for example, describe changes in your syllabus, strategies, processes, curriculum, format, style, assessment, etc. Did you measure any change in student learning? What are your plans along these lines for next year?

I. Describe how your teaching and your perception of yourself as a teacher have changed (if they have) as a result of your involvement in this faculty learning community.

J. Additional comments

APPENDIX D

Final Focus Group Protocol
SOTL Faculty Learning Community

About the proposed goals:

During the first FLC meeting, you completed the Faculty Learning Community Goals Inventory. The following goal was found as the most frequently reported among the FLC participants:

___ Thinking teaching beyond the classroom.
___ Learning more about an specific pedagogical tool or strategy.
___ Companionship and learning from others.

_X_ Developing greater teaching skill and capacity.

_____ Carry out a shared teaching project in the teaching community.

To what extent do you believe you achieved this goal?
What factors contributed to the achievement of this goal?
What factors challenged the achievement of this goal?

About the learning generated during this period:

How do you think you have changed as a teacher due to your participation in the FLC? (*If yes, probe about how these changes have happened and if the answer is no, investigate why he/she believes that his/her participation in the FLC has favored their current conceptions on teaching and practices.*)

Specifically probe for changes in:
  o pedagogical practice
  o Conception of teaching
  o self-perception as a teacher

Has your participation in the SOTL FLC changed your view/conception of the large lecture course? How? (*If the teacher says no, inquire why he/she considers that their conception hasn't changed.*)

Thinking a bit on your students and their learning, do you consider that participation in this FLC has changed your conception of your students? (*If yes, probe about the way the professor has changed and if he/she says no, probe why he/she believes the experience has not changed their concept of teaching.*)

    o What do they think you learned from your students during the development of their project associated with SOTL FLC?

All are teachers from different subject areas and are not experts in educational research. However, the SOTL (scholarship of teaching and learning) project undertaken this semester is a form of educational research.

    o What have you learned about SOTL in the university context?

    o How has your discipline and training in it contributed to your undertaking of SOTL?

    o Has your participation in the SOTL FLC changed your views on SOTL? In what way?

Has working together with other teachers on similar interests around teaching impacted somehow the way in which you understand or address those interests? How so?

So far, we have addressed the learning you consider you obtained during your participation in the SOTL FLC. We have referred to your teaching, students and SOTL. Beside these, what other things do you consider you learned during your participation in the SOTL FLC?

Suggestions:

What aspects of this FLC could be changed in order to improve this experience for future opportunities? And for future participants? Do you have any suggestions (add, delete, replace, restructuring, etc.) in terms of content or form of the FLC program? (for the group, for the coordination and management of the FLC program).

HOME AND AWAY: A CASE STUDY ANALYSIS OF A LEARNING AND TEACHING PROGRAMME SUPPORTING THE DEVELOPMENT OF A 'TRANSFORMATIVE' PARTNERSHIP WITH A PRIVATE HEI IN SRI LANKA

Hazel Messenger, Digby Warren and Wendy Bloisi

ABSTRACT

Transnational arrangements between different types of higher education institutions provide an interesting example of partnership working, being business arrangements with learning as a core organising principle. Successful partnerships both learn and work together and can become mutually transformative, sources of growth for the individuals and institutions involved. Individual projects early in the lifecycle of a

University Partnerships for Academic Programs and Professional Development
Innovations in Higher Education Teaching and Learning, Volume 7, 141–157
Copyright © 2016 by Emerald Group Publishing Limited
All rights of reproduction in any form reserved
ISSN: 2055-3641/doi:10.1108/S2055-364120160000007018

partnership can support this development, enabling both organisations to take responsibility for relationship building and the demonstration of trust. This approach has the advantage that it takes the focus away from the home/away dichotomy often apparent in discussions of transnational partnership working and instead attention turns to the development of a new hybrid organisation, a 'third space' characterised by reciprocity, commitment, effective communication, competence and trust.

This chapter provides a case study analysis of a learning and teaching programme which provided the opportunity for a partnership between a London-based university and a private provider in Sri Lanka to have transformational potential. It uses multiple sources of data to identify practical characteristics associated with developing a culture of transformative partnership working which includes the experiences of the 'boundary spanner' responsible for its development and leadership.

Keywords: Partnerships; transformative; university; learning; teaching

INTRODUCTION

Transnational arrangements between different types of higher education institutions provide an interesting example of partnership working, being a business arrangement with learning as a core organising principle. In a recent document from the Higher Education Academy relating to creating partnerships in a learning and teaching context (HEA, 2014a, p. 2), partnership is understood as; 'a relationship in which all involved are actively engaged in and stand to gain from the process of learning and working together to foster engaged student learning and engaging learning and teaching enhancement'. Partnerships represent a 'wicked' issue (Rittel & Webber, 1973; Trowler, 2012) giving institutions complex issues to resolve (Wagstaff, 2013), but can become mutually transformative, sources of growth for the individuals and institutions involved (Sutton, 2010).

Sutton (2010) describes partnership activity in transnational education (TNE) as operating on a relational continuum from transactional to transformational. She suggests that a transactional partnership is a business relationship, mainly concerned with the product of the relationship, with little impact beyond financial benefit being experienced by the home institution. By contrast, a transformational partnership has the potential to have a wide and long-lasting influence on both institutions, going far beyond what was originally planned. She suggests that transformational partnerships are characterised by being more relationship-orientated, have a long-term expansive perspective and acknowledge that development will involve individual and organisational change, 'expanding the capacity for each institution for educating its students, conducting research and serving communities' (Sutton, 2010, p. 62).

Despite the high institutional risks involved, Wagstaff (2013, p. 8) considers that little is known about what contributes to the successes or failures of TNE partnerships and suggests that organisations should be more proactive in learning from them, including reflecting on changes resulting from being in partnership and how 'individual partnerships are contributing to its own evolving ecology'. Williams (2010) suggests that ethnographic and case study approaches could help with identifying the factors that contribute to the success or failure of partnerships. These types of studies can also include the experiences of the 'boundary spanners' (Williams, 2010, p. 7) who are responsible for their development (Whitchurch, 2008; Williams, 2010, 2012). Citing Kanter (1996), Williams (2010, p. 30) proposes that these individuals have a value-base which encourage 'personal relationships, building trust, communication, negotiation and managing without power' and are also capable of coping with ambiguity and personal stress.

This chapter provides an evaluation of a learning and teaching development programme which contributed positively to the transformative potential of a TNE partnership between higher education institutions in the United Kingdom and Sri Lanka. Using data collected in situ during the programme as well as the reflective account of the coordinator, it proposes that this 'partnership within a partnership' involving partners-as-students provided what Bhabha termed a 'third space' (Rutherford, 1990, p. 211). In this context the colonial authority of 'home' and 'away' was replaced by a hybrid space and a heightened opportunity for an 'expanded form of learning and the creation of new knowledge' (Gutiérrez, 2008, p. 152). By including reflections from the 'boundary spanner' responsible for the development and implementation of the programme, evidence is also included which may be useful for the professional development of colleagues working in TNE partnerships, an area that Hoare (2013) comments is lacking.

TRANSNATIONAL PARTNERSHIPS IN HIGHER EDUCATION

TNE provision is defined by GATE (2000, p. 1) as:

> Any teaching or learning activity in which the students are in a different country (the host country) to that in which the institution providing the education is based (the home country). This situation requires that national boundaries be crossed by information about the education and by staff and/or education materials (whether the information and the education, and the materials travel by mail, computer network, radio or television broadcast or other means)

This rapidly developing phenomenon involves universities internationally working in partnership with overseas education providers (Bohm et al., 2004; British Council, 2013; HEA, 2014b; Montgomery, 2014). Partnership working is common in many sectors, with success at progressing beyond the contractual stage being underpinned by generic relational principles including developing clarity, trust, commitment and organisational learning (Wildridge, Childs, Cawthra, & Madget, 2004). Healey, Flint, and Harrington (2014) in writing about partnerships in learning and teaching in higher education, indicate that success is based on *learning* in partnership as well as *working* in partnership (emphasis in original). It follows therefore, that to develop effective and potentially transformative partnerships, the *working* relationship needs to incorporate a *learning* relationship. There is widespread acknowledgement that partnerships in education are highly contextual with their own 'learning culture' (James & Biesta, 2007, p. 21), influenced by many factors including 'the experiences and expertise of the partners involved, the culture and history of the setting for partnership and the wider social and political context of higher education' (Healey et al., 2014, p. 14). 'Culture' also refers to a cultural theory of learning, which assumes that learning 'is something that happens in and through social practices' (James & Biesta, 2007, p. 21). These definitions help to identify the factors that might contribute to a culture which has a focus on developing the partnership from a business transaction to something with wider impact. Appreciating the significance of context therefore helps to challenge the polarities often found in discussions relating to TNE, something that Djerasimovic (2014) suggests helps to overcome issues relating to cultural or ideological imperialism.

PARTNERSHIP DEVELOPMENT IN TRANSNATIONAL EDUCATION

In their work on transnational partnerships between Australian universities and institutions in the Far East, Heffernan and Poole (2005) suggest that although a partnership may originally be set up as a business transaction, paying attention to the process of developing good relationships from the outset is fundamentally important for high-quality outcomes. In the United Kingdom the Quality Assurance Agency for Higher Education (QAA) demand a focus on the 'ends rather than the means' (QAA, 2012, p. 17), but as Keay, May, and O' Mahony (2014, p. 265) point out:

> working in partnership in TNE contexts goes beyond what can be recorded through a pre-defined partnership agreement ... crucial attention needs to be paid to the process, that is, the way in which partners interact and engage collaboratively over time in order to achieve the best possible outcomes for students.

A number of authors from different sectors consider that partnership development should be seen as a relational and practical lifecycle; for example by Dwyer, Schurr, and Oh (1987) and Child and Faulkner (1998) (for business-to-business partnerships) and Hardy, Hudson, and Waddington (2000) and Gray (1989) (for public sector partnerships). Healey et al. (2014) emphasise the significance of *learning relationships* and *learning communities* (emphasis in original) to the development of partnerships in educational contexts, suggesting that a culture of partnership is characterised by a number of critical relational factors including shared vision and values, effective communication, developing trust and personal commitment. Similarly research into successful international business partnerships has identified that communication, trust and commitment are essential influencing features (Ahmed, Patterson, & Styles, 1999), with the development of trust being the most important of these (Dowell, Heffernan, & Morrison, 2013). Sutton and Obst (2011) echo this by explaining how transnational partnerships need to focus on the partnership relationship itself and the relationships between the individuals involved as much as on the product of the relationship. They suggest that partnerships require care and nurturing, with patience, flexibility, a focus on relationship building, trust and rapport all essential factors that help to move them forward. However, MacFarlane (2009) identifies that the development of trust in relationships has received less attention in educational literature compared to that in business and psychology, and emphasises that this particularly relates to practical and operational factors.

Heffernan (2004), Heffernan and Poole (2004, 2005) and Dowell et al. (2013) suggest that it is helpful to see the relational process that characterises transnational partnership development occurring within a five-stage lifecycle. These five stages progress as follows; firstly there is awareness or pre-relationship stage, which is followed by an exploratory, early interaction stage then an expansive, relationship growth stage. Once the partners have established mutual trust and respect and have identified areas of mutual benefit and growth, the lifecycle proceeds to a mature committed stage, finally ending when there is dissolution. This approach, with the partnership seen as an ongoing relational exchange, is based on the relationship marketing model of Dwyer et al. (1987). It has the advantage that it enables identification of ways in which transnational partnership activity may be encouraged to move beyond the initial business transaction, and anticipates that 'establishing, maintaining and developing successful relational exchanges' (Morgan & Hunt, 1994, p. 20) through effective communication, trust and commitment are significant at all stages. This takes the focus away from a colonialist home/away dichotomy and towards the creation of a reciprocal relationship of mutual benefit where both partners take responsibility for relationship building and exploring possibilities for growth. In a learning and teaching context this would be seen as developing a sense of community between those involved (Healey et al., 2014, p. 28) forming a 'partnership learning community' which 'facilitates deep connections … leading to enhanced learning and motivation for all community members'.

Heffernan and Poole (2005) consider that the five stages of the lifecycle mark major transitions in how the partners relate to and have regard to each other. Developing a sense of community in the lifecycle of the partnership should not anticipate a smooth, unidirectional path as each of the stages will be influenced by the past and influence the future. Heffernan (2004) suggests that the early interaction stage of a partnership (Dwyer et al., 1987) may be quite fragile because the partners do not know each other well. Heffernan and Poole (2005) consider that it is this stage that is the most significant in partnership development, as it is when impressions and expectations are formed, boundaries established and the possibilities for growth explored. To progress to the next stage there needs to be a high degree of mutual learning, with a high level of interaction and engagement increasing mutual knowledge and reducing uncertainty (Heffernan, 2004). In this way trust is demonstrated and developed with demonstrations of rapport, confidence and goodwill showing a commitment to the partnership working. Specific projects can facilitate this process, especially if they are introduced with the anticipation that there will be more projects as time progresses. This is a multi-layered process involving the organisational and individual changes that Sutton (2010) suggests contribute to the development of a transformative partnership.

The remainder of this chapter provides a case study analysis of how a learning and teaching development programme contributed to the transformative potential of a partnership between a UK university and a private higher education institution (HEI) in Sri Lanka. It reviews the programme and reports on the experiences of the development team, indicating the potential for the programme to have a wider impact than what was originally conceived.

CONTEXT

Sri Lanka has been identified as a region in need of investment to support the development of quality higher education provision (British Council, 2013; The Economist Intelligence Unit, 2013; World Bank, 2009), as state-funded universities are currently only able to provide for 16% of those eligible to take up places. With a publicly intended aim for Sri Lanka to be an international hub of excellence for higher education by 2020 (Ministry of Higher Education, Sri Lanka, 2012) the Sri Lankan government is therefore encouraging partnerships between non-state (private) HEIs and overseas universities in order to help with this shortfall. Acknowledging the traditional reliance on a transmission style of teaching, they have also stated that they wish to encourage more active learning 'to produce students who think broad and can have open discussions and learning' (Ministry of Higher Education, Sri Lanka, 2012, p. 23).

The partnership arrangement discussed here is between a London-based university and a private educational organisation in Sri Lanka. The university wanted to expand the number of students enroled on its courses and had been actively seeking a partner in a stable south Asian country. This partnership would provide a source of offshore income for the university from the fees being paid and also publicise the university in Sri Lanka. Sri Lanka had been stable since the civil war ended in 2009 and a 'due diligence' investigation (UKHE, 2012, p. 42) had shown that the organisation had a reliable profile which indicated that it would be able to deliver the financial aspects of the relationship. The partner also had extensive experience of delivering high-quality pre-degree and professional qualifications, which gave confidence in their ability to deliver the courses to meet the appropriate quality standards. The QAA anticipates that students in the home or partner institution will have equivalent experiences which means that although partnerships may start as a business transaction it is necessary to develop effective collaborative arrangements in order to provide a quality experience for the students (QAA, 2012).

The arrangement started in 2014 when the partner was validated to deliver undergraduate courses in two subject areas, computing and business and postgraduate provision through an executive MBA at its campuses in Colombo and Kandy. Partnership working had been a feature for many years in all of the faculties within the university, with business and law having 15 partners offering a total of 48 courses involving over 1,000 students. Since 2013 these had been brought together and managed by an academic Partnerships Manager with responsibility for monitoring their quality and financial contribution.

The conditions of the validation included the requirement for the university's Centre for the Enhancement of Learning and Teaching (CELT) to provide staff development in teaching and learning in higher education for the staff involved in the business programmes. This requirement resulted in two programmes, both developed in collaboration with CELT and delivered in Sri Lanka by the UK course leader for the MBA (herself an experienced academic developer) with support from the faculty's Partnerships Manager. The first undergraduate-focused programme was delivered over five days at the Colombo campus. The second two-day programme concentrated on postgraduate provision and the new MBA in particular. This was delivered in both Colombo and Kandy in order that members of the staff team who worked in the business sector and taught part-time could attend. Details of both programmes were agreed in advance with the CEO of the Sri Lankan organisation who indicated that he and his senior team would be actively participating.

METHODOLOGY

Healey et al. (2014, p. 29) explain how it is very difficult to 'see' partnership as a process when it is committed to paper indicating that 'it is essentially experiential'. This chapter aims to reveal some of the processes involved in the development of a partnership by presenting a case study analysis of the implementation of the learning and teaching programmes, with a view to identifying how they might contribute to the potential for the partnership to develop from a business transaction to something more transformative. A case study approach is appropriate for building understanding around a particular issue (Merriam, 1998) with Yin (2009) emphasising the need to take into account context. This is particularly relevant to educational environments (Chickering & Reisser, 1993) therefore the possibilities for generalising from the case to other contexts needs to be considered. Hodkinson and Hodkinson (2001, p. 11) consider that they prefer not to think about generalisations because of the statistical connotations of the term, instead preferring to propose that findings may be transposed elsewhere if they 'ring true' to the reader.

A case study approach anticipates using multiple sources of data and here these include prepared resources, participants' responses to activities, photographs, formal and informal feedback and the reflective records of the course coordinator. The analysis also includes a narrative account of partnership working in action, providing a 'rare tale' from a 'cross border traveller' (Trahar, 2013, p. 302).

A PARTNERSHIP WITHIN A PARTNERSHIP: AN ANALYSIS OF THE TRANSFORMATIVE POTENTIAL OF A LEARNING AND TEACHING PROGRAMME WITH A PARTNER ORGANISATION IN SRI LANKA

Sutton (2010, p. 62) emphasises that transformative partnership working understands the reciprocal nature of the relationship and the capability for 'expanding the capacity for each institution for educating its students, conducting research and serving communities'. She suggests that the transformative potential of partnerships can be enhanced through specific projects which enhance mutual learning. Although the learning and teaching development programme appeared to be focused 'away' into the Sri Lankan organisation, its transformative impact was felt in the United Kingdom first as it would reach into the 'home' organisation before it would reach out into the partner. The collaborative development of the programme involved a new partnership between the faculty and CELT which has resulted in involvement in other initiatives within the university. Had

CELT been able to take sole responsibility for the development programmes the relationships developed would have been quite different. Prior to the start of the programme each organisation had established a view of the mutual benefit of the partnership and of each other's integrity and competence. Requiring development in learning and teaching could have been perceived as the university lacking trust in its new business partner. However the CEO of the organisation regarded the outcome positively, indicating that he felt that it gave his staff team an excellent opportunity and provided the organisation with a competitive advantage compared to other private HEIs in Sri Lanka. Communication with him during the development of both programmes regarding their style and content helped to communicate the university's commitment to the events, as did the involvement of coordinators who both had high levels of experience and expertise in partnership working and learning and teaching development.

The planned programmes consisted of a blend of formal and informal presentations, group activities, discussions and collaborative feedback. The aim was to encourage a high degree of interaction and engagement between the participants as well as between the organisers and their Sri Lankan colleagues in order to maximise the learning that could occur through this unique opportunity. At the end of each day the rooms where the programmes took place had transformed into working environments where the collaborative work of learning was apparent on flipcharts and sticky notes. Permission had been given to use a camera and the resulting images and their use in further presentations in the United Kingdom and overseas have been a key factor in contributing to the wider reach of the programmes. Photographs of the participants engaged in collaboration and feedback provided a permanent record of the development of inclusive active learning communities where collaboration and sharing knowledge were the norm. This was important as the participants had different backgrounds, different levels within the organisations involved and different types of relationships with each other. Introducing photographs into the pre-prepared formal presentations also provided a humanising element into resources that could have appeared sterile and distant. They also provided amusement, especially around the issue of 'who ate all the sweets'. This collaborative style of working and using photographs as a record has been adopted since by one of the senior members of the Sri Lankan staff team in his work on technology-enhanced learning with colleagues at a local university.

Each programme spanned several days and it was important to receive immediate feedback in order to inform subsequent activities. Feedback on the first day of the undergraduate programme gave confidence in the approach being adopted. Participants documented their thoughts regarding professional practice; *'Learnt* (sic) *different perspectives of others in the lecturing field'*, and awareness of the coordinators modelling an active style of teaching; *'Today's session initiated an opening to practically experiencing different teaching styles and ways of keeping the students engaged with what is being done'*. Similarly, responses to the postgraduate programme identified that the programme was creating the right sort of vibe; *'Interesting, interactive, most useful and appreciated. Much thanks!'* and it was possible to note that a hybrid space for mutual learning was emerging; *'It's good experience sharing knowledge with someone from a different context'*.

With participants having a wide variety of backgrounds and representing all levels of the Sri Lankan organisation, it was important for the coordinators to recognise the significance of hierarchies and other factors, like gender. Although in the United Kingdom it may have been possible to 'mix things up', in this unfamiliar environment this was not appropriate. An early decision was made to allow groups to form themselves, which meant, for example, that the senior management team worked together. Senior management commented that although they met frequently to discuss business issues, they rarely had the opportunity to discuss learning and teaching. They signalled their personal and organisational commitment to the programmes by remaining involved throughout and indicated the practical value they found in particular concepts, like the work of Chickering and Gamson (1987) and Hounsell, McCune, Hounsell, and Litjens (2008) which could be clearly situated in their own context.

Showing care and respect for the needs of the other is an important part of developing trust in partnership development. The Sri Lankan organisation provided refreshments for everyone during each day which provided informal opportunities for talking and finding out more about each other. Being comfortable and confident in formal and informal settings is an important part of the role of those working in transnational contexts as is having a genuine and ongoing interest about local culture, history, families and hobbies. These informal sessions did not just contribute to the development of relationships between UK and Sri Lankan colleagues, but also to relationships between those employed by the Sri Lankan organisation itself. Although the Sri Lankan team worked for the same organisation, because they worked in different locations and with different contractual arrangements, they did not have many opportunities to get to develop the types of close relationships which help to develop trust. The learning and teaching programme helped individuals to get to know each other, providing the chance for the development of 'active trust' (Giddens, 1991, p. 136) between colleagues separated by time and space. This type of 'professional trust' (Hargreaves, 2002, p. 395) is essential for professional effectiveness especially in partnership arrangements involving individuals separated by distance, national boundaries, and status.

By the time the second, postgraduate programme began, each organisation could predict its success based upon the commitment and responsibility already demonstrated throughout the first programme. There was practical demonstration of the values that Healey et al. (2014) suggest should be brought to working in partnership and new ways of working and learning together were beginning to show. By the end of the first programme the type of language being used to talk about learning and teaching had changed; '*Don't just give the task and expect good work from them ... be aware of the feedback cycle*' and '*Some students like coursework because they can complete them leisurely with deep learning*' and the influence of this was being seen in the collaborative development of the new degree courses.

Although the programmes were dealing with a serious topic, the way in which they had been constructed had allowed all the participants from both partners to relax and get to know each other. There was practical demonstration of being on the same wavelength in what they were aiming to achieve. As time progressed the daily feedback became more natural and in the formal programme evaluation the participants commented that the style adopted was '*interactive*', '*interesting*' and '*friendly*' with comments about the university's coordinators including '*their experience evident from the way they spoke and acted*'. That the participants had enjoyed the opportunity to develop and share their ideas was apparent as comments like '*awesome*', '*fantastic*', '*wonderful*' and '*productive*' appeared more than once in the feedback sheets. However, one of the participants commented that although they had really enjoyed the opportunities for interaction and debate, their students would be expecting the didactic style that they were accustomed to, which was somewhat deflating.

A NARRATIVE ACCOUNT OF PARTNERSHIP WORKING IN ACTION BY THE DEVELOPMENT PROGRAMME COORDINATOR

Although the development programme was a requirement of the university and had involved a lot of preparation, including rearranging university responsibilities, not all colleagues had seen this programme in a positive light, regarding it as a bit of a holiday. What they might not have realised was the significant sense of responsibility involved in working on the university's behalf in an unfamiliar environment and the personal demands in making it look easy and seamless. However, the first visit to the organisation for the validation had been characterised by goodwill and good humour and had included tours of each campus, formal and informal meetings with the staff and a celebratory dinner with the senior management team. All of this contributed to getting a 'feel' for the organisation and for what it would be like to work together.

Williams (2010) comments on the importance of networks in managing effective collaborations and colleagues around the country had been generous in providing specialist resources and advice during the preparation of the learning and teaching programme. By the time the flight took off to Colombo, a full five-day programme including presentations, activities, handouts and certificates had been prepared, the content had been agreed with the partner's CEO, day-to-day responsibilities were as up-to-date as possible and arrangements had been made for the family's pets. The fact that there had been time to pack clothes in the suitcase alongside flipcharts, sticky notes, felt tips, packs of sweets and delegate packs was an added bonus.

Williams (2010) and Sutton (2010) identify that working in a boundary spanning role involves having an entrepreneurial spirit and an eye for creating new opportunities. Having a dual identity as a teaching academic and educational developer/researcher plus a genuine interest in the 'human experience of being with another' (Wagstaff, 2013, p. 12) provided the background to wanting to learn more from the implementation of the development programme. Being on the periphery of the organisation was advantageous as it gave the opportunity for initiative and creativity. Although the university did not seem too concerned in how the programme fared, by the end of the year it would be the subject of an international conference presentation, a book chapter and a workshop for other partnership workers funded by an academic development body.

The development programme provided a space for knowledge exchange and learning and the opportunity to work collaboratively with experienced colleagues who had revealed themselves as deeply committed and fun to work with. The second day of the undergraduate programme happened to be April 1, and the fact that one of the senior managers was taken in by a spoof 'Mini Cooper T' introduced in the presentation just before the mid-morning break continues to be a source of great delight to everyone who was present. These colleagues are now co-professionals and friends who just happen to be on the other side of the world. Although information technology has shrunk the distance between the United Kingdom and Sri Lanka they could still be a million miles away if they were not on the same wavelength. Far from being a 'jolly', the programme represented a type of pilgrimage which enabled revisiting and reinforcing the values associated with learning and working relationships in higher education.

CONCLUSIONS

To summarise, the key factors that influenced the transformative potential of the learning and teaching programmes were the *value* in it seen by the management of the partner organisation and the representatives of the university and its capability for demonstrating and reinforcing the *values* of partnership (Healey et al., 2014). These in turn were influenced by the stage in development of the partnership, the genuine care and respect towards each other of the key organisers and recognition of the importance of relationship building between all those involved. Collectively these might be described as constituting a culture for transformative partnership working.

Having the concept of 'partnership' at the centre of all work transforms individuals and organisations and the ways in which they work with others. Organisational boundaries become fluid and the programme in Sri Lanka had been neither 'home' nor 'away' but a physical, temporal and relational third space (Bhabha in Rutherford, 1990) where the requirements of the validation were translated into practical outcomes which transcended the original purpose. It provided the catalyst for a new co-created culture of partnership learning and working together. This transitional and galvanising space is now helping to create a new hybrid organisation based on relationships rather than structures and processes.

REFERENCES

Ahmed, F., Patterson, P., & Styles, C. (1999). The determinants of successful relationships in international business. *Australasian Marketing Journal, 7*(1), 5—21.
Bohm, A., Follari, M., Hewett, A., Jones, J., Kemp, N., Meares, D., ... Van Cauter, K. (2004). *Vision 2020. Forecasting international student mobility: A UK perspective.* London: British Council.
British Council. (2013). *The shape of things to come: The evolution of transnational education: Data, definitions, opportunities and impacts analysis.* Retrieved from https://

ihe.britishcouncil.org/sites/default/files/import-content/the_shape_of_things_to_come_ 2.pdf

Chickering, A. W., & Gamson, Z. F. (1987). Seven principles for good practice in undergraduate education. *American Association of Higher Education Bulletin, 39*(7), 3–7. Retrieved from http://www.aahea.org/articles/sevenprinciples1987.htm

Chickering, A. W., & Reisser, L. (1993). *Education and identity* (2nd ed.). San Francisco, CA: Jossey Bass.

Child, J., & Faulkner, D. (1998). *Strategies of co-operation: Managing alliances, networks and joint ventures.* Oxford: Oxford University Press.

Djerasimovic, S. (2014). Examining the discourses of cross-cultural communication in transnational higher education: From imposition to transformation. *Journal of Education for Teaching, 40*(3), 204–216.

Dowell, D., Heffernan, T., & Morrison, M. (2013). Trust formation at the growth stage of a business-to-business relationship. *Qualitative Market Research: An International Journal, 6*(4), 436–451.

Dwyer, F. R., Schurr, P. H., & Oh, S. (1987). Developing buyer-seller relationships. *Journal of Marketing, 51*(2), 11–27.

GATE. (2000). *Trade in transnational education services: A report by the global alliance for transnational education.* Washington, DC: GATE Publications.

Giddens, A. (1991). *Modernity and self-identity.* Cambridge: Polity Press.

Gray, B. (1989). *Collaborating: Finding common ground for multiparty problems.* San Francisco, CA: Jossey Bass.

Gutiérrez, K. D. (2008). Developing a sociocritical literacy in a third space. *Reading Research Quarterly, 43*(2), 148–164.

Hardy, B., Hudson, B., & Waddington, E. (2000). *What makes a good partnership? A partnership assessment tool.* Leeds: Nuffield Institute for Health.

Hargreaves, A. (2002). Teaching and betrayal. *Teachers and Teaching: Theory and Practice, 8*(3–4), 393–407.

HEA. (2014a). *Framework for partnership in learning and teaching in higher education.* York: Higher Education Academy. Retrieved from https://www.heacademy.ac.uk/sites/ default/files/resources/hea_framework_for_partnership_in_learning_and_teaching.pdf

HEA. (2014b). *Internationalisation.* York: Higher Education Academy. Retrieved from https:// www.heacademy.ac.uk/enhancement/themes/internationalisation

Healey, M., Flint, A., & Harrington, C. (2014). *Engagement through partnership: Students as partners in learning and teaching in higher education.* York: Higher Education Academy.

Heffernan, T. (2004). Trust formation in cross-cultural business-to-business relationships. *Qualitative Market Research: An International Journal, 7*(2), 114–125.

Heffernan, T., & Poole, D. (2004). "Catch me I'm falling": Key factors in the deterioration of offshore education partnerships. *Journal of Higher Education Policy and Management, 26*(1), 75–109.

Heffernan, T., & Poole, D. (2005). In search of 'the vibe': Creating effective international partnerships. *Higher Education, 50*(2), 223–245.

Hoare, H. (2013). Swimming in the deep end: transnational teaching as culture learning? *Higher Education Research & Development, 32*(4), 561–574.

Hodkinson, P., & Hodkinson, H. (2001). The strengths and limitations of case study research. Paper presented at the Learning and Skills Development Agency Conference 'Making and Impact on Policy and Practice', Cambridge, 5–7 December.

Hounsell, D., McCune, V., Hounsell, J., & Litjens, J. (2008). The quality of guidance and feedback to students. *Higher Education Research and Development, 27*(1), 55–67.

James, D., & Biesta, G. (2007). *Improving learning cultures in further education.* Abingdon: Routledge.

Kanter, R. M. (1996). Beyond the cowboy and the corpocrat. In K. Starkey (Ed.), *How organisations learn* (pp. 43–59). London: International Thomson Business Press.

Keay, J., May, H., & O' Mahony, J. (2014). Improving learning and teaching in transnational education: Can communities of practice help? *Journal of Education for Teaching: International Research and Pedagogy, 40*(3), 251–266.

MacFarlane, B. (2009). A leap of faith: The role of trust in higher education teaching. *Nagoya Journal of Higher Education, 9*(14), 221–238.

Merriam, S. (1998). *Qualitative research and case study applications in education.* San Francisco, CA: Jossey Bass.

Ministry of Higher Education, Sri Lanka. (2012). *National higher education strategic management plan of Sri Lanka: 2012–2015 mid term plan.* Retrieved from http://planipolis. iiep.unesco.org/upload/Sri%20Lanka/Sri_Lanka_National_Higher_Education_Strategic_ Management_Plan_2012-2015.pdf

Montgomery, C. (2014). Transnational and transcultural positionality in globalised higher education. *Journal of Education for Teaching, 40*(3), 198–203.

Morgan, R., & Hunt, S. (1994). The commitment – Trust theory of relationship marketing. *Journal of Marketing, 58*(3), 20–38.

QAA. (2012). *UK quality code for higher education, part B: Assuring and enhancing academic quality, chapter B10: Management of collaborative arrangements.* Retrieved from http://www. qaa.ac.uk/publications/information-and-guidance/uk-quality-code-for-higher-education-chapter-b10-managing-higher-education-provision-with-others1#.VdxnJvlVhBc

Rittel, H., & Webber, M. (1973). Dilemmas in a general theory of planning. *Policy Sciences, 4*(2), 155–169.

Rutherford, J. (1990). The third space. Interview with Homi Bhabha. In Ders. (Hg) (Ed.), *Identity: Community, culture, difference* (pp. 207–221). London: Lawrence and Wishart. Retrieved from http://www.wsp-kultur.uni-bremen.de/summerschool/download%20ss%202006/The%20Third%20Space.%20Interview%20with%20Homi%20Bh abha.pdf

Sutton, S. B. (2010). Transforming internationalisation through partnerships. *International Educator, 19*(1), 60–63.

Sutton, S. B., & Obst, D. (2011). The changing landscape of international partnerships. In *Developing strategic international partnerships: Models for initiating and sustaining innovative institutional linkages.* New York: Institute for International Education. Retrieved from https://www.google.co.uk/url?sa=t&rct=j&q=&esrc=s&source=web&cd=7&cad=rja&uact=8&ved=0CEgQFjAG&url=http%3A%2F%2Fwww.iie. org%2F~%2Fmedia%2FFiles%2FCorporate%2FPublications%2FPartnership-Intro. ashx&ei=HEPrU4mKCISV7AbD34H4DA&usg=AFQjCNFhb718QwmUUOAuVMjl ZQfLq4MmtQ&sig2=IwMw4brnsrnt-rDtLfeR-A

The Economist Intelligence Unit. (2013). *Higher Education in South Asia: Trends in Afghanistan, Bangladesh, India, Nepal, Pakistan and Sri Lanka. A custom research report for the British Council.* Retrieved from http://www.britishcouncil.in/sites/britishcouncil. in2/files/sapd_british_council_south_he_report.pdf

Trahar, S. M. (2013). Autoethnographic journeys in learning and teaching in higher education. *European Educational Research Journal, 12*(3), 367–375.

Trowler, P. (2012). Wicked issues in situating theory in close-up research. *Higher Education Research and Development, 31*(3), 273–284.

UK HE International Unit. (2012). *International partnerships: A legal guide for UK universities.* London: UK HE International Unit. Retrieved from file:///C:/Users/Hazel/Downloads/Useful%20info%20-%20Eversheds%20guide%20to%20partnerships%202012.pdf

Wagstaff, D. (2013). *What do we know about collaborations and partnership in higher education?* London: The Leadership Foundation for Higher Education.

Whitchurch, C. (2008). *Shifting identities, blurring boundaries: The changing role of professional managers in higher education.* Research and Occasional Paper Series, CSHE.10.2008. Berkeley, CA: Centre for Studies in Higher Education, University of California.

Wildridge, V., Childs, S., Cawthra, L., & Madget, B. (2004). How to create successful partnerships – A review of the literature. *Health Information and Libraries Journal, 21*(1), 3–19.

Williams, P. (2010). *Special Agents: The nature and role of boundary spanners.* Paper to the ESRC Research Seminar Series 'Collaborative Futures: New insights from intra- and inter-sectoral collaborations', University of Birmingham, February 2010.

Williams, P. (2012). *Collaboration in public policy and practice: Perspectives on boundary spanners.* Bristol: The Policy Press.

World Bank. (2009). *Towers of learning: Performance, perils and promise of higher education in Sri Lanka.* Retrieved from http://documents.worldbank.org/curated/en/2009/07/11137864/towers-learning-performance-peril-promise-higher-education-sri-lanka

Yin, R. K. (2009). *Case study research: Design and methods* (4th ed.). London: Sage.

BY DESIGN AND BY CHANCE: THE STORY OF ONE INTERNATIONAL PARTNERSHIP

Inese Berzina-Pitcher, Punya Mishra and S. Giridhar

ABSTRACT

Emerging economies are becoming less reliant on funding from foreign agencies. One of the consequences of this is the formation of more self-funded international partnerships offering new models of inter-university partnerships. This chapter offers a perspective on such an on-going collaborative international partnership between two institutions of higher education — one in the United States and the other in India. It describes the context in which the partnership was formed, the manner in which it evolved over time as both partners faced barriers, and challenges to the instantiation of the original vision. Sakamoto and Chapman's (2010) Functional Model for the Analysis of Cross-border Partnerships is used to analyze and organize the key factors that have played roles in the development and success of the partnership. In addition, the chapter focuses on one component of the partnership activities, the short-term professional development visits to the United States for educators from Indian partner institution. Drawing on participants' experiences from both sides of the partnership, this chapter presents the expectations, challenges, and opportunities this partnership has offered to members of both

University Partnerships for Academic Programs and Professional Development
Innovations in Higher Education Teaching and Learning, Volume 7, 159–179
Copyright © 2016 by Emerald Group Publishing Limited
All rights of reproduction in any form reserved
ISSN: 2055-3641/doi:10.1108/S2055-364120160000007019

universities. The chapter ends with recommendations to establish or improve international collaborative university partnerships.

Keywords: International; collaborative; university; partnerships; teaching

INTRODUCTION

This chapter offers a perspective on an evolving collaborative international partnership between two institutions of higher education – one in the United States and the other in India. International university partnerships that connect two universities in different countries are not a new phenomenon in higher education; however, creating and sustaining international university partnerships has become an important concern of 21st century higher education (Altbach & Knight, 2007; De Witt, 2002). Depending on the specific purposes for establishing them, university partnerships can be broadly divided into three main categories. The first category includes academic partnerships, such as joint degree and study abroad programs, which are programs where students and faculty participate for curricular or co-curricular purposes. Then, there are research partnerships that are built on faculty research interests and activities. The third category could be called "capacity building" partnerships that are focused on institutional and individual faculty and staff development. This chapter focuses on the third category, the capacity building partnership, that is also a self-funded partnership, and, in this instance, describes one that is mostly funded by the institution outside the United States. Historically, these partnerships that link U.S. institutions with institutions abroad have been funded by U.S. government agencies, most notably the U.S. Agency for International Development (USAID), or by U.S.-based private foundations. The focus of these partnerships has been institutional development, training of academic, research and administrative staff, and introduction of new technologies (Cohen, 2010; Coleman & Court, 1993; King, 2009). This has allowed the U.S. universities to not only become a model for many new institutions in developing countries (King, 2009), but also has led U.S. universities to adopt a specific partnership model that satisfies the requirements and priorities of the donor institutions, sometimes above the needs or interests of overseas partners.

The economic growth in many countries has led to rapid expansion in higher education, especially in the BRIC (Brazil, Russia, India, and China) countries (Altbach, 2005; Carnoy, Loyalka, Androushchak, & Proudnikova, 2012), where there is not only a growing demand for higher education, but also where governments have increased their efforts to advance research and technology. It has led to the development of new universities as well as changes in existing ones. The eagerness of governments and individual institutions to establish world-class universities with international recognition and availability of funding has led to increased interest in partnerships with highly regarded universities in the United States. Many of these partnerships are not different from the earlier ones, as they are funded by government or private donor agencies and are focused on individual and organizational capacity building. The main difference is that the funding is attached to the university located outside the United States.

While the donor-agency funded capacity building partnerships seem to dominate, a number of international university partnerships have emerged that are funded by one or both institutions. The sustainability of such partnerships depends on institutional collaboration and commitment to the partnership and provides opportunities to explore different approaches to both partnership planning and implementation.

In this case study, the U.S. partner is the College of Education at Michigan State University (MSU), well known for its international work and ranked education programs. The Indian partner is Azim Premji University, a new private, not-for-profit university established in 2010 by the Azim Premji Foundation, recognized in India for its work in the public school education sector. Azim Premji University has been established with a clear social vision – "to contribute to the realization of a just, equitable, humane and sustainable society" (Azim Premji University, Vision). Through its programs that prepare committed professionals in the area of education and development and cultivate research and service to the field, Azim Premji University aspires to advance changes in the education sector in India. MSU's land-grant tradition and its commitment to research grounded in practice and service to community, "that seeks to answer questions and create solutions in order to expand human understanding and make a positive difference, both locally and globally" (MSU Mission Statement), aligns closely with the mission and vision of Azim Premji University and became the foundation for the partnership.

This chapter describes the context in which the partnership was formed, the manner in which it evolved over time as both partners faced barriers and found ways to negotiate and steer the association through these roadblocks. This chapter will specifically focus on one component of the partnership activities, the short-term professional development visits to MSU for the Indian partner institution's staff and faculty. We document the nature of participants' experiences from both sides of the partnership and through that seek to understand the expectations, challenges, and opportunities that this program offered to members of both universities. We use Sakamoto and Chapman's (2010) Functional Model for the Analysis of Cross-border Partnerships to analyze and organize the key factors that have played roles in development and success of the partnership. Through this we identify factors that have both challenged and contributed to the successful development of the partnership and offer our recommendations. The chapter ends with us identifying three imperatives essential for establishing international collaborative university partnerships.

CONTEXT AND PARTNERSHIP DESCRIPTION

Within the context of this chapter we define international collaborative partnerships as arrangements between two or more institutions with the goal of obtaining a shared objective (Eddy, 2010). In this we include both the organizational and human aspects of the project. This "partnership" is constituted by two organizations (in this case College of Education, MSU and Azim Premji University) working together to achieve a goal, while "collaboration," in our framework describes the faculty working together (either as individuals or in groups) (Eddy, 2010). Collaborative partnerships provide social structures (Psaltis, 2007) for building collaborations and, as such, shape individual experiences. Thus, we acknowledge that although individual faculty from each institution may work independently, there are also formal and informal agreements that tie each institution together and define the partnership.

The Azim Premji Foundation (operational since 2001), built on a belief that education is a powerful medium to influence change in society, has engaged with several state governments in India and at the ground level with issues such as teacher education, school leadership development, assessment reforms, curricular material development, institutional development for pedagogical and administrative reform. The Azim Premji University emerged from the Foundation's nearly decade-long experience on the ground with large scale intensive interactions with state-run government public school systems. The university is a unit (or a part) of the overarching organization – the Azim Premji Foundation. It is important to clearly visualize the Foundation as an organization with two broad strategic footprints. One is its deep and established field institutions working on the ground to contribute to improving the state-run public school systems, while the other is the University that is specifically established recognizing the urgent need in India for well qualified and deeply committed professionals who will work and contribute to the education and development sector.

The institutionalized nature of work of the Foundation's Field Institutes is informed by the reality that long term and consistent engagement with multiple stakeholders is necessary for educational change. On-the-ground engagement includes capacity development of teachers, head teachers, and other education functionaries, as well as work on curriculum, assessment, and policy issues at the state and national level. These field institutes are currently in 46 districts across eight states in India, with a team of over 1,000 members.

It was on the basis of the learning and experience with their work on the ground with public school education systems that the Foundation saw a clear, urgent, and important need for well-trained, qualified, and committed professionals in the education and development sector. This is how the idea of a University was formed and this genesis is perhaps unique. As it established the university, members of the Foundation visited and studied the best institutions of education and teacher preparation to inform their plans and preparations. One of the institutions that the Azim Premji University staff visited was the College of Education at MSU. It stood out not only for its national and international reputation and for the quality of its faculty, but also for the land-grant tradition, a commitment to research that is grounded in practice. This tradition aligned closely with the mission of the Foundation and its vision for Azim Premji University and became the foundation for building the partnership.

The other organization in this partnership, the College of Education at MSU, is well known for its five-year teacher preparation program, nationally ranked graduate programs, and internationally recognized faculty. For more than a half century, College of Education faculty have engaged in international programs sponsored by external funding agencies, such as USAID, National Science Foundation (NSF), and private foundations, as well in short-term consulting opportunities and research projects with colleagues at different universities across the world. Since the early 2000s, MSU has emphasized and promoted the international mission of the University, which led to more organized efforts by the College of

Education to support development of new international programs and for faculty to integrate international experiences and perspectives into their teaching, research and service. For example, the graduate-level Fellowship for Enhancing Global Understanding program was established to provide international experiences to graduate students. The College established an international scholars exchange and study program with the Faculty of Education of Southwest University (SWU) in Chongqing, China, which includes SWU students and faculty groups visiting MSU for an extended time. In addition, a partnership program with Nelson Mandela Metropolitan University in South Africa provides Department of Educational Administration graduate students with a short-term international professional consulting experiences.

When key members of Azim Premji Foundation and the College of Education met and discussed, they saw the potential benefits from an association or partnership between both institutions, an opportunity to contribute to the development of a new university, to form connections between faculty and students at MSU with educators in India, and an opportunity to gain valuable insights from a region that was distant from their own.

The partnership was formalized in March of 2011. In the ensuing years, the College of Education at MSU explored possible areas for working together, such as curriculum development, student welfare, faculty development, and the use of educational technology. Dr. Donald Heller, then the dean of College of Education, and several faculty visited Azim Premji University and interacted with its faculty members. The Chief Executive Officers (CEOs) of Azim Premji Foundation, Dileep Ranjekar and Anurag Behar (who is also the Vice Chancellor of the University), visited MSU a number of times. The faculty at MSU and members of the Foundation identified some research projects located in the field institute's work and jointly presented the research at international conferences.

It is important to note that the programming of the partnership has been constantly evolving to meet the interests of both institutions (details below). One of the first insights was the realization early on by both partners that to move from a vague and unsubstantiated desire to engage in various aspects of the University to a more meaningful partnership required both sides to identify one, or at most two, areas for tangible, concrete collaborations and thus create conditions for ownership and commitment. Over time this led to a focus on the Azim Premji University educator short-term professional visits to MSU and how it became the central element of the partnership project. We believe that this program not only showcases a different approach to professional development, but also highlights the strengths of this partnership. In this section we will outline the program, share feedback from participant surveys and, finally, provide more information on the factors that have contributed to the success of this program.

UNDERSTANDING THE "EXPOSURE VISITS"

The Azim Premji University educator (which include both university faculty and members of the field institutes) short-term professional development visits to MSU, also known at Azim Premji University as "exposure visits," were developed to support Azim Premji University's efforts to improve the quality of current and future education professionals in India. These visits are planned and developed in coordination with the participants, taking into account their backgrounds, professional interests, and needs. What started out as one-week individual or small group visits has evolved into a two-week program of scaffolded experiences, as explained below, which provide opportunities for the participants to expand their knowledge on a range of topics. These include topics such as teaching and learning philosophies and approaches; teacher education; leadership; technology integration; and school-level policies and practices. They also include opportunities to explore specific areas related to the professional interests and needs of the visitors. These visits of four to six educators from Azim Premji University take place twice a year, one in April and the other in October/November, at times convenient to the faculty involved at MSU's College of Education and when Azim Premji University educators could take time off from their teaching or field work schedules.

Although the central focus of these visits is to expand Azim Premji University educator perspectives on teaching and learning through the context of K-12 and teacher education in the United States, in practice they benefit both MSU and Azim Premji University educators. The opportunity for the MSU faculty and staff to reflect on their own work and learn about education in India, more specifically how the Indian education context affects areas of their own expertise and research, has become an important aspect of these visits as well.

In the past four years, 34 Azim Premji University educators have visited the College of Education, and more than 50 faculty, staff, and graduate students at the MSU College of Education have been actively involved, sharing their expertise in teacher education, both at elementary and secondary level, in the content areas of literacy, mathematics, science, social

166 INESE BERZINA-PITCHER ET AL.

studies, and special education, as well in disciplines of educational technology, educational policy, research methods, and assessment. While the program is mostly financed by the Azim Premji University, the majority of MSU faculty and staff meet with visitors without financial (or any other) compensation.

This program does not include formal lectures or workshops. Instead it focuses on in-depth conversations with MSU faculty members structured around specific topics. The program also includes visits to undergraduate and graduate classrooms, K-12 schools and districts, the state of Michigan Department of Education, organizations that offer informal learning opportunities (such as after-school programs for students and museums), and other educational organizations. Although there are no formal lectures, the visits are structured and start with conversations about the U.S. education system, K-12 schools, and teacher education, followed by an overview of the Teacher Education programs at MSU, then visits to schools that include classroom observation opportunities, and discussions with school administrators, mentor teachers, and student teaching interns. Each visit and conversation is meant to provide opportunities for the visiting faculty to fulfill two goals: first, to learn about the practices in the context of schooling in the United States, including how issues of equity and social justice that are so important to the Foundation play out in the U.S. schools and classrooms of teacher education programs, as well as how they are included into teacher education curriculum; and second, to share their own experiences in the context of Indian schooling with MSU faculty, staff, and students, and anyone else they interact during their visits to different schools and organizations.

THE VALUE OF THE EXPOSURE VISITS

We recently conducted an online survey of all the Azim Premji University and MSU College of Education participants in this program to provide us with their feedback about their experiences with the program. The findings confirm that the partnership is achieving our goal to provide new social and educational experiences that deepen professional understandings of their own practice for both MSU College of Education and Azim Premji University educators. Two findings especially stood out from the MSU College of Education faculty responses. When asked about their role during the meetings, words such as "share," "engage," "discuss," and "learn" were used frequently. One faculty member simply described their meeting with Azim Premji University educators as "professional colleagues having conversations." Another faculty member said:

> ... I have learned a lot about teacher preparation, the education system, and community work in India through these interactions. I am always very interested in engaging in these conversations because they help me understand our own program in new ways.

Another interesting finding was the majority of MSU College of Education faculty, both junior and senior, regardless of their prior international experience, are interested in continuing these relationships with the Azim Premji University educators they have met, and most mentioned that they would like to visit Azim Premji University in India.

Additionally, a majority of MSU faculty were interested in future research opportunities; several mentioned their interest in collaborating with Azim Premji University faculty. Expanding research collaboration was also mentioned by Azim Premji University participants, though in terms of opportunities to develop research skills for junior and senior faculty. As one Azim Premji University participant mentioned, "structured opportunities if built, can help younger faculty in their professional development."

Several findings from Azim Premji University educators' survey responses highlight the strength of this program. One of the most memorable experiences for the Azim Premji University educators was visits to different schools in Michigan. One educator remembered "the images of engaged children, structured classrooms and dedicated teachers, quite vividly to this day." Another mentioned, "the second most memorable experience was interacting with the kids and the teachers in U.S. schools. That was quite different from what we experience every day here." It was not surprising, then, that the participants listed increased time in schools as one of the suggestions for program improvement.

When asked how Azim Premji University educators have benefitted from their visits to MSU, most mentioned developing a better understanding of U.S. higher education, teacher education programs, and K-12 education: "Observation of schools helped me with getting the pedagogical aspects of US schools"; and, "Understanding the US school system and teacher education programs were of high value." Similar to MSU faculty, Azim Premji University participants used words to describe the collaborative meetings such as "conversations," "exposure," "engaging," "and learning." Azim Premji University educator responses show that these visits provide valuable learning experiences not only about the United States and MSU, but they also provide opportunity to broaden their perspective on their own system and practices. In the words of one of the educators, "this visit gave a comparative framework to understand what we do in our practice of teacher education." In addition, it was interesting to see that two Azim Premji University educators specifically mentioned that the visit gave them assurance and validation of their own work.

Key suggestions to improve the program of "exposure visits" recommended from Azim Premji University participants were to include more school visits, more conversations with school teachers and MSU faculty, and more college classroom observations. This was not surprising, as earlier conversations had changed the program from a one- to two-week program. Another alternative expressed by both MSU and Azim Premji University participants was having pre-visit preparation. Overall the survey results confirm that our design for the program is meeting the goals and objectives.

ANALYSIS OF THE PARTNERSHIP DEVELOPMENT AND ACTIVITIES

A lot has been learned about partnership development in the past five years. We use Sakamoto and Chapman's Functional Model for the Analysis of Cross-border Partnerships (2010) to analyze and organize the key factors that have played roles in development and success of the partnership. The framework identifies the following factors that influence higher education institution participation in international partnerships – (a) organizational, (b) financial, (c) individual (faculty), and (d) context for collaborative venture (political and regulatory environment). We loosely follow the framework as laid out (i.e., we maintain the four broad categories though we do not necessarily include all the sub-categories that Sakamoto and Chapman included in their approach). As will become clear, many of the key factors identified support the findings of other partnership projects. At the same time there are factors that have been crucial in the MSU and Azim Premji University partnership development process that have been less emphasized in the current literature or in the framework. Under each broad category of Sakamoto and Chapman's (2010) framework we present our main recommendation, followed by a more detailed description and/or examples. The fact that the authors play leading roles in each of these institutions allows us to provide the perspectives of both institutions.

ORGANIZATIONAL FACTORS

Centrality of Content to Institutional Mission

Recommendation 1: Build partnership programs on trust and shared vision. Partners may have different priorities at different times. Trust will help to overcome differences. Shared vision, written or unwritten, will establish why the partnership exists in the first place and will allow the partnership to grow and develop or will help identify when the partnership has reached its full potential.

One of the strengths of the partnership between MSU's College of Education and the Azim Premji University was shared key values and perspectives. MSU is one of the first land-grant universities built around the Morrill Acts of 1862 and 1890. The expectation was that these publicly-funded institutions would expand their focus from an abstract liberal arts curriculum to a broader commitment to applied education and social good in the communities in which they exist (Thelin, 2011). Though much has changed in terms of how land-grant universities are funded and how they operate, the original democratic mandate for openness, accessibility and service to people still exists today, and is particularly strong in the vision of the College of Education at Michigan State.

The commitment to the land-grant mission on MSU's side was met with a parallel set of organizational values that form the basis for the work of the Azim Premji University and the Foundation. Azim Premji University, in its mission, is committed to the development of a just, humane, equitable and sustainable society and on a foundational belief that education is a powerful medium to influence positive change in society.

In early conversations between faculty and leadership of both universities, this commonality of purpose was clear and, over time, served as a way of bringing both teams together around a shared set of values and broader social purpose, as well as a way of sustaining connections and partnerships when faced by challenges. The focus on practice on the ground (in the case of MSU, represented in its commitment to teacher education and practical research; and in the case of Azim Premji University, through being a unit of the overarching Foundation whose field institutes are core to its vision), combined with a parallel commitment to the development of a research agenda that would inform practice, were important to creating a shared set of values and commitments.

Sufficient Comparative Advantage

Recommendation 2: Each partner will benefit in different ways. The motivation to remain in a partnership depends on benefits received. Recognize
that and build on it instead of seeing it as a barrier.

Despite the alignment of broader values, there were also significant
differences between what the two partner institutions brought to the partnership. The College of Education at MSU is a highly ranked college of
education, with years of expertise in the fields of teacher education and
research, as well as a strong foundation in international work. That said,
MSU had not had any significant prior international work with India.
Thus, when the project started, one of the strong motivations from the side
of MSU was a willingness to learn and be part of the growth and development of education in the largest democracy in the world.

For Azim Premji University, it was an opportunity to interact with a
much respected university whose purpose of public good resonated with its
own clear purpose. As much as the reputation of the College of Education,
its value-based commitment to public good was an important factor. Since
the Azim Premji University was established and had a plan to introduce
degree programs in the area of teacher education, it found the College of
Education at MSU as an appropriate institution to interact with and learn
from as it established its own programs.

Capacity of Institution to Absorb Extra Demands on Faculty Time and Work

Recommendation 3: Institutional support, in the form of resources and
expertise, is essential for establishing and advancing an international
partnership. The success of a partnership depends not only on developing
external relationships, but, most importantly, also builds on existing internal relationships. Seek out expertise, advice and support from others at
your institution who have experience with international work.

The College of Education at MSU is a large unit that has been historically engaged with research on the practice and policy of education on a
large scale. It has, over the years, developed extensive expertise in developing international relationships; an Assistant Dean for International
Education coordinates these various projects and activities. Thus, there was
both a large number of faculty participating in international projects as
well as strong institutional memory of various models and funding structures that have worked in the past. There was also an understanding that

international work takes time and requires support – the size of the college allowed for such support to be provided. For instance, during the years that this partnership was being negotiated and structured, the office of the Dean and the department of Counseling, Educational Psychology, and Special Education often picked up the costs of travel and other basic expenses. Individuals such as Dr. Jack Schwille, Assistant Dean (since retired), his extensive experience with global partnerships, and his unstinting support for this particular project meant that the individual faculty members who were pursuing this could always feel supported.

Having said this, to a very large extent the strength and tempo of activities depends on the time that individual faculty on both sides can give to the partnership. At Azim Premji University, the schedule of teaching, institution building, research, and field practice meant that faculty could only contribute at specific times of the year. The local environment and context, specific objectives, and student backgrounds limit the nature of what can be exchanged and absorbed. It is not as much skepticism as the limitation of relevance.

Existing Institutional Relationships

Recommendation 4: Communication is the key to building relationships. Maintaining any relationship requires effort, but especially international relationships.

In the case of this partnership, there were no specific existing relationships that could be leveraged. This meant that the first part of the process, almost four years, was spent in developing and nurturing a shared understanding of what each organization had to offer and take from the partnership. Key to this were the personal relationships that were formed (described in greater detail below). As Cooper and Mitsunaga (2010) have emphasized, "staying in touch and listening are both key to faculty collaborative efforts" (p. 80). Keeping this in mind, the initial conversations were general, seeking to better understand the needs and priorities of the two institutions. Initial meetings were also supported by the use of Internet and Communication Technologies (ICT), though it soon became clear that these technologies, despite the potential, did not offer the same level of connection that face-to-face meetings provided. There were, of course, some "hiccups" along the way – misunderstandings of intent, scope of the project, budgets involved and so on. In fact, there were often times during which it appeared this partnership would never see the light of day. It was only through constant communication and interaction that both organizations and the individuals working within them could build a foundation of trust in each other and their respective goals to make this partnership a reality.

One of the stumbling blocks on MSU's end was misunderstanding the very nature of Azim Premji Foundation. The use of the word "Foundation" implied to faculty and administrators at MSU that Azim Premji Foundation was an organization with resources that were awarded in the form of grants, similar to those in the United States (such as the Bill and Melinda Gates Foundation). This is in contrast to Azim Premji Foundation, which is an organization that actually does the work on the ground. This misperception of the purpose of the Azim Premji Foundation led to MSU proposing a multi-million dollar five-year plan for faculty development. This plan was so far removed from the reality of what the partnership could be that it was the biggest challenge faced by this nascent partnership and could have been a deal-breaker. It was only continual communication by individuals on both sides that managed to salvage this near debacle into a functioning partnership.

One key way that trust was restored was by scaling back the scope of the project, making it an annual project that would be continually reviewed and extended only if both parties felt there was something worth continuing. This removed the pressure of a multi-year and multi-million dollar commitment and allowed the project to evolve over time.

In such a situation, the enthusiasm and commitment of the CEOs of the Foundation and the key faculty at MSU was of critical importance. As the conversations continued, it became clear that it was strategically crucial to identify one or two key realistic initiatives that can be immediately implemented. It became clear that rather than attempt to have MSU contribute ideas to program curriculum or course curriculum – something that was tried and did not work as planned – it would make sense to focus on issues related to student support and exposure visits for Azim Premji faculty to the College of Education at MSU. To arrive at this kind of wisdom and action was not easy. This is where patience, trust, transparency and candor between the key players on both sides was vital. The frank and candid conversation about what worked and what did not were important and allowed the partners to drop the efforts in areas that were not generating traction and focus instead on areas that were showing promise of success.

The other important aspect is that, ultimately, identification of initiatives depends on the individuals involved, not just the key personnel. For example, in the area of student support, a MSU College of Education faculty member and the head of student support at the Azim Premji University formed an association of mutual respect, friendship, and willingness to learn. It led to a basis of successful interactions in which the various suggestions were seriously considered in order to decide what to implement in the context and environment of Azim Premji University and also allowed both parties to acknowledge that they had done as much as was possible together. This part of the project emerged not out of design but rather a chance meeting between an MSU faculty member and members of the Azim Premji University when they visited the MSU campus. Once an alignment of needs and capacities was identified both sides worked quickly to make issues related to students' affairs a key part of the partnership.

Similarly, it took a detailed discussion between Foundation CEOs Dileep Ranjekar and Anurag Behar, and Dean Heller and Professor Punya Mishra, of MSU's College of Education, to agree that going forward – from 2013 on – the partnership would focus on small groups of faculty (including members of the Field Institutes of the Foundation) visiting MSU for two weeks of interaction, exposure and learning that could cover specific aspects of education, such as teacher education, school management, assessment and pedagogy.

Organizational Depth of Interest (Number of Faculty Who Want to Participate)

Recommendation 5: Utilize your internal network and your knowledge about your institution – successful partnerships need a range of faculty and administrator support.

A multi-year, multi-threaded partnership of this nature needs a range of faculty and administrators to ensure its growth and development. One of the advantages of this partnership has been that most of the people involved share a commitment and passion for education, for sharing ideas, and for learning from each other. This support has ranged from that of the leadership at both institutions, from the Vice Chancellor of Azim Premji University to the President of Michigan State, as well as the Dean of the College of Education. This interest has been indicated by the number of visits by key faculty and leadership from MSU to India and vice versa.

One of the most important factors in the success of this partnership has been the key role played by individual faculty members or administrators, so called "internal champions" (Eddy, 2010), who took on the role of nurturing and supporting this arrangement even when things were not going very smoothly. At MSU, the charge was led by one of the authors of this chapter. Though his research interests did not include international or comparative education, he was deeply interested in fostering a partnership between the two organizations – primarily because India was his country of origin. In some ways his lack of a research agenda in India was a benefit since there was no conflict of interest in his research and outreach agenda. Thus he became a crucial point of contact for all the work in which the partnership would be engaged. Having received tenure (and soon promoted to Professor) he was under less pressure than an untenured faculty member to "prove himself" and, thus, could take on longer-term projects and devote his time over years to making this project a success. Having been at MSU for over a decade, Mishra had well-developed contacts (and social capital) across the university that helped move things along. Over time, the addition of a deeply committed graduate student (the first author) brought not only extensive international experience, but also a network of professional connections and innovative ideas about program development; this led to the expansion of this project to individuals and groups across the university and the broader community. From the Azim Premji University, the Registrar and Chief Operating Officer – also one of the authors of this chapter – played the nodal point-person role to facilitate the partnership. In his case, he had been at the Foundation from its very early days, having contributed to building its field work and programs. He then moved to the university at its inception, which helped bring an overall perspective and understanding to the association. Individual rapport, friendship and mutual respect amongst the two nodal persons in the two institutions was a key contributor to the partnership.

Certain organizational changes also helped move the partnership along. For instance, in 2014, the Azim Premji University reorganized itself into five schools and a research center. These are the School of Education (SOE), School of Development, School of Policy & Governance, School of Liberal Studies (SLS), and the School of Continuing Education, each responsible for its own programs. This reorganization is relevant in the context of our discussion here. It meant that now the School Director took the responsibility of selecting the faculty who would attend the two-week program at MSU. It also means that any initiative that may be considered under this participation would get a buy-in/rejection from the School Director thereby ensuring complete ownership once an initiative was accepted. For anyone from the Field Institute nominated for the two-week program, the Foundation's Director of Field Institutes would decide the nominations.

FINANCIAL

Recommendation 6: Recognize that funding can define a partnership. Who is funding and what is being funded are central questions for any partnership. The financial structure of the partnership has important consequences for the nature of the relationship between partners and sustainability of the partnership.

The partnership between MSU and Azim Premji University is somewhat unique in that the bulk of the funding comes from Azim Premji University. Mr. Premji's endowment has ensured that the Foundation (including the University) has a strong financial structure in place. Some initial funding came from both organizations independently but, over time, there has been a clear shift to the funding coming from the international partner to the U.S. university. This is in contrast to most other partnerships between U.S. universities and universities in the developing world, which are typically funded by U.S.-based funding agencies (such as NSF, USAID, and the World Bank). This partnership has a different structure with important consequences for the nature of the relationship developed. The fact that the funding is coming from the University in India has meant that (a) the U.S. partner has to ensure that the partnership is truly serving the needs of the partner institution (the funder) and that money is not being misused on irrelevant matters that do not extend the work in fruitful directions, (b) that the project is not burdened by bureaucratic reporting requirements of external funding agencies, and (c) as mentioned earlier, the scope of the work is not predefined at the beginning of the partnership, but can grow and be adjusted as new needs arise.

INDIVIDUAL

Recommendation 7: Find the right faculty members on both sides as things expand. Faculty not only need to be passionate about their work, they need to be flexible, able to think on their feet, open to challenges and opportunities, and embrace working collaboratively with colleagues from different cultural backgrounds and traditions, as well.

From the point of view of faculty at the College of Education at MSU, this partnership has provided opportunities to both learn more about the educational system in India and to contribute to it, as well as reflect on one's own practice from a comparative perspective. A range of faculty members have visited the University in Bangalore and many more have met the visitors who have come from India to spend time at MSU. Interestingly, faculty for the most part have volunteered their time or participated in these projects once their travel and other incidental expenses have been met. A large part of this is because the Indian partner universities have been able to truly inspire the faculty at MSU with the breadth of their vision, the depth of their passion, and the scale of their ambitions.

Not all faculty members who have attempted to work with the partners have been completely successful, however. For those unable to navigate this partnership well, it was not because of any lack of interest or passion, it was more to do with style of operating. International work is messy and complex, and though planning may be important to success it does not guarantee it. A willingness to improvise and be opportunistic (in the best sense of the word) is essential. Design is important as is a willingness to be open to chance and the unexpected. Things seldom go as planned and it is important that faculty who want to work in an international context be willing to change their plans and be open to thinking on their feet to come up with alternative plans. As Amey, Eddy, and Ozaki (2007) emphasize, the flexibility and adaptability are key to successful partnerships. Learning to listen, to hear alternative points of view, is of critical importance. Taking a humble stance of a co-learner and participant, rather than that of an expert flying in to offer "gyan" (Hindi word for "knowledge"), is key.

Finding such people can be a challenge particularly as the scope of work expands. The key factor here is flexibility – at multiple levels. Over time there have been more than a few sub-projects that have started, grown and then, somewhat naturally, faded away. For instance, two areas that took a great deal of time and effort by faculty from MSU working with faculty and staff at Azim Premji University were developing processes of faculty evaluation and promotion. There were multiple meetings between experts at both universities, including visits on both sides, with full day workshops and so on. This work progressed steadily over two years and then, as Azim Premji University developed its own policies for faculty evaluation, this line of work gradually came to an end. A similar story could be seen in the development of the department of student affairs at Azim Premji University. The leadership at MSU had to continually monitor these sub-projects to ensure that they were moving along and be willing to have open conversations with partners at Azim Premji University regarding when each of these lines of work had reached its culmination and needed to be gradually phased out, even while keeping lines of communication open to envisage new sub-projects for the future.

CONTEXT FOR COLLABORATIVE VENTURE (LEGAL/ REGULATORY), INTELLECTUAL PROPERTY RIGHTS, POLITICAL STABILITY, CULTURAL CONTEXT

Recommendation 8: Relationships based on trust and collegiality will help navigate and overcome obstacles created by policies or practices at the institutional level, or external environments in which institutions operate.

The fact that both organizations saw the value in this partnership and, at least at the beginning, focused on overarching goals rather than specifics, combined with the fact that there was not a third party involved with its own goals and objectives (as often happens when external funders are involved) meant that the process of signing the partnership documents was relatively easy. The initial contract that was signed between the two organizations was for 18 months and was repeatedly extended for over five years. This has been possible mainly due to the development of a relationship based on trust and collegiality. In the Indian context, the fact that the Azim Premji University is a private institution has helped since it has a greater level of freedom than other government-supported public institutions in India. At the same time, while being a private, autonomous not-for-profit institution, it forms and conducts these kinds of collaborative partnerships in compliance with the requirements of the University Grants Commission, the central body that guides higher education in India.

CONCLUSION

This chapter has provided an example of what we consider to be a successful partnership between MSU and Azim Premji University. Both institutions came to the partnership with previous experiences, MSU with many years of experience with international projects, Azim Premji University with the experience of Foundation that for many years in its work on the ground has partnered with a number of other organizations. The cardinal principles that applied to Azim Premji Foundation partnerships also applied here. The principals of mutual trust, respect, candor, and openness were understood by MSU College of Education and become a basis for the partnership between both institutions.

Through the analysis of our experiences we arrived at several key realizations that we believe are important to the establishment and development of successful collaborative partnerships and that we have described in the previous section. These can be summarized in three imperatives for anyone considering developing or participating in international collaborative partnership:

1. *Change the perspective.* Shift the focus from "capacity building," which has dominated international partnerships for decades, to partnerships that are built on mutual learning. It is an opportunity to look beyond traditional forms, think creatively, and be innovative and expand on past partnership experiences.
2. *Build relationships.* Relationships among individual people are the foundation of every partnership, especially those that are self-funded and collaborative in nature, and make each partnership unique and different.
3. *Be flexible.* Be flexible with modes of communication, with choice of faculty, and with needs of projects. As the title of the chapter says, design and planning are important to success. But equally as important is an openness to the unexpected – to take a chance when things do not go according to plan. In this context steady small steps make more sense than putting all your resources into one large project.

Over the past five years, this partnership has involved over 100 people from MSU and the Azim Premji Foundation. We are hopeful that this partnership will continue to grow and evolve with time. The strength of this self-funded, collaborative partnership lies in multiple threads of connections that, at their foundation, have a strong connection in shared values and goals.

ACKNOWLEDGMENTS

We are deeply thankful to our colleagues at the College of Education, Michigan State University and Azim Premji Foundation (which includes the Azim Premji University). Without their support the partnership and, consequently, this chapter would not have been possible. We also thank the editors of this volume and reviewers for their feedback.

REFERENCES

Altbach, P. G. (2005). The private higher education revolution: An introduction. In P. G. Altbach & D. C. Levy (Eds.), *Private higher education: A global revolution* (Vol. 2, pp. 1–9). Rotterdam: Sense Publishers.
Altbach, P. G., & Knight, J. (2007). The internationalization of higher education: Motivations and realities. *Journal of Studies in International Education, 11*(3–4), 290–305.

Amey, M. J., Eddy, P. L., & Ozaki, C. C. (2007). Demands for partnership and collaboration in higher education: A model. *New Directions for Community Colleges, 139*, 5–14.

Azim Premji University. (Vision). Retrieved from http://azimpremjiuniversity.edu.in/ SitePages/vision-mission.aspx

Carnoy, M., Loyalka, P., Androushchak, G. V., & Proudnikova, A. (2012). *The economic returns to higher education in the BRIC countries and their implications for higher education expansion.* Higher School of Economics Research Paper No. WP BRP, 2. Retrieved from http://reap.fsi.stanford.edu/sites/default/files/Does_Expanding_Higher_ Education_Equalize_Income_Distribution.pdf

Cohen, C. L. (2010). *Developing institutional and human capacity for agricultural research.* Retrieved from https://agrilinks.org/sites/default/files/resource/files/Cohen_Human% 20and%20Institutional%20Capacity%20Development%20for%20Agricultural%20 Research_2010.pdf

Coleman, J. S., & Court, D. (1993). *University development in the third world: The Rockefeller foundation experience.* New York, NY: Pergamon.

Cooper, J., & Mitsunaga, R. (2010). Faculty perspectives on international education: The nested realities of faculty collaborations. *New Directions for Higher Education, 2010*(150), 69–81. doi:10.1002/he.391

De Witt, H. (2002). *Internationalization of higher education in the United States of America and Europe.* Westport, CT: Greenwood Press.

Eddy, P. L. (2010). Institutional collaborations in Ireland: Leveraging an increased international presence. *New Directions for Higher Education, 150*, 19–29. doi:10.1002/he.387

King, K. (2009). Higher education and international cooperation: The role of academic collaboration in the developing world. Higher Education and International Capacity Building: Twenty-Five Years of Higher Education Links, 33–49.

Michigan State University. (MSU). Mission Statement. Retrieved from http://president.msu.edu/mission/#sthash.oG7avkXU.dpuf

Psaltis, C. (2007). International collaboration as construction of knowledge and its constraints. *Integrative Psychological and Behavioral Science, 41*(2), 187–197.

Sakamoto, R., & Chapman, D. W. (2010). Expanding across borders, the growth of cross-border partnerships in higher education. In R. Sakamoto & D. W. Chapman (Eds.), *Cross-border partnerships in higher education: Strategies and issues* (pp. 3–15). London: Routledge.

Thelin, J. R. (2011). *A history of American higher education.* Baltimore, MD: JHU Press.

COMMUNITY COLLEGE-UNIVERSITY CROSS-BORDER PARTNERSHIP THROUGH FACULTY EXCHANGE

Iddah Aoko Otieno and Tom Otieno

ABSTRACT

Institutions of higher education are increasingly facing a myriad of challenges emanating from a fast changing higher educational landscape. One strategy colleges and universities adopt as they pursue their missions in a progressively competitive global environment is to form strategic partnerships with other colleges and universities locally and globally. This chapter examines a partnership, anchored in faculty exchange, between an American metropolitan community college, and a public university in the Republic of Kenya, East Africa. The issues discussed include the rationale for the formation of a partnership between a two-year institution and a doctoral-granting institution in spite of their differing missions, the partnership formalization process, types of activities undertaken in each country, program outcomes, and program management and challenges. The chapter concludes with some recommendations that would be useful to anyone considering starting a cross-border faculty

University Partnerships for Academic Programs and Professional Development
Innovations in Higher Education Teaching and Learning, Volume 7, 181–199
Copyright © 2016 by Emerald Group Publishing Limited
All rights of reproduction in any form reserved
ISSN: 2055-3641/doi:10.1108/S2055-364120160000007020

exchange program, especially at an institution where infrastructure for internationalization activities is limited.

Keywords: Faculty; exchange; international; university; partnerships

INTRODUCTION

Institutions of higher education (IHEs) are increasingly facing a myriad of challenges emanating from a fast changing higher educational landscape, particularly in the areas of funding, research, faculty development, information technology, competition for students, demographic changes in student body, and the need to graduate a globally competent labor force. Consequently, colleges and universities have to strategically position themselves to operate in a progressively competitive global environment. Recognizing that institutions can do more together than they can do alone, one strategy that is commonly adopted by IHEs is to form partnerships with other colleges and universities locally and globally. The increasing significance of such partnerships has resulted in the publication of a number of books on the subject in recent years (Romano, 2002; Sakamoto & Chapman, 2012; Sutton & Obst, 2011; Van de Water, Green, & Koch, 2008). These books cover a wide range of topics pertinent to the purposes, underpinning values, planning, developing, and implementing international partnerships, the range of activities involved, and the different ways in which different types of institutions are exploring the potential for international partnerships. They are a useful resource to any institution considering forming international partnerships. This chapter examines a partnership, anchored in faculty exchange, between an American metropolitan community college and a public university in the Republic of Kenya. Since the motivation for initiating this partnership was to contribute to the "cultural and global awareness" component of the community college's mission, we begin with a couple of illustrations as to why such awareness is important.

The 2014 Ebola epidemic was the largest in history, affecting multiple countries in West Africa. A man who traveled to the United States from Liberia in September 2014 became the first patient to be diagnosed with Ebola in the United States. In a matter of days, two healthcare workers who had provided care for this patient tested positive for Ebola. The fourth case of Ebola diagnosed in the United States was in a medical aid worker who had returned to New York City from Guinea. These occurrences led to apprehension among the American public. For instance, in Louisville, Kentucky, a middle school teacher was forced to resign after her school demanded she takes a 21-day (incubation period for Ebola virus) leave because parents and staff of the school were concerned she would expose students to Ebola, since she had recently traveled to Kenya. This nervousness was despite the fact that no cases of Ebola had been reported in Kenya, and the East African country is over 3,000 miles away from the Ebola epidemic in Western Africa.

On September 11, 2001, members of the global Islamic terrorist group, al-Qaeda, used four hijacked passenger airplanes for suicide attacks targeting symbolic United States landmarks. The attacks claimed about 3,000 human lives and caused billions of dollars in property and infrastructure damage. The Ebola epidemic and the terrorist attack are just two examples that underscore the fact that no country can exist in isolation in the 21st century. The world is a global village, with interconnected economies, politics, education, environmental concerns, and security concerns, among others. To understand the causes and effects of world events and to appropriately shape our personal, communal, and national responses requires an understanding of other cultures rather than building defensive walls around national borders.

Higher education has the responsibility to graduate students who have the knowledge and skills to live and work in an interdependent world. Our graduates need to have a better understanding of global issues and world events and be able to appreciate other cultures. They need to develop intercultural communication skills to be able to cope with an increasingly culturally and ethnically diverse workplace. In other words, our graduates need to be globally competent. Conferees at a meeting sponsored by the American Council on International Intercultural Education (ACIIE) and the Stanley Foundation (1996) defined global competency as existing when "a learner is able to understand the interconnectedness of peoples and systems, to have a general knowledge of history and world events, to accept and cope with the existence of different cultural values and attitudes and, indeed, to celebrate the richness and benefits of this diversity" (p. 4).

RATIONALE FOR THE FORMATION OF BCTC-MU PARTNERSHIP

This chapter examines a partnership between an American community college and a doctoral-granting public university (state-supported) in Kenya,

East Africa. Bluegrass Community and Technical College (BCTC) is a multi-campus two-year institution (offers degrees primarily at the associate's level) in the Commonwealth of Kentucky and awards associate degrees in both academic and technical areas. In the fall 2013 semester, BCTC reported a total student headcount enrollment of 12,367 (Bluegrass Community & Technical College [BCTC], 2013). BCTC is a member of the Kentucky Community and Technical College System (KCTCS) comprising 16 colleges spread over 68 campuses across Kentucky.

While the focus of BCTC's mission is on excellence in teaching and learning, the mission also calls upon the institution to promote "regional economic vitality and quality of life through diversity and inclusion, cultural and global awareness, critical thinking, civic responsibility, professional competence, and sustainability" (BCTC, 2014). Programs and services that contribute toward BCTC's fulfillment of the "diversity and inclusion" and "cultural and global awareness" components of its mission include the recruitment and enrollment of international students and the occasional hosting of international speakers. The college also convenes an annual international education week during which international students showcase their cultures through speaking engagements, music, food, clothes, and artifacts. Students and faculty also have opportunities to experience and learn about other cultures through participation in the activities of the Kentucky Institute for International Studies (KIIS), a consortium formed by several IHEs in Kentucky to organize and coordinate study-abroad programs for college students (KIIS, 2015). Additionally, BCTC has had an active linkage with Changsha University in China since 1990. Through this exchange program, BCTC faculty make short visits to China and Chinese scholars visit BCTC where they stay for up to one year and contribute to the teaching of Chinese language at BCTC.

Considering the existence of the China Exchange Program, and the fact that KIIS study-abroad programs are held primarily in European, South American, and Asian countries, there clearly was a need to initiate a program that infuses African experiences into the "cultural and global awareness" agenda at BCTC. The first author of this chapter began holding informal discussions with her faculty colleagues at BCTC in the fall of 2001 semester. A 12-member advisory board composed of faculty members with interests in international travel and/or internationalization of higher education was established to brainstorm and make recommendations to the college president. An exchange program was considered more desirable than at-home activities because of the experiential learning that accrues from cross-border partnerships (Farnsworth, 2002; Van de Water et al., 2008, p. 22). The next point of discussion was the choice of an African institution of higher education with which to form a linkage. Maseno University (MU) was selected as the first institution to approach because the first author is an alumnus of the university and the discussants agreed her knowledge of both MU and BCTC and local cultures would be of great value to the success of an exchange program. Maseno University is a relatively young institution. It was founded in 1991 as a constituent college of Moi University and achieved university status in 2001. It is a multi-campus public university with the main campus located in Maseno Township, Kenya. The University has a total student enrollment of 8,000 and awards bachelors, masters, and doctoral degrees.

Naturally, there were concerns about the compatibility of BCTC and MU, with the former being a two-year institution and the latter a doctoral-granting institution. The approach taken was to focus on common grounds in the missions of the two institutions. Both institutions are committed to excellence in teaching and learning. BCTC has long been committed to the promotion of cultural and global awareness as stated in its mission statement. This commitment has been reiterated in its strategic plan through objective 3.2.1, which stresses creating "more awareness of and sensitivity to diversity in BCTC community" (BCTC, 2010). Among the actions steps for achieving this objective are to "provide multicultural and inclusion experiences that enhance multicultural awareness and competencies of faculty, staff and students" and to "support international student enrollment and enhance global awareness activities." The mission of Maseno University also includes a cultural component. Maseno University (2013) Charter states that "the mission of the University is the promotion of excellence in undergraduate and postgraduate studies, basic and applied research for the enhancement of economic, social, cultural, scientific, and technological development of Kenya, with special emphasis on training practically oriented graduates" (p. 7). The philosophy of the university underscores the cultural component of its mission even more as stated in the Maseno University Charter: "Maseno University fosters the belief that communities are enriched by the diversity of human knowledge, ingenuity and experiences ... we strive to promote an environment in which ideas are shared and intellectual diversity embraced" (Maseno University, 2013, p. 7). Clearly, there was sufficient overlap in the missions of the two institutions that could support the establishment of an exchange program.

PARTNERSHIP FORMALIZATION PROCESS

Having established the need for a partnership with an African IHE that is consistent with the mission of BCTC, and having identified a potential partner, the next step was to sell the idea to the institution and secure support for the initiative. This process involved a series of meetings during the fall 2001 semester with various stakeholders including faculty colleagues, Director of International Students and Visiting Scholar Services, Vice President for Multiculturalism and Inclusion, Vice President for Academics, and the President. The president gave the green light for official communication with Maseno University on the possibility of a partnership to begin toward the end of the spring 2002 semester. The initial communication was conducted electronically. MU responded positively and the process of drafting a Memorandum of Understanding (MOU) was initiated.

As had been anticipated when Maseno University was selected as a potential partner, the fact that the two institutions had overall different missions came into play. Being a doctoral-granting institution, research is an integral part of MU's University mission. Furthermore, its charter lists 21 functions of the university, one of which is to "provide opportunities for development and further training for staff and students of the institution" (Maseno University, 2013). How could a partnership with BCTC, a two-year institution, help Maseno University meet these aspects of its mission? Three requirements MU negotiators put on the table were particularly tricky for BCTC: (i) Assurances that there would be opportunities for professional development for MU faculty, including research collaboration, (ii) Opportunities for MU students to advance their education in America at no cost to MU, (iii) Donations of scientific equipment and books to MU.

The solutions came from informal relationships with other institutions within Kentucky. Bluegrass Community and Technical College has a long-standing association with University of Kentucky (UK), a doctoral-granting institution. In fact, BCTC is physically located within University of Kentucky grounds. BCTC promised to facilitate research collaboration with UK faculty once MU visiting scholars to BCTC had been identified. Additional non-research based professional development opportunities would also be available to the visitors through participation in social, academic, and cultural enrichment activities at BCTC and within the Commonwealth. At the time of these negotiations, the second author of this chapter was the coordinator of the Graduate Program in the Department of

Chemistry at Eastern Kentucky University (EKU), a comprehensive public institution located about 30 miles from BCTC. When contacted by BCTC, he agreed to facilitate the admission of, and award of teaching assistantship to, qualified MU students to EKU to pursue master's level education, particularly in the Department of Chemistry. As for the third request, BCTC negotiators indicated their willingness to donate books, but expressed regrets for not being in a position to donate scientific equipment. Other issues that were negotiated included accommodation and transportation of visiting scholars. The e-mail "negotiation" phase took the entire fall 2002 semester by the end of which a draft MOU, detailing the responsibilities of each party and the general time-line for implementation, was submitted to the BCTC president.

The final phase of the partnership formalization process was a visit to Maseno University in the summer of 2003 by the first author, as the designated Director of the Kenya Exchange Program at BCTC. The purpose of this trip was to complete the finer points of the negotiations and secure the signature of the Maseno University Vice Chancellor on the MOU. After many meetings and deliberations with members of Maseno University's International Relations and Links Committee, a formal MOU between BCTC was signed by the Vice Chancellor. Upon the director's return to the U.S.A., the MOU was signed by both the President of BCTC and the Chancellor of KCTCS. The Kenya Exchange Program at BCTC had become a reality.

PROGRAM ACTIVITIES

Classroom Instruction

Student contact has been a key component of the Kenya Exchange Program at BCTC. The first two visits by MU faculty to BCTC were characterized by heavy classroom instruction. The visiting scholars were each given four classes to teach in their respective areas of expertise: Mathematics, Psychology, and Biology. One scholar was also involved in team teaching a course with a BCTC colleague, providing the MU scholar the opportunity to learn to navigate an unfamiliar teaching environment in which he had to share control of course material and classroom management with someone else. The scholars credited classroom instruction experience as one of the most rewarding part of their visit, as one of the scholars put it, "the interchange of ideas resulting from these interactions is at the core of what the exchange program is about, exposing BCTC students to other cultures of the world" (L. Othuon, personal communication, October 6, 2006). In addition, teaching in a new cultural environment exposed the scholars to cultural differences in student-teacher classroom interactions. One of the scholars observed that "Maseno university students see me more as an authority figure than the BCTC students. At BCTC, the teacher is more of a facilitator. They know that the instructor knows more than they do, but that does not cut them off from talking with you directly, sometimes addressing you by your first name" (B. Owuor, personal communication, October 10, 2006). Visiting BCTC faculty stayed in Kenya for only two to three weeks and, as a result, they could not be assigned any courses to teach.

Classroom Observation

Learning through observation is one of the best ways to experience how things are done in a different cultural environment. The Kenya Exchange Program requires faculty from both partner institutions to observe classroom instruction at the host institution. The visiting scholars are normally paired with a faculty member who serves as a guide and host. Scholars credit this form of mentorship as the best way to learn and network with peers on pertinent issues surrounding classroom management across cultures. This perspective is consistent with the use of mentoring programs to enhance the professional development and socialization of new faculty at IHEs (Otieno, Lutz, & Schoolmaster, 2010). Useful feedback gleaned from these classroom observations have certainly helped faculty in their own practices at home and abroad. For instance, one of the scholars appreciated the fact that, in contrast to the common practice at his home institution, both the class textbook and his BCTC counterpart used examples with local themes that students could relate to in explaining new concepts and principles to students.

International Dialogue Series

The BCTC International Dialogue Series is a set of open forums that was created to provide a platform for interchange of ideas between the visiting scholars and BCTC faculty, students, and staff. Each dialogue is conducted in a format in which the speaker makes a brief presentation, followed by a discussion with the audience. Selected examples of topics that have been discussed over the years are provided below, with titles of presentations given in parenthesis. Presentations by visiting Kenyan scholars exposed the BCTC community to the education system in Kenya ("Maseno University At-A-Glance," "Kenyan Educational System,"), research ("From Tea Plant to Tea Cup"), contributions of women to the Kenyan society ("The Role of Women in National Development"), and ongoing changes in Kenyan families as a result of global influence ("Kenyan Families in Transition"). In this reciprocal arrangement, BCTC scholars who traveled to Kenya shared with the Maseno University community information about education in America ("Educational Opportunities in USA," "Navigating the Doctoral degree Program in the USA," "The American Community College"), race relations ("The Un-united State of America Post-Obama"), personal growth and wellbeing ("Which Way Do I Go?," "We Are What We Eat," "Motivation Will Get You There"), agriculture in the Appalachian region ("Global Sustainable Agriculture: Knowledge through Sharing"), and history and natural resources of Kentucky ("The Uncommon Wealth of the Commonwealth of Kentucky").

The International Dialogue Series has been institutionalized at BCTC and it continues even when there are no visiting scholars on campus. Faculty who have traveled abroad and international students have stepped in to share their experiences with international travel, research, music, food, and culture. Countries covered in these discussions in recent years include Nepal, India, Morocco, Congo, Kenya, Venezuela, Nicaragua, Korea, and France.

Cultural Enrichment

Cultural enrichment opportunities have been a significant tool in exposing the visiting scholars to the way people live in the host country. Enrichment activities include visiting families in their homes, preparing meals and eating together, participation in community events, visiting churches, educational tours, and other local excursions. Examples of local excursions in Kentucky for visitors from Kenya include visits to football and basketball games, local points of cultural and historical interest such as Kentucky State History Museum, Shaker Village (restored village that is home to a collection of architecture, furniture, and artifacts of the Shaker community), Mohamed Ali Center (Museum and cultural center built as a tribute to the champion boxer Muhammad Ali), Mammoth Cave National Park, Kentucky Horse Park, and a visit with the Governor at the State Capital in Frankfort. Local excursions in Kenya for visitors from America have included visits to Bomas of Kenya (tourist destination in Nairobi that displays traditional homes belonging to several Kenyan ethnic groups), Kisumu Museum, Kogelo Village (Ancestral home of the father of Barack Obama, the 44th President of the United States), Lake Nakuru and Amboseli National Parks, and Maasai Mara National Reserve. These avenues have provided program participants with alternative views about the host culture through first-hand experiences and participant observation. The stories that returning visitors bring home and share with their students and families are stories that touch on the humanity in us all, despite our cultural backgrounds. These educational journeys and experiences stick with the scholars for a lifetime. The hosts, too, are enriched by these trips, as they see familiar events and sites afresh, through their guests' perspectives.

Research

As discussed earlier in the section on partnership formalization process, BCTC agreed to facilitate research collaboration between MU and University of Kentucky faculty in order to meet the research needs of MU scholars. One MU visiting scholar took advantage of this opportunity to conduct research in the Department of Plant Pathology at the University of Kentucky. In a reciprocal arrangement, a faculty member from the same department visited MU to explore additional research collaboration and student exchange opportunities between the two institutions. With regards to Maseno University's request for opportunities for its students to advance their education in America at no cost to MU, an informal arrangement was made with Eastern Kentucky University as described earlier in this paper. As part of this arrangement, three MU students have, to date, secured graduate assistantships and successfully obtained thesis-based M.S. degrees in chemistry at EKU. EKU has since signed a formal memorandum of understanding with MU.

OUTCOMES

Knight (2001) pointed out the importance of monitoring and evaluating internationalization initiatives and suggested appropriate tracking measures. Among the tracking measures relevant to a faculty exchange program proposed by Knight are, (1) the number of faculty/staff participating in international institutional exchange through exchange agreements and (2) the number of visiting international faculty/staff collaborating with domestic personnel. While no specific goals were set for the Kenya Exchange Program for these measures, the number of participants was noted. Between 2005 and 2013, eight BCTC faculty and staff, 3 Eastern Kentucky University faculty, and one Somerset Community College faculty have visited MU as part of the Kenyan Exchange Program in a total of four trips, each led by the program director. During the same time frame six MU faculty visited BCTC in three separate trips. Additional monitoring, the results of which are summarized below, included interviews with participants and observations by project director.

Enriched Learning Experience for BCTC Students

Because of factors such as work, family obligations, and travel costs, most American students, as elsewhere, are unable to visit other countries, even with the availability of study-abroad programs. The Kenyan Exchange Program has provided BCTC students with numerous opportunities to experience the world at home through their interactions with the visiting scholars in and out of the classroom. In addition, the BCTC faculty who have participated in the exchange program have been able to infuse some of their experiences into their courses, further enriching the learning experience for BCTC students, as one BCTC faculty participant observed, "I have traveled to many parts of the world, but the Kenya trip by far exceeds my experiences elsewhere. Even the pictures I took in Kenya have been a useful visual aid in my Geography 160 class on Lands and Peoples of the Non-Western World" (R. Kelley, personal communication, September 23, 2005). These experiences shared by faculty participants in their classrooms certainly broadened the students' minds on multicultural issues impacting our fast changing world.

Professional Development for Faculty

Being an effective academician means being a lifelong learner. The rapid advances in information technology, the increasing diversity of student populations, and the need to graduate a more internationally competitive work force require faculty to be continually learning to ensure their curriculum and pedagogical approaches keep pace with the changing times. The Kenya Faculty Exchange Program provides many professional development opportunities for faculty. Participation in the program requires cultural orientation workshops and the ability to work coopera-tively with people from diverse cultural backgrounds. Several BCTC faculty have traveled to Kenya which, like any foreign travel, is an invalu-able learning experience. They have attended the International Dialogue Series, served on the international advisory committee, and generally inter-acted with the visiting scholars in a number of ways. As a result of these experiences, they have gained new intercultural skills and are better prepared to teach their courses from a more global perspective.

Similarly, MU scholars at BCTC have had several opportunities for professional development. Teaching in a new cultural environment can be challenging. When the first batch of Maseno University visiting scholars arrived on campus in 2006 with full teaching responsibilities, it became necessary to establish an International Faculty Mentoring Program to help the scholars navigate the unfamiliar territory of teaching at an American community college. The program pairs the visiting scholars with their American counterparts. Mentoring activities include syllabus preparations, peer evaluations, and opportunities to observe their American counterparts teaching and advising students. Participants in this program credit it as an important avenue for professional development and growth. It provided a platform for scholars from BCTC and MU to dialogue on pertinent issues in classroom instruction and management from a cross-cultural perspective. As is typical of faculty mentoring programs (Otieno et al., 2010), the mentoring program was mutually beneficial for faculty participants, as observed by one BCTC faculty: "Mentoring the visiting scholars was such an enriching experience. I learned from my mentee as much as he learned from me. We exchanged notes and teaching techniques throughout the semester. We visited each other's classes periodically. We became such good friends within a very short time" (L. Miriti, personal communication, October 11, 2006).

Cultural Enrichment for Faculty

One of the goals of the Kenya Exchange Program is to expose participant to other cultures of the world through educational travel. The visiting scho-lars have been provided an opportunity to visit, and some cases, live with American families, observing first-hand how Americans live. BCTC scho-lars have also visited Kenyan homes and participated in activities provided by host families. Participants note that these avenues have provided them a window into cultural practices unfamiliar to them. It has also made them more comfortable with people from diverse cultural backgrounds. Through these interactions, long lasting relationships have been forged across cultures. Recalling a series of "international dinners" hosted by American colleagues during one of the exchange visits, a Kenyan scholar observed:

> That is another gem if I may call it so. Kentucky and Kenya are distances away. And you come here and you get into this program of dinners every so often. Really there is no other better way to know colleagues than to be able to talk to them in an atmosphere that is devoid of a working office environment. And we have been treated very well. These are really social evenings in which we get to talk very casually with our colleagues. I think there is no better way in which you can enhance friendship between diverse communities in the world. I think you guys are creating an opportunity here, which not many people have thought of. (B. Owuor, personal communication, October 6, 2006)

Increased Dialogue on International Issues

The presence of Maseno University faculty on BCTC campus for a whole semester during the 2006 and 2008 visits, and one month in 2011 has enriched both faculty and student experiences in significant ways. Through the International Dialogue Series, BCTC and MU faculty have been able to learn from each other by sharing teaching experiences in both African and American classroom contexts, as one visiting scholar succinctly put it: "I have the conviction that the world is but a small global village and for us to succeed, we have to put in place corporate measures to ensure that we understand global issues as they affect our day-to-day lives. It is only though this that we can be able to appreciate cultural diversities of humankind" (L. Othuon, personal communication, October 6, 2006). These dialogue forums have most certainly enhanced the global awareness at BCTC. The International Dialogue Series is a lasting legacy to the Kenyan Exchange Program.

Service Opportunities for BCTC Faculty and Staff

Faculty responsibilities in American IHEs is typically comprised of teaching plus research and/or service (Otieno, 2013). The Kenya Exchange

Program has provided BCTC faculty with numerous opportunities to meet the service component of their professional responsibilities. Examples of volunteer service responsibilities include making trips to the airport to pick up or drop off the visiting scholars, serving as mentors to the scholars, and taking them to sporting events, churches and educational and cultural tours, and hosting the scholars in their homes.

Increased Visibility for BCTC

In the fall of 2010, the Director of the Kenya Exchange Program was appointed by the president as BCTC's representative to the Kentucky Community and Technical College System's Global Studies and International Partnerships Work Group – a team of international educators from the sixteen community and technical colleges within Kentucky – whose main goal is to advice the KCTCS administration on internationalization initiatives. Membership on this group has provided increased visibility for BCTC within KCTCS with regards to the international dimension. The Kenya Exchange Program was also featured as one of the top three best programs to be emulated system-wide at the KCTCS' 2012 New Horizons Conference in Louisville, Kentucky.

Maseno University Book Project

During the negotiation of the partnership agreement with BCTC, Maseno University representatives identified lack of scientific equipment and books as needs, which they hoped their new partners would help them meet. In response, the Maseno University Book Project was launched at BCTC as part of the Kenya Exchange Program. Every other year, a call for book donations is sent via e-mail to BCTC faculty, staff, and students. The project has provided a unique avenue for BCTC students and staff to donate books to the MU library. Since its inception in 2005, over 2,000 books in the social and behavioral sciences, natural sciences, and computer information technology have been donated to MU. Through this project, the BCTC community has responded to one of the greatest challenges facing African IHEs: lack of books (Books for Africa, n.d.). It has also created a campus environment with a shared understanding of global citizenship and international cooperation.

Expanded Reach

The Kenya Exchange Program was initiated as a BCTC initiative but over the past 10 years, it has expanded to include all the sixteen colleges within the Kentucky Community and Technical College System. For example, in 2013, a faculty member from Somerset Community and Technical College visited Maseno University. In 2009, a faculty member from the University of Kentucky's Department of Plant Pathology visited Maseno University to explore research collaboration and student exchange opportunities. Additionally, three Eastern Kentucky University faculty members from the departments of English & Theatre, Chemistry, and Occupational Therapy have traveled to MU under the umbrella of the program.

PROGRAM MANAGEMENT AND CHALLENGES

The Kenya Exchange Program at BCTC is a collaborative effort comprising many units and key stakeholders in the internationalization process. Some of the offices directly involved in the planning process include the offices of the President, Vice President for Academics, Vice President for Multiculturalism and Inclusion, Director for International Students and Visiting Scholar Services, and the Human Resources Department. The International Advisory Committee, whose members are drawn from various academic units across campus, also plays a central role. The day-to-day management of the program falls under the purview of the program director. The director's responsibilities include corresponding with the partner institution, scheduling visits between the partner institutions, providing orientations on etiquette and travel issues to both BCTC and MU scholars, and working with a variety of offices in planning for scholar visits, including letters of invitation, compensation, accommodation, and local transportation of the scholars. The Office of the President makes decisions regarding finances, duration of stay, and remuneration for the scholars and provides resources for the implementation of the program. The office of International Students and Visiting Scholar Services is responsible for immigration issues, including visa application and Student and Exchange Visitor Information System (SEVIS) compliance. The Human Resources department is responsible for processing scholar compensations and benefits. The international advisory committee works out the details of each visit, including program activities, transportation, and accommodation.

The involvement of all these units has given the exchange program a campus-wide feel and ownership necessary for the success of any program.

Managing the Kenya Exchange Program has not been without challenges. On occasions, in response to student concerns about their learning, it became necessary to remind some of the visiting scholars to be cognizant of the fact that BCTC and MU are different types of institutions serving different student populations. Being a doctoral-granting institution, MU typically admits highly motivated traditional college students and instructor expectations are generally high. By contrast, BCTC is a two-year institution with a more demographically diverse student population, including non-traditional students with work and family obligations, as well as some students that may not be college ready.

The biggest challenge in managing the program is the dearth of resources needed to sustain a program of this magnitude. There is no specific budget allocated for exchange programs at BCTC. Consequently, the program director has to negotiate financial support with the administration each time a visit is scheduled. During the last decade, the resources for funding program activities, inviting scholars on campus, and accommodating them have dwindled, with the unintended consequence of fewer visits between the two institutions. Lack of incentives for participation is yet another challenge. Most of the participants in this program are self-funded, a factor that has reduced the number of interested participants significantly. In numerous occasions faculty, students, and even staff have expressed interest in participating in the program, but have not followed through on finding out that there is no funding to help defray travel costs. Even at the programming level, there is no money allocated to fund program activities. Hence the program relies heavily on volunteers to serve as mentors, guides, hosts, and drivers, for the visiting scholars.

Hosting visiting scholars has been particularly challenging. "Having visiting scholars on campus is a wonderful thing. Hosting them is a nightmare," a presenter at a national conference once lamented. We can certainly identify with this colleague. BCTC has experimented with two models to address the issue of hosting visiting scholars. The first model involved providing the scholars with a stipend and assisting them in finding accommodation within walking distance from campus. Such an arrangement was expected to eliminate the need for personal transportation and allow them to fully participate in program activities, including cultural immersion. The scholars paid for their accommodation from their stipend. While this arrangement seemed attractive from our perspective, the scholars were not particularly pleased with the idea of living in an apartment by themselves and without the conveniences of laundry and food services. They were confronted with the reality of cooking and cleaning for themselves, chores some of them had not performed in years. They complained of being homesick, especially during the winter months. In addition, they had to walk to work without having the luxury of a car – a real culture shock for some of them. This model also created more complications for the program director. The apartment was not furnished and she had to rely on personal resources and donations of furniture and kitchen ware from friends and colleagues for the scholars to use.

In subsequent years, the length of stay for the visiting scholars has been reduced to one month and, at the same time, a new model for hosting them was adopted. The scholars were hosted by American families for periods of one week with each family. This option presented invaluable opportunities for cultural exchange, global awareness, and also eliminated the feeling of loneliness and isolation that the previous scholars had expressed. However, this model also created several challenges revolving around time management, host/visitor expectations, accommodation arrangements, and transportation. The scholars also cited switching homes on a weekly basis as a nuisance. BCTC faculty, while at MU, were provided with room and board at the institution's guest house. The major concern expressed by these scholars was lack of activities in the evening hours in the semi-rural setting. MU has since revised its accommodation arrangements and visiting BCTC faculty now stay in the nearby city of Kisumu in a hotel owned and operated by the university.

CONCLUSION

As stated earlier in this chapter, the motivation for initiating BCTC/MU partnership was to contribute to the "cultural and global awareness" component of the community college's mission. Romano (2002) provides examples of other community colleges' involvement in international education through a variety of activities such as curricular commitment to internationalization, faculty development, study-abroad programs, the recruiting of international students to the campus, and extracurricular programs of international/intercultural nature for both on- and off-campus groups.

Establishing and managing community college-university cross-border partnership through faculty exchange can be fulfilling but at the same time challenging. Below are some recommendations that would be helpful to anyone considering starting a cross-border faculty exchange program, especially at an institution where infrastructure for internationalization activities is limited.

- Articulate the need for such a program and how it will further the mission of the institution.
- Seek broad support for the proposal. This requires a collaborative approach that actively engages key stakeholders in the conversation as early as possible.
- Choose the partner institution judiciously. There has to be a relevant common ground in the missions of the two institutions so that each party can derive some benefits from the partnership.
- Resources are limited. Despite an institution's good intentions to enhance the international dimension, the support for international programs is not always guaranteed. It may be instructive to look for external grants to supplement institutional resources.
- Flexibility is key. Be ready to adjust the breadth and scope of the program to meet new challenges and prospects.
- Be innovative in designing program activities. Include both at-home and cross-border initiatives that appeal to participants from diverse cultural backgrounds.

In addition to above recommendations, Van de Water et al. (2008) have compiled a list of elements that may be included in a formal written partnership agreement (p. 41). Barnes (2011) has also provided several MOU and exchange templates. Formalizing a partnership and documenting the agreement in writing is valuable for positioning the partnership within institutional missions, clarifying expectations and responsibilities of parties involved, and establishing guidelines for implementation of program activities.

REFERENCES

American Council on International Intercultural Education and The Stanley Foundation. (1996). *Educating for the global community: A framework for community colleges.* Conference Report. Stanley Foundation, Muscatine, IA.
Barnes, T. (2011). Beyond handshakes and signing ceremonies: Leveraging institutional agreements to foster broad and deep international partnerships. In S. B. Sutton & D. Obst (Eds.), *Developing strategic international partnerships: Models for initiating and sustaining innovative institutional linkages* (pp. 177–204). New York, NY: Institute of International Education.

Bluegrass Community & Technical College. (2010). *Strategic plan 2010–2016: Focus on the future*. Retrieved from http://www.bluegrass.kctcs.edu/IPRE/Strategic_Planning.aspx. Accessed on July 15, 2015.

Bluegrass Community & Technical College. (2013). *2013–2014 BCTC Factbook*. Retrieved from http://www.bluegrass.kctcs.edu/IPRE/Factbooks.aspx. Accessed on August 1, 2015.

Bluegrass Community & Technical College. (2014). *BCTC mission*. Retrieved from http://www.bluegrass.kctcs.edu/en/About/Our_Mission_and_Vision.aspx. Accessed on August 16, 2015.

Books for Africa (n.d.). *Books for Africa*. Retrieved from http://www.booksforafrica.org/index.html. Accessed on October 25, 2015.

Farnsworth, K. A. (2002). Forward. In R. M. Romano (Ed.), *Internationalizing the community college* (pp. VII–X). Washington, DC: Community College Press.

Kentucky Institute for International Studies [KIIS]. (2015). *KIIS history*. Retrieved from http://kiis.org/portal/index.html. Accessed on July 20, 2015.

Knight, J. (2001). Monitoring the quality and progress of internalization. *Journal of Studies in International Education, 5*(3), 228–243.

Maseno University. (2013). *Charter for Maseno university*. Retrieved from http://maseno.ac.ke/index/index.php?option=com_content&view=article&id=148&Itemid=161. Accessed on August 2, 2015.

Otieno, T. (2013). Navigating the tenure and promotion processes at regional comprehensive universities: Challenges and coping strategies. In D. Mack, E. D. Watson, & M. M. Camacho (Eds.), *Mentoring faculty of color: Essays on professional development and advancement in colleges and universities* (pp. 26–41). Jefferson, NC: McFarland & Company.

Otieno, T., Lutz, P. M., & Schoolmaster, F. A. (2010). Enhancing recruitment, professional development and socialization of junior faculty through formal mentoring programs. *Metropolitan Universities Journal, 21*(2), 77–91.

Romano, R. M. (Ed.). (2002). *Internationalizing the community college*. Washington, DC: Community College Press.

Sakamoto, R., & Chapman, D. W. (Eds.). (2012). *Cross-border partnerships in higher education: Strategies and issues*. New York, NY: Routledge.

Sutton, S. B., & Obst, D. (Eds.). (2011). *Developing strategic international partnerships: Models for initiating and sustaining innovative institutional linkages*. New York, NY: Institute of International Education.

Van de Water, J., Green, M. F., & Koch, K. (2008). *International partnerships: Guidelines for colleges and universities*. Washington, DC: American Council on Education.

SMALL IS BEAUTIFUL – HOW A YOUNG UNIVERSITY CAN SUCCESSFULLY ESTABLISH UNIVERSITY PARTNERSHIPS – THE CASE OF FH JOANNEUM UNIVERSITY OF APPLIED SCIENCES

Thomas Schmalzer and Doris Kiendl-Wendner

ABSTRACT

This chapter provides an example of how a young higher education institution, with only 20 years of existence and around 4,000 students, located in a small town in central Europe, has established and has been maintaining high profile networks and international collaborations with universities and industry. This case focuses on one particular department within the university, the "Institute of International Management," which has spearheaded this development over the past decade. The initiative

University Partnerships for Academic Programs and Professional Development
Innovations in Higher Education Teaching and Learning, Volume 7, 201–220
Copyright © 2016 by Emerald Group Publishing Limited
All rights of reproduction in any form reserved
ISSN: 2055-3641/doi:10.1108/S2055-364120160000007021

originated on the departmental level and subsequently produced spillover effects for the entire university.

Despite budgetary constraints and a locational disadvantage compared to universities in large urban agglomerations of developed countries, a broadly based international mobility alongside intense collaboration in research has been achieved. This has been reached through an integrated strategic approach combining specific teaching activities (study abroad, project classes, joint degrees, quality assurance, massive open online courses, and more), R&D, networks as well as motivated and qualified staff.

This case illustrates how universities from developed countries in Europe, the United States, Australia, parts of Asia, and Latin America, irrespective of size, brand name, location, and financial endowments, are able to internationalize and build sustainable partnerships to the benefit of students, faculty, and a wider group of stakeholders.

Keywords: Faculty; teaching; international; university; partnerships

INTRODUCTION

A major trend in the internationalization of higher education (HE) is the increasing expansion of student and faculty exchange across the globe, going beyond the immediate neighboring countries towards a full coverage of the world. The main trends and corresponding implications from a cross-cultural perspective are discussed for instance in Schmalzer and Neubauer (2010) or Corrales, Ramirez, and Schmalzer (2008). Only strong and sustainable partnerships can ensure a successful implementation of such types of institutional and personal interaction and an effective harnessing of potential synergies and learning effects. Developing such networks, however, is difficult, time intensive, and costly.

Furthermore, research and education are the two main objectives of universities. Both objectives can best be achieved through intensive partnerships. Establishing and maintaining collaborations with other higher education institutions (HEI) on the national and international level as well as with industry, primary and secondary schools, policy makers, and other stakeholders enables universities to reach out to additional knowledge, resources, networks, multipliers as well as to provide complementary skills and competences.

This chapter is dedicated to providing a case study on how a small and young university faced with budget constraints and a geographical disadvantage, being away from large urban agglomerations, is able to establish successful partnerships on an international scale. The case is based on qualitative information and experience of the authors and follows along well-trodden case study research paths (Hartley, 2004; Remenyi, Money, Price, & Bannister, 2002).

Particularly, this case is about a "University of Applied Sciences" (UAS) in Austria, Europe. UAS typically focus on teaching from a practical angle centered on the labor market and conducting applied research. In 1993 the Austrian parliament passed a law on the establishment of UAS (Federal Law number 340/1993). This legislation deliberately provides only a lose framework for UAS, giving a lot of freedom to the HEIs as regards the legal form of establishment and the organization of the university.

Federal legislation in Austria defines the main aim of UAS as education of students for the demand of the labor market. Thus, each degree program is based on a needs analysis of the labor market with respect to the competencies required in specific industries. Employability of graduates is the objective of each degree program. In addition, UAS are required to conduct applied research with companies and other organizations.

This case study elaborates on the partnerships which have been established at a specific UAS in Austria, namely the FH JOANNEUM (FHJ). In particular, it shows the strategic development of the Institute of International Management (IIM), one unit within the FHJ, which has been spearheading the international development and the establishment of partnerships of the whole university in the past decade.

ABOUT FH JOANNEUM – UNIVERSITY OF APPLIED SCIENCES

The institution was founded in 1995 and is a public and state accredited UAS. Its legal form is that of a limited liability company like most other UAS in Austria with the regional government of the province of Styria, one of nine Austrian provinces, being its main shareholder.

The vision of FHJ puts special emphasis on partnerships. The university aims to act as an interface between society, industry, and science. New synergies in the tertiary education sector should be generated through cooperation. In addition, the university is dedicated to promoting inter-cultural competence by strengthening the regional and international focus in equal measure to make an effective contribution to the European educa-tion and research landscape (FH JOANNEUM, 2015).

Facts and Figures

While the university started with only four degree programs in 1995, it has grown tremendously within the last twenty years. In 2015 FHJ had about 4,000 students in 46 bachelor's and master's degree programs. The univer-sity employs 550 full-time faculty and staff as well as over 1,000 adjunct faculty members.

The degree programs of the university are organized in six departments. Fig. 1 shows the allocation of students to the departments.

Below the level of the departments, institutes have been created at FHJ. An institute usually includes at least one bachelor's and one master's

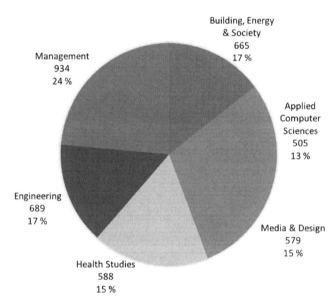

Fig. 1. Number and Relative Share of Students at Departments of FHJ in 2014. *Source*: FH JOANNEUM.

program and one "transfer center," which is responsible for applied research projects with industry and other external partners. The IIM as of 2015 comprises the following integrated parts:

- Bachelor's degree program "International Management" (60 students per year, 180 ECTS)
- Master's degree program "Business in Emerging Markets," (30 students per year, 120 ECTS)
- Master's degree program "European Project and Public Management," (25 students per year, 90 ECTS, executive education)
- "Transfer Center," managing R&D projects, funded by industry or grants (e.g., national, European Union, or other)

Institutes within the university enjoy a high degree of freedom within the framework determined by the legal norms and the organizational structure of the UAS. Each institute manages its own budget, designs curricula, establishes, and manages its partnerships.

The IIM at FHJ was founded in 2001. It serves as a good example as to how something can be built out of nothing on a practical level, where the nucleus is a small scale organizational unit, with only limited resources and no natural advantages.

At the early stages after the foundation, the challenge included not only the curricula, internal structures, and processes but also the development of a stable faculty and market recognition from scratch. All international and national networks, partnerships with other HEIs, businesses, and further stakeholders had to be established, maintained, and grown. The latter has always been one of the key strategic objectives of the institute. The following subchapters describe the various practices applied within the IIM and the strategic approach behind these practices.

International Cooperation and Exchange Programs

The employability of graduates in the area of international management depends on their competencies and skills. Studies have shown that the labor market does not only expect specific skills of graduates, but also "generic" competencies, such as leadership, self-determination, team work, and inter-cultural communication (Azevedo et al., 2012). The programs offered at universities must be fit for this purpose to meet future demands. The purpose must align with the curricula and qualifications of faculty and staff members. Thus, only faculty and staff members possessing these "generic" competencies can train students to develop these skills as well.

Consequently, faculty and student exchange programs are at the core of the mission of the IIM. The institute has concluded over sixty partnership agreements with universities worldwide (Fig. 2).

Developing and fostering inter-cultural competencies, language skills, self-determination, and problem-solving capabilities can, however, only work if these partnerships come to life by faculty and students using them both ways (incoming and outgoing) on a regular basis. Therefore, incentives have to be created and barriers have to be overcome so that students and faculty use those opportunities.

Student Mobility

While, in principle, many students are interested in studying abroad to broaden their horizon, to enjoy a different culture, and to add international experience to their resumes, there are many obstacles to mobility. In particular, language barriers, financial constraints, lack of recognition of credits obtained abroad, family issues, and safety concerns impede student mobility. According to a study conducted in several EU member states (Souto-Otero, Huisman, Beerkens, de Wit, & Vujić, 2013), the lack of information about existing opportunities, personal background, financial barriers, and the compatibility of studying abroad with the HE system hinder student mobility. Nevertheless, the benefits of exchange semesters for the development of crucial skills are widely acknowledged.

The internationalization strategy of the IIM aims at lowering those barriers through numerous activities and measures, such as trainings before students study abroad, a wide network of partner institutions and incoming international faculty, and students serving as mentors and buddies. In addition, the institute chose to integrate a mandatory study abroad semester in its bachelor's program.

Therefore, the curriculum requires each student to spend one semester at a partner university. Students and faculty who select a partner university in the European Higher Education Area (EHEA) can benefit from EU mobility grants via the Erasmus+ program. To support student and teacher mobility to countries outside of the EHEA, national as well as EU funds and scholarship programs exist. The institute actively applies for such support and encourages its incoming and outgoing students as well as faculty members to use the programs available to them.

Fig. 2. Map of Partner Universities of IIM at FHJ. *Source:* FH JOANNEUM.

Apart from financial constraints, other obstacles to student mobility have to be overcome. When it comes to language barriers, the IIM prepares students well for their exchange semester by teaching most courses in English language. Mandatory inter-cultural trainings and additional language courses (Spanish, French, Italian, Chinese, Russian, and Croatian) complete the services offered.

Concerning the recognition of credits obtained during the exchange semester, the curriculum at the home university is deliberately flexible and enables students to make their choice among the courses offered abroad. An entire semester is reserved for the exchange with no courses taking place at the home university for the student cohort on exchange. Therefore, students do not have to make up for courses missed at home while studying abroad.

The partnership agreements with other HEIs are based on the principle of balance of incoming and outgoing students. This balance can be uneven in the short-run and may endanger the sustainability of these agreements if the uneven balance persists over more years. In order to avoid the risk that partner universities discontinue the agreements on the grounds of an imbalance, the IIM has created various attractive options for the partner universities. Among them is the "Global Business Program" (GBP) of the institute, which offers courses in English on a modular basis (two weeks of intensive teaching with 5 ECTS for each course) for incoming students.

Since academic calendars vary across countries, the modular system enables incoming students to collect enough credits during their exchange semester on subjects they need or want in an efficient manner also allowing for time to travel and widen their personal horizons.

The institute cares for its exchange students by offering a special orientation program and buddy system where international students team up with local students, thus creating benefits for both sides. Austrian students receive insights into a foreign culture while studying at home ("internationalization at home"), and exchange students feel more comfortable during their semester abroad. At the same time, they gain first-hand experience with local peers, which often proves difficult for incoming students.

Another specific offer of the institute is the "Applied Summer School doing business in Europe" providing the opportunity to students from partner universities to gain international experience within a three-week intensive program. The summer school includes seminars, company visits, and excursions and is especially attractive for students who cannot afford to study abroad for an entire semester due to financial and/or time constraints.

These initiatives lead to increases in student mobility, both incoming and outgoing, and results in around 230 outgoing and around 215 incoming students per year. In terms of incoming students, the GBP accounts for about half of all incoming students from around 25 different countries worldwide. Since its inception in 2003, the GBP has had well over a thousand students enrolled.

Internationalization @ Home: Distance Learning in a Diverse Classroom — The Example of MOOCs

Technological developments have made it possible to learn from practically any location on the globe. Thus, distance learning has become widely used. To exploit new opportunities in creating and fostering partnerships, the IIM has engaged, in addition to classic e-learning offerings, in experiments with Massive Open Online Courses (MOOCs). In 2014 and 2015, the institute ran a six week MOOC on "Competences for Global Collaboration" (www.cope15.at). This online learning scenario has been offered to the institute's own students as well as participants from partner universities. In both MOOCs, over 500 participants from more than 30 countries participated actively (Kiendl-Wendner & Pauschenwein, 2015).

A MOOC provides a large degree of freedom to learners and enables them to improve not only their specific knowledge but also their self-organization skills, since the learners connect with other participants. Autonomy, diversity, interactivity, and openness are the key drivers of the learning process in such open learning scenarios (Siemens, 2005).

From the perspective of establishing and maintaining partnerships, MOOCs and other kinds of distance learning scenarios are excellent opportunities to overcome some mobility barriers, especially financial ones. Still, the inter-cultural differences and language issues must not be underestimated. This requires sophisticated e-moderating skills of faculty and facilitators (Salmon, 2004).

For international partner universities this constitutes an additional added value as they can provide experience on working and studying with peers from abroad at no cost. This strengthens institutional linkages and serves as an excellent marketing tool to attract future foreign students.

Key lessons learnt in this respect are that the set-up of such an initiative is rather costly and the execution period is moderation intensive to keep participants active. However, due to the scalability of MOOCs, it does present a viable option to efficiently deliver courses in an online form and at the same time cultivate existing partnerships, establish new ones, and generate added value for the university's brand.

Joint Academic Programs

Apart from "simple" student exchange programs, the institute has established strategic partnerships with selected universities, in particular in
Russia (Voronezh State University), Taiwan (NKFUST), and Chile
(USACH), to create double degree programs on the level of its master's
program (Business in Emerging Markets). The establishment of these joint
programs has to take into account national regulations on the recognition
of credits obtained abroad as well as necessary adaptations in the curricula
of the partnering institutions. In Austria, the national regulations on recognition of credits follow the rules of the EHEA. These rules aim at promoting mobility while defining quality criteria through the European Credit
Transfer system (ECTS) and the European qualifications framework. A
certain flexibility with respect to the courses and credits is necessary, especially for partnerships with universities with different educational systems,
but at the same time strong quality criteria and effective quality assurance,
and management are required.

Faculty Mobility

An intensive partnership among universities can best be established and
maintained through faculty mobility for joint research projects and teaching exchange. This enables partnerships to become deeper, since common
ground on values, teaching methods, research topics, understanding of
quality in HE, and methodology can be reached.

The partnership agreements between FHJ and its numerous partner
institutions have created opportunities for lecturers to meet their colleagues
from other universities. In addition, the university creates incentives for
full-time faculty and research associates to participate in international conferences by cost coverage and career paths.

In total, around 35 faculty members of the UAS as a whole participate in
outgoing programs each year. Incoming faculty mobility has been made possible especially in the framework of the GBP mentioned above, in the course
of which professors from strategic partners have been invited to teach intensive courses. This opportunity is positive not only for students who benefit
from international lecturers. The high degree of faculty mobility has also had
a substantial impact on mutual research activities with international partners.
From joint projects to publications in core thematic areas of the institute
(e.g., Schmalzer & Smolarski, 2006), spill-overs have been utilized.

Industry Collaboration through Classroom Projects

The mission of the university is strongly focused on the role of the UAS as an engine of innovation for companies and other stakeholders in the region. Thus, the university has been actively involved in projects of various kinds with industry in research and teaching. Classroom projects with industry are usually conducted in the way that a company identifies a task which the students perform under supervision of a lecturer. Such a task is embedded in a project where students generate results used then directly by the companies. The companies on their part usually provide input from a content perspective in terms of requirements and recommendations and contribute financially for the results delivered.

Such classroom projects are demanding for all parties involved, for students, lecturers, and companies alike. Students may find it challenging to adapt to industry standards and apply theoretical knowledge to a practical case. Therefore, coaching by qualified and motivated faculty members as well as company representatives to overcome these challenges is essential for the success of the project, both with respect to the quality of the results and with respect to the learning outcomes of the students.

Companies have to consider that such classroom projects require at least one employee of the company prepared to spend time with the students and the lecturers, at least for the project kick off and the presentation of the final results. For lecturers, classroom projects are often more time consuming than "ordinary" teaching, especially since the planning of such classes has to integrate a considerable degree of flexibility.

Still, classroom projects with industry are mutually valuable, since they generate numerous positive effects. In particular such projects

- enable students to directly apply their skills and knowledge on a specific topic; this deepens the understanding of students and generates learning outcomes for the students;
- enable students to get to know companies for future employment and internships;
- may give students the additional opportunity of writing their master's theses jointly with the company;
- provide companies with an opportunity to obtain results which they can use in their business processes;
- often enable companies to get to know excellent students for future recruitment;
- enable the university to generate additional funds;

- enable the university to extend its network for future projects and internship opportunities.

The establishment of partnerships with industry has always been of high importance for FHJ because its situation as a university with relatively low financial resources makes the university dependent on links to companies and organizations. Classroom projects constitute a low threshold and low risk activity with a high potential of positive effects.

In the past years, this asset has been actively used to also collaborate on projects for companies with other partner universities. Similar project based classes were identified at partner universities, such as in India (BIMTECH). International teams and cross-border collaboration were introduced to project classes on both sides. Although it was a challenge to ensure efficiency and effectiveness of such teams across borders, the international dimension enabled students to learn about cross-cultural differences in learning and working styles and deliver results that were more out of the box than usual.

Apart from projects with companies conducted within the framework of teaching activities, the institute has been focusing on the establishment and maintenance of strategic research partnerships with universities and other research institutions worldwide. One example of such projects has been the development of a methodology for the internationalization strategy of the Internationalization Center of the Chamber of Commerce of the province of Styria in Austria. The following section describes these activities more in detail.

Joint Research Initiatives

In terms of research collaboration, the institute in the past years has been actively working on between 15 and 25 research projects simultaneously. Successful initiatives include projects on the internationalization of small- and medium-sized enterprises (Schmalzer & Smolarski, 2006), the Austrian contribution to the Global Entrepreneurship Monitor (Schmalzer, Wenzel, Mahajan, & Penz, 2015) as well as numerous projects on HE development in fields such as financial and quality management.

The average budgets of these projects (for the institute alone excluding all other partners) range from 30,000 EUR to 150,000 EUR with project durations of between one and three years. Through these projects, the institute generates roughly 400,000 EUR of annual revenues from third parties. This currently finances a considerable number of research staff working at the institute. Most financing stems from projects funded via European Union programs. This is followed by national programs and direct R&D contracts from industry or public clients (see above). The core topics covered in this respect are:

- Entrepreneurship and Innovation
- Internationalization of Business and Market Entry
- Employability
- Management in HE

These projects are mostly implemented in international consortia of between five and 25 partner organizations from all over the world. This allows staff to work on topics the institute alone would not be able to cover in terms of expertise as well as resources.

Project development and fundraising are centered around three to five core strategic partners with who the institute has been collaborating intensely for a number of years. These strategic partnerships were established first through intensive networking and subsequently through mutual trust which has emerged due to several successful projects. Additional projects are done on a looser yet reciprocal basis of collaboration. The pool of strategic partners also contains triple accredited and internationally renowned universities. The projects are managed by specialized staff (research associates and administrative staff) dedicated mostly to R&D to a large extent being freed from teaching. This staff is mostly financed directly via the projects.

A special case are the institute's activities in the area of joint quality assurance initiatives, where the institute also actively pursues projects focusing on quality management in HE. The main reason behind is to raise the level of quality as well as the compatibility of quality assurance and recognition systems not only within the institute itself but also throughout the network of international partners. A crucial problem in this respect is to ensure similar standards when sending students abroad to different countries and HEIs (as has been elaborated above). Through dedicated projects such as UNIQUE (University Quality Exchange, funded by the European Commission), the institute is able to promote European quality standards together with its strategic partners in emerging markets with main hubs in China, Mexico, India, Russia, and Namibia. These activities benefit not only the bachelor's program, where students have to spend a mandatory semester abroad but also benefits the joint master's program (Business in Emerging Markets).

Other projects on quality management in HE developed an expertise in the area of competence based curriculum development and teaching as well as on how to increase employability of graduates in the labor market through reforms in quality management. These results were directly fed into the curriculum reaccreditation and reform processes and serve as a basis for the new development of degree programs at the institute and within the organization as a whole. Instrumental in this respect were the meta-level indicators on measuring competence gaps between HE graduates and actual industry needs developed in the project MISLEM (see also Azevedo et al., 2012) as well as competence based teaching and curriculum reform results from the project COMPETENCE.

Thus, the strategies of FHJ to establish and maintain university partnerships in research, on the one hand, and in teaching, on the other hand, are strongly linked. Output from applied research projects feeds back into teaching and vice-versa. While such collaborations generate benefits and positive spill-overs on various levels, challenges such as cross-cultural communication barriers as well as a large coordination and administration effort exist. These must be managed pro-actively to ensure success.

The following sections summarize the overall strategic approach and draw conclusions from the practices described above. This provides further insight into how a non-top-tier university with adverse starting conditions can achieve international recognition and increase key performance indicators in teaching and research.

STRATEGIC APPROACH TO ESTABLISH
UNIVERSITY PARTNERSHIPS

The IIM at FHJ defined its main goal to become an outstanding regional player in the field of international business linked with a variety of international high profile academic institutions as well as corporations. Concrete actions were planned and implemented to achieve this overarching goal. Along the lines of Porter (1996), who states that "strategy is the creation of a unique and valuable position, involving a different set of activities," the following sections provide a short account of the chosen strategic approach focusing on academic partnerships and attempt to interlink the various activities needed to operationalize the strategy.

Strategic Approach via Selected Teaching Activities

Starting the creation of the strategic networks by recruiting skilled and dedicated staff and faculty is a key success factor in the strategic approach to establish partnerships for and through teaching activities. The initial networks of partner universities came into existence through active participation in organizations such as the Academy of Management, the European Association for International Education, the World Association for Cooperative & Work-Integrated Education as well as through the personal relations of the first Chair of the Institute, Gerhard Apfelthaler. Later, some of the networks which had been created for R&D projects became very fruitful for teaching collaboration as well; among them the Latin American PILA network, which was one of the sustainable results of a project funded by the European Union.

It became evident from the early development of the institute on that university partnerships need a high level of trust among the participating institutions and enough flexibility from all participating HEIs. Direct contact with representatives of the partners through faculty exchange, joint publications, joint conferences, and other academic collaboration, such as exchange of teaching materials, substantially supported the growth of trust among the IIM and its strategic partners in teaching.

A university which makes studying abroad mandatory for its undergraduate students has to provide a large network of partner universities to enable the students of the home university to select an appropriate partner university. To achieve sustainability in the university partnerships, the institute has paid special attention to its teaching activities to make them as attractive as possible for incoming international students so that the balance of incoming and outgoing students is even and the long lasting effect of the partnership is guaranteed. The institute has, thus, come up with a special educational offer for incoming international students, the GBP, which has been running for more than 10 years now.

The GBP does not only provide attractive study options for international students; in addition, this program has enabled the UAS to invite guest professors from its international partner universities to come and teach. This again has substantially supported the establishment of trust as a crucial component in partnerships, the mutual understanding of the various educational systems in different nations, the creation of joint degrees, the joint application for R&D projects, joint publications, and friendships among faculty members of FH JOANNEUM and its partner universities.

Strategic Approach via Funded Projects in R&D

The general aim of the institute and FHJ as a whole, at the point of inception, was and still is to develop into an internationally recognized degree program and internationally recognized UAS. However, the budgetary situation endows only standard teaching activities with per capita funding depending on the number of students. These funds are provided by the federal government for approved degree programs. Although applied research is a legal obligation for UAS in Austria and internationalization as well as partnerships are high on the agenda, no basic funds are dedicated toward developing these. Subsequently, additional financing has to be acquired through competitive calls for project proposals and international student and faculty mobility.

The IIM started out with a strategic focus on obtaining third party project based financing by hiring a part time staff member from its regular budget for half a year. During these six months, the staff member's task was to write project proposals and acquire research projects from industry. The aim was to subsequently finance this position and additional research associates via the project funds that came in. The first grant was successfully acquired, and since then the research unit has grown to a headcount of 10 staff members with around seven full-time equivalent positions still following this strategy.

In order to achieve high success rates in acquiring third party financing, a number of critical success factors have to be met. First, specialized, dedicated, and motivated staff has to be selected to work on project proposals to increase its effectiveness. Due to the fact that small UAS typically do not provide a lot of central research administration services to its operative units, also internal systems and procedures have to be established to ensure effective and efficient administration, financial management, and documentation of funded projects. Moreover, it is crucial in this respect to train and develop one's own staff to become experts in these activities to lower the administrative costs. While in earlier years the institute administered only four medium sized projects with a staff equivalent to a 1.5 full-time position, 25 simultaneously running projects are currently handled by an equal number of staff. The learning curve in this respect is steep in the beginning and must be harnessed to strategically pursue this additional pillar of financing.

An additional success factor is to broaden the scope of possible funding programs to apply for. If one focused only on pure research oriented funds, two problems would arise. During a typical annual call cycle, only a few suitable calls for project proposals are available to apply for. Furthermore, these are highly competitive, thus lowering the average success rate in such programs. Consequently, the institute did not restrict itself in terms of the type of program aimed for but rather defined clear thematic areas in which to develop research excellence. This experience and knowledge then serves as the unique selling proposition through which self-written projects as well as invitations to act as partners in projects are generated and success rates are boosted. Wherever the thematic area matches a priority of a funding program, the institute is actively submitting proposals. With generally low success rates, financing can be secured only through generating a large number of submissions. To achieve this, it is impossible to rely solely on self-written proposals. By establishing a strong network within academia and private businesses, NGOs, and public institutions, where all network members actively work on securing third party financing and partner invitations are done on a reciprocal basis, the necessary funds to secure stable operations can be acquired.

Apart from the aspects mentioned above, another key feature of the strategy is the harnessing of synergies, cross-fertilization, and actively seeking by-products or spillover benefits from the projects acquired.

A classical project, even outside of traditional research funds, involves a research work package through which the academic mission and goals of the institute can be fulfilled directly (research funding, publications, visibility, and more). However, through international collaboration in most of these projects, new networks are established, which serve as potential future partners and applicants in projects to come. This increases the capacity for financing one's operations in the future.

Moreover, the academic partners in such projects are the pool for establishing student and faculty exchange relations. The advantage by using projects to get to know each other on an institutional and personal level ensures an effective implementation of additional agreements in the future.

In terms of collaboration with businesses, funded projects are a door-opener to industry. A research organization can present its skills and expertise in a risk and cost minimized environment from the perspective of the industry partner. If performance is seen as good, it often also leads to follow-up research contracts directly originating from the industry partner.

Through larger projects also comes international visibility of the organization. Where typically HEIs in smaller cities are less visible on an international level, this is a tremendous support of branding and marketing activities at an institutional level. Furthermore, it helps to attract high profile guest professors as well as full-time staff from abroad as they see value in establishing contacts to an institution successfully acquiring larger amounts of third party research funding. At the same time, it also opens the door to institutional collaboration with universities that would otherwise have chosen a more renowned institution in the capital city for its exchange of students and faculty.

From a long-term perspective, the network development through funded projects also facilitates the creation of long lasting strong relationships. Those personal and institutional contacts that have worked best over a number of years transform into strategic partnerships where constant faculty and student exchange as well as joint research and acquisition of funds is a common priority. These strategic partnerships then serve as the backbone of financing operations as well as thematic development in key areas of expertise.

A positive spillover for the operations of the institute is that staff members mainly working as research associates and assistants on projects as well as fundraising are actually also taking over higher level academic work in teaching and publications. Furthermore, a benefit for the institute is that they also support administrative work reducing the overall burden for other academic staff. The budgetary constraints, which most European HEIs have been encountering in the past decade or more, could therefore be mitigated via this strategy.

Additional synergies are generated through the topics covered in the projects as such. Research outputs are integrated into teaching, and students as well as full-time faculty are working on research projects. This increases quality and applicability of the educational offering provided.

To conclude, this process can be viewed as self-reinforcing mechanism. The more proposals are being submitted and consequently partners invited, the more an institution will be asked to act as partner in other projects. Once projects are granted the network expands and its quality increases as relationships deepen. This again fuels the future development of the research unit and institutional collaborations. To see this as a strategic process and invest the necessary seed money to get it started with dedicated people is the crucial lesson learnt from the experience of the IIM at FHJ.

CONCLUSION

UAS in Austria have been created only rather recently for the purpose of applied higher education and research. This business model per se includes partnerships as both teaching and research need to be done jointly with partners. This inherent necessity – in conjunction with internationalization as major development trend worldwide as well as being a key institutional priority of FHJ – lead the IIM to strategically develop its partnerships and collaborations with academic and business partners on a global scale.

Faced with all sorts of adverse conditions, such as financial constraints, lack of brand name, and a locational disadvantage, several key factors have lead to the successful establishment and maintenance of a sustainable network in teaching and applied research.

The main drivers to establish and maintain successful international partnerships in HE identified in the above account are:

- initial personal relations alongside membership in professional organizations to start the process
- secure third party funding (e.g., R&D)
- align curriculum to reflect strategic objectives (compulsory study abroad semester and internships, practical projects, etc.)
- hire and develop dedicated, motivated and highly skilled staff
- harness internal and external synergies from R&D projects and teaching initiatives to intensify collaborations and institutional interaction
- integrate and align activities at the organizational unit level following the overarching strategic objective.

Apart from these core factors, a number of environmental aspects have only found limited space in this discussion. The institution in which the IIM is embedded granted extensive freedom in the establishment of university partnerships, and this has been used with a high degree of enthusiasm and creativity. Additionally, the institute has been given freedom to develop and implement its own strategy in this respect and adapt its business model and respective approaches as needed. The lack of financial resources has been compensated by creative ideas that were the result of a well-composed team of experts and enthusiasts. Personal factors and leadership skills combined with excellent networking has contributed its own fair share. And ultimately, the constant fundraising activities and skillful application of knowledge on EU funds and building of working partnerships in this area have been crucial to the implementation of the strategy described. The biggest difficulty, however, following a long-term strategic objective is not to lose focus and to flexibly adapt toward changing conditions and opportunities.

While these findings are based on an experiential account of the case of FHJ, they show the significance of using positive spill-over effects and synergies to reduce costs and maximize benefits as well as the exploitation of institutional and individual learning. This case can provide a model for strategic development of international collaborations and development for non-top-tier universities in developed countries. It presents possible avenues to integrate initiatives in teaching and research, fundraising, and internationalization to harness the positive effects of partnerships within academia as well as collaborations with industry and other external stakeholders. Replication along these general lines is feasible given the availability of qualified and motivated staff, infrastructure as well as third party financing possibilities.

REFERENCES

Azevedo, A., Omerzel, D. G., Andrews, J., Higsen, H., Caballero, A., & Frech, B. (2012). Satisfaction with knowledge and competencies: A multi-country study of employers and business graduates. *American Journal of Economics and Business Administration*, (1), 23–39. doi:10.3844/ajebasp.2012.23.39

Corrales, E. M., Ramirez, J., & Schmalzer, T. (Eds.). (2008). *Building bridges across educational communities: World class practices in higher education*. New Delhi: Macmillan India Ltd.

FH JOANNEUM. (2015). *About us*. Retrieved from Mission and Vision https://www.fh-joanneum.at/aw/home/~cwd/leitbild/?lan=en. Accessed on December 10, 2015.

Hartley, J. (2004). Case study research. In C. Cassell & G. Symon (Eds.), *Essential guide to qualitative methods in organizational research* (pp. 323–333). London: Sage Publications Ldt.

Kiendl-Wendner, D., & Pauschenwein, J. (2015). MOOCs on Competences for Global Collaboration – A method to contribute to business education for sustainability and to improve the employability of graduates on the labour market. In T. I. Education (Ed.), *SIEC ISBE Conference* (p. 4). Krakow. Retrieved from http://www.siec-isbe.org/uploads/8/9/6/2/8962951/2015_proceedings.pdf. Accessed on December 10, 2015.

Porter, M. E. (1996). What is strategy? *Harvard Business Review*, (6), 61–78.

Remenyi, D., Money, A., Price, D., & Bannister, F. (2002). The creation of knowledge through case study research. *Irish Journal of Management*, 2, 1–17.

Salmon, G. (2004). *E-moderating: The key to teaching and learning online*. London: Francis & Taylor.

Schmalzer, T., & Neubauer, M. (2010). Cross-cultural implications of academic mobility. In M. Neubauer, N. S. Anuradha, & S. Keuchel (Eds.), *Cross-cultural approaches to learning and studying: A comparative study of Austria, Germany and India* (pp. 1–16). New Delhi: Macmillan Publishers India Ltd.

Schmalzer, T., & Smolarski, J. (Eds.). (2006). *Internationalisation of small to medium-sized enterprises*. Valašské Meziříčí: Aldebaran Publishing.

Schmalzer, T., Wenzel, R., Mahajan, L., & Penz, E. (2015). *Global entrepreneurship monitor 2014: Bericht zur Lage des Unternehmertuns in Österreich*. Graz: FH JOANNEUM.

Siemens, G. (2005). Connectivism: A learning theory for the digital age. *International Journal of Instructional Technology and Distance Learning*, 1, 3–10.

Souto-Otero, M., Huisman, J., Beerkens, M., de Wit, H., & Vujić, S. (2013). Barriers to international student mobility: Evidence from the Erasmus program. *Educational Researcher*, 42(2), 70–77.

UNIVERSITY PARTNERSHIPS FOR ACADEMIC PROGRAM AND PROFESSIONAL DEVELOPMENT: BUILDING FACULTY CAPACITY FOR 21ST CENTURY TEACHING AND LEARNING

Alia Sheety, Elizabeth Moy, Judith Parsons, David Dunbar[†], Kathleen C. Doutt, Elizabeth Faunce and Leslie Myers

ABSTRACT

In an environment of constrained resources and related quality assurance efforts, a growing number of American institutions are tapping collaborative relationships to develop creative ways to advance institutional outcomes. The Southeastern Pennsylvania Consortium for Higher

---

[†]We dedicate this work to the deceased Dr. David Dunbar, whose contributions to this work, and to the fields of science and science education, are innumerable.

University Partnerships for Academic Programs and Professional Development
Innovations in Higher Education Teaching and Learning, Volume 7, 221–241
Copyright © 2016 by Emerald Group Publishing Limited
All rights of reproduction in any form reserved
ISSN: 2055-3641/doi:10.1108/S2055-364120160000007022

Education (SEPCHE), a non-profit organization incorporated in 1993, is a collaborative of eight private colleges and universities located in the Greater Philadelphia region. SEPCHE's institutions are small to mid-sized colleges and universities, and like other institutions of higher education, they are increasingly challenged by several environmental factors including diminished growth in enrollment; reduced family financial capacity; limitations in availability and types of funding; and greater demand for accountability.

This chapter highlights the challenges faced by faculty to ensure that students are learning at the highest levels while balancing teaching, research and institutional responsibilities, and the role that collaborative professional development can play in helping faculty attend to these challenges. Several examples illustrate how faculty-led professional development efforts have expanded professional and research capacity efforts across institutions.

The chapter includes faculty perspectives on what has helped and hindered adoption of these efforts within and across institutions. It assesses institutional conditions and supports for sustained collaborations. These efforts are part of an initiative examining faculty work and student learning in the 21st century funded by the Teagle Foundation.

Keywords: Faculty; teaching; international; learning; partnerships

INTRODUCTION

American institutions of higher education are increasingly challenged by several environmental factors including: diminished growth in enrollment; reduced family financial capacity; limitations in availability and types of funding; and greater demand for accountability (Lawlor Group, 2012). In response, a growing number of colleges and universities are tapping collaborative relationships to develop creative ways to advance institutional outcomes.

This chapter describes a faculty-led, multi-institutional professional development effort helping faculty ensure that students learn at the highest levels. The chapter shares (1) the challenges of teaching in the current environment; (2) the collaborative foundation upon which this work rests; (3) the initiative's theoretical underpinnings; (4) the process of faculty development and narrative examples to illustrate how faculty made use of model elements; and (5) discussion of the elements that helped and hindered adoption of evidence-based teaching approaches.

TEACHING CHALLENGES IN THE CURRENT ENVIRONMENT

Twenty-First Century Teaching and Learning

Over the last 15 years, the American Association of Colleges and Universities (AAC&U) has developed detailed learning outcomes that will better prepare students for the increasing complexity, diversity, and change occurring now and in the future. Developed through a multi-year process with hundreds of universities, employers and accreditation agencies for engineering, nursing and business, the outcomes articulate specific goals and skills, such as "teamwork and problem solving, intercultural knowledge and competence, synthesis and advanced accomplishment across general and specialized studies" (The LEAP Vision for Learning, 2011).

Over that same time period, recent discoveries about how students learn combined with ever expanding roles in teaching and research (that include knowledge curation and co-creation) and growing emphasis on robust assessment to ensure institutional accountability, have challenged traditional faculty approaches to teaching and learning. The skills required by students to learn at the highest levels require faculty to model and foster capacities for which they themselves have not been trained (Bissonette, 2011).

Changing Demographics

In the United States, a growing share of students attending college are first from their families to attend. More students work and provide care for family members while going to school; this proportion is higher for students of color (Mangan, Chronicle Higher Education, 2015). More than half of all students work while in college (Mendoza, 2012), while one in four students raise children while in college (Gault, Reichlin, & Román, 2014).

The combination of pressures balancing school while working and caring for family undermine student achievement and college completion:

Whereas half of all individuals from high income families possess a bachelor's degree by age 25, only 1 in 10 individuals from low-income families do. (Bailey & Dynarski, 2011)

At the same time, the American Association of Colleges and Universities estimates that roughly half of students arrive to college academically underprepared. (AAC&U, 2002). Working with issues of diversity and academically under-preparedness are critical challenges cited by faculty developers (Sorcinelli, 2007).

Faculty

While demographic changes in the classroom are changing the ways that faculty work with students, technological advances are shifting how teachers and learners relate to knowledge creation and application. Co-creation of knowledge requires faculty to know how to facilitate such a process and demands greater student ownership of learning – both for which most faculty and students have not been trained.

Institutional expectations for teaching and research have accelerated. For faculty in small institutions, the ability to advance research can be severely limited by heavy teaching loads and service commitments. For example, it is typical in institutions like these for faculty to teach four courses per semester. It is also typical for these institutions to expect faculty to produce peer reviewed research publications as part of their promotion and tenure processes as well as to engage in service to the institution.

What has become clear is the need for continuous faculty development to help faculty with the many changes impacting the professorate. As an institutional support, faculty development can help faculty balance and address the roles they play – shifting teaching toward more student-centered learning; shifting research to involve learners in the scholarship of teaching and learning; and supporting service commitments through intra- and inter-institutional learning communities.

COLLABORATIVE FOUNDATIONS FOR THIS EFFORT

The collective challenge to provide stronger educational outcomes more efficiently has been at the heart of activities of the Southeastern Pennsylvania Consortium for Higher Education (SEPCHE) since its forma-tion in 1993. Member institutions include: Arcadia University, Cabrini University, Gwynedd Mercy University, Holy Family University, Immaculata University, Neumann University and Rosemont College. Located in metro-politan Philadelphia, they are competitors in a hyper-competitive market. With over 100 colleges and universities, the Philadelphia region is second only to Boston in its number of high education institutions. Collectively, SEPCHE members educate over 22,000 students.

SEPCHE academic collaborations include cross-registration, library borrowing privileges, cross-institutional faculty-student research, student honors conference and various academic symposia, annual faculty professional development, and shared coursework to name a few. Other SEPCHE collaborations include shared career and alumni professional development events and diversity conferences engaging faculty, staff and students on a variety of topics that have included race and culture, interfaith dialogue, valuing different abilities, and immigration.

SEPCHE collaborations have proven efficient and effective in strengthening the quality of teaching and learning and in providing a range of student programs that individually institutions might not be able to offer. Because collaborative program expenses are shared, member institutions pay a fraction of what they collectively produce in transformative learning experiences.

Beyond financial efficiencies, SEPCHE students, staff and faculty value the networks and relationships developed over time that have improved their mastery, motivation, sense of belonging and contribution, in some cases, to innovative initiatives that have been transformative for students and faculty.

This work builds upon prior research of the consortium investigating the extent to which research-based teaching strategies can impact learning. In 2008, 16 faculty across eight SEPCHE institutions introduced active teaching strategies fostering "learning how to learn" skills that included reflection, prediction and analyses of thinking processes, actions and consequences. Overall results suggest that these efforts produced a protective or stabilizing influence against typical declines in learner confidence in classes that employed these methods (Moy, O'Sullivan, Terlecki, & Jernstedt, 2014).

THEORETICAL UNDERPINNINGS FOR THIS WORK

Active Learning

Active learning is an outgrowth of constructivist theory that suggests that learning is actively constructed and acquired through experience. Active learning generally involves metacognitive strategies that emphasize learning processes.

Metacognition focuses on building skills and habits that deepen learning, such as self-awareness, self-regulation, goal setting, evaluation and adjusting to meet goals; metacognition diagnoses and guides learning through the use of feedback. (Jernstedt, 2011)

Metacognitive processes that include self-assessment and reflection have been shown to increase the degree to which students transfer learning to new situations (Bransford, Brown, & Cocking, 2000). Developments in the learning sciences have renewed attention to the role that metacognition plays in strengthening learning development and learning transfer.

Developments in Neuroscience

Over the last two decades, discoveries in neuroscience have reinforced widespread calls for more active teaching approaches. Knowledge about how learning develops in the brain supports constructivist theory approaches such as active teaching and learning. For example, it is now known that learning circuitry becomes more durable when learning requires effort and when it is emotionally relevant to the learner (Brown, Roediger, & McDaniel, 2014). Likewise, neural networks are shaped and organized by exposure to different experiences (Bransford et al., 2000).

The implications for teaching include the shift toward active teaching and student-centered learning, in which the student takes an active role in learning. As knowledge is constructed, a critical role of the teacher is to diagnose the learner's prior knowledge and correct misunderstandings in order to strengthen the learner's conceptual foundation upon which new learning will be built. Likewise, formative assessment skills enable the teacher to check the learner's progress. (Bransford et al., 2000).

Supporting Faculty in the Shift toward Active Teaching: The Process of Faculty Development

Given the challenges that exist in shifting faculty teaching practices that have been documented in the literature, this effort sought to understand the extent to which metacognitive approaches may help faculty adopt teaching approaches that strengthen evidence-based practices. With support from the Teagle Foundation, this effort pursued answers to three questions:

- *How can faculty leverage the metacognitive framework to foster teaching practices that strengthen the range of skill sets for 21st century learning?*
- *How can faculty employ metacognitive strategies in a way that makes the processes of teaching and learning more efficient over a longer period of time?*
- *Autonomy, mastery and purpose contribute to human motivation for complex processes (Pink, 2012). How can institutions support these factors in ways that yield new recommendations for rewarding faculty in an environment of diminishing resources?*

THE PROCESS OF FACULTY DEVELOPMENT

To answer these questions, SEPCHE developed and launched a scalable professional development model with several parts: short infusions of professional development given regularly, faculty application of strategies to an aspect of teaching, peer discourse and ongoing coaching support with a faculty development specialist (Moy et al., 2014).

Model elements reflect what the learning sciences have found help people learn. Recognizing that learners learn by engaging in "hands on" experiential learning, a major part of this initiative supports faculty engagement in action research – applying what they learn in the classroom, measuring its efficacy, and learning through parallel engagement in the scholarship of teaching.

In addition, faculty professional development is intentionally chunked into smaller units to enable application and spacing of learning. In this way, teachers break from learning to apply what they have learned before resuming professional development. Regular gatherings enable faculty to apply learning to teaching practice, gather evidence and receive valuable feedback from colleagues and a faculty development specialist.

Chief academic officers (CAOs) established an innovation fund and invited faculty proposals from all disciplines for funded research of an aspect of teaching and engagement using metacognitive approaches. At the start of each semester, CAOs announced a call for proposals during a faculty-led workshop on active learning and metacognitive teaching strategies. Following the session, faculty developed research proposals with support from faculty conveners and the SEPCHE executive director. CAOs reviewed and awarded proposals. Award letters were sent to faculty outlining the requirements of the award: reimbursement procedures, attending required meetings with colleagues and the professional development specialist, and completing reporting requirements. In order to complete their research, most faculty were required to obtain clearance from their institutional review board (IRB) that reviews and approves research involving human subjects.

Faculty with awarded research gathered every six weeks during the semester to engage together in web sessions with faculty development expert Dr. G. Christian Jernstedt, professor emeritus of psychological and brain sciences, director emeritus of the Center for Educational Outcomes at Dartmouth College, and an active researcher with over 45 years of experience exploring the cognitive, behavioral, and social factors associated with learning. Through a master class format, faculty described their ongoing research and received feedback from peers and Dr. Jernstedt. Dr. Jernstedt wove into sessions small infusions of professional development on the science of learning enabling faculty reflection and application of principles. At the end of each semester, faculty submitted an interim or final report on their research question stating what they learned and what they will do next to advance their learning and teaching practices.

The following are four faculty narratives that illustrate how faculty applied learning to improve their practice at the course, program, institution and cross-institutional levels:

Course Initiative: Gauging Learning in a Course-Based Undergraduate Research Experience

Engaging large numbers of undergraduates in authentic scientific discovery is desirable but difficult to achieve. A growing body of literature suggests that early engagement in a research experience has positive impacts on student performance in the first year and improves student retention into the second year. Course-based undergraduate research experiences (CUREs) have drawn national attention in American biology education as a promising way to address this challenge.

In a CURE, research is embedded into the course. This affords many more students to engage in research, but is it better? This research seeks to understand the learning taking place in a CURE through the introduction of reflective practice to learn how students may be learning in a CURE.

Teaching Challenge
Research suggests that reflection strengthens learning (Ambrose, Bridges, DiPietro, Lovett, & Norman, 2010; Brown et al., 2014). Knowing this, how

might an instructor integrate more reflection into teaching? Can it help to measure how student learning changes over time?

Process

The course syllabus provided an entry point to integrate more student reflection. Careful review of the syllabus with a faculty coach yielded suggestions for syllabus format and structuring changes. The result – a simpler, more streamlined syllabus reflecting a research-based principle: organization facilitates learning (Ambrose et al., 2010; Bransford et al., 2000).

Second, a set of weekly reflective prompts gauged how students perceived the course changing their thinking both inside and outside the class. To advance the measurement of student learning along several dimensions, a Learning Dimensions Survey was constructed with the assistance of a faculty development expert and administered to students on a weekly basis.

Third, as students engaged in the weekly reflection survey, the instructor completed the same reflective prompts to capture his own impressions of student learning as a way of triangulating what was occurring in student learning. Below are representative comments:

> Students are continuing the need to trouble-shoot experiments and are **therefore looking back at past experiments in their notebooks for guidance with ongoing trouble-shooting with their current experiments.** I am finding students paging through their lab notebooks to understand how what they did earlier in class has a connection to what experiments they are currently conducting.

The reflection observes how students construct learning by building upon prior learning (Ambrose et al., 2010; Bransford et al., 2000; Brown et al., 2014). It also reflects what the literature has shown about the various functions of reflection, from thinking about the past, cementing current actions to projecting into the future and drawing meaning from all of these ideas (Fade, n.d.).

Instructor reflection also reveals the kind of iterative problem solving that demands and strengthens critical analysis to identify what went wrong in order to correct experiments:

> Students are beginning to learn that mastering techniques takes **time and practice.** After the second or third round of streaking bacteria out on an agar plate or streaking phage particles on an agar plate their streaking skills continue to improve. **Students indicated that they rarely get to do a technique more than once in their other classes and value the ability to truly master techniques in this course.**

Mastery results from the sheer practice of doing an experiment over and over again, they become much more confident testing new ideas and taking risks. This contributes to learner confidence and agency.

Outcomes
While data from this recent effort continues to be compiled and analyzed, the integration of reflection as a tool contributes a more nuanced picture of exactly what and how students may be learning than what typical forms of assessment can capture.

Reflection additionally enables the instructor to see where students may need additional support in the course of practice. It is common for novice learners to bring prior knowledge to a subject that is incorrect. Uncovering prior knowledge in order to correct it is a critical practice that shapes students' learning (Ambrose et al., 2010; Bransford et al., 2000; Brown et al., 2014). Reflective prompts can be designed to tease out prior knowledge; in this way, reflective prompts can improve diagnosis and facilitation of learning.

Regular student reflection not only allows students to obtain a much better grasp of what they do or don't know but it also enables the instructor to better gauge student understanding. Given initial findings, one can see how making time for reflection helps students learn the material on a much deeper level.

Program Initiative: Integrating Online and Blended Teaching

Teaching Challenge
Data collected on adult learner preferences from graduate students in an educational research course indicate a positive correlation between assignment complexity (cognition) and a preference to learn with an instructor (Sheety & Melton, 2013, 2014). Results show that when the same students rank their feelings about online learning, they perceive online learning to be similar to learning on their own. Participants report higher anxiety and less confidence in learning online compared to learning in groups, with an instructor or even learning alone.

Based on this prior research and while developing the college's first graduate education hybrid program integrating face-to-face, hybrid and online coursework, two questions formed the basis for research:

1. What challenges do faculty and students encounter in the transition to online/hybrid learning and what strategies address those challenges?
2. What metacognitive aspects of existing learning theories should and can be integrated into online course offerings to improve teaching and learning?

Process

The project consisted of three stages: (1) literature review of existing research on online teaching and learning; (2) hybrid course design and data collection; and (3) faculty professional development for part-time (adjunct) faculty interested in teaching in the program.

This research addresses a perennial question of how students learn best in various settings. This work appraises various assessment methods and strategies used to measure and enhance students' learning processes, a common topic across disciplines and projects.

Research on Online Teaching and Learning

Review of the literature provides important evidence of the shifts to which faculty must attend as they move from traditional approaches to online teaching: the shift in instructor role (Zheng & Smaldino, 2003), use of technology (Pallof & Pratt, 2000), and the shift in student role (Palloff & Pratt, 2003; Yang & Cornelious, 2005). When redesigning courses for online teaching, a primary recommendation includes aligning assessment to course measurable goals first before choosing the appropriate technology to achieve identified goals (Boettcher & Conrad, 2004).

Pallof and Pratt (2000) underscore the importance of participation and engagement as a "collaborative learning process form[ing] the foundation of a learning community. When collaboration is not encouraged, participation in the online course is lowered and can be seen in the form of queries to the instructor, rather than dialogue and feedback" (p. 6).

Hybrid Course Design and Data Collection

Two courses were designed with these insights in mind: (1) an online course for part-time faculty to prepare them to be effective online facilitators by experiencing a course as a student and (2) shifting a face-to-face educational research course to a hybrid format.

Developing and assessing the hybrid course became the primary focus for this effort. Keeping in mind the role of cognition, affect and behavior in the learning process and the goal of building a learner-centered classroom where adult students are able to share and clarify their knowledge, and build creative problem solving capabilities (Weimer, 2002), this effort made use of two metacognitive strategies: (1) engagement and satisfaction from the new learning environment (affect and behavior) and (2) thinking about thinking (metacognition).

To measure changes in learning, students responded twice during the semester to reflective on questions providing formative feedback to adjust the course. In addition, they completed a survey that included items, such as "I'm anxious to take a hybrid course," or "I received feedback from the course instructor in a timely manner," and "I received feedback from other students in the course in a timely manner." A focus group in the last day of class contributed to a summative assessment that will inform design of future courses. In the faculty online course, they completed weekly journal reflecting on their experience as online learners.

Outcomes
In response to challenges that faculty and students encounter in the transition to online/hybrid learning both faculty and students journals reported time management as the main challenge.

> I learned that time management is essential. Students and instructors must focus on time management because of the nature of an online course, I believe instructors must be committed to checking online more frequently and students must manage their time appropriately so that all requirements are met and goals are achieved.(Amy, May 2014)

As a result, we developed an introductory short video that shares students and faculty experiences with time management to support students in planning and managing their time as online learners. In addition syllabus includes detailed information, including estimated time required per unit, to allow students to plan ahead of time.

Institutional Initiative: Building a Faculty-Led Learning Community

Teaching Challenge
The teaching challenge addressed through this research was twofold: (1) develop habits of higher order thinking as faculty members, specifically as evidenced in course preparation and (2) promote habits of higher order

thinking in students. Through an institution-based learning community entitled the Academy for Metacognition, this effort invited teachers to assess and strengthen their metacognitive habits.

Collaboratively, Academy members began: applying suggestions from a common reader on student engagement strategies; recording weekly our reflections in a course-specific journal; sharing insights at biweekly meetings; and critiquing specific aspects of our teaching using the Immaculata University Cross-disciplinary Rubric for Faculty Metacognition.

Cognizant of institutional accreditation evaluation standards and discipline-specific criteria, the process of communicating, measuring, and documenting student learning outcomes was a major part of the teaching and learning process. Academy for Metacognition members from multiple disciplines focused heavily on student learning outcomes demanded by their respective areas of expertise. Collaboration with persons of varied disciplines generated insights on course content and creative ways of engaging students. Conversations with peers helped to identify the skills that students needed to master and ways of promoting the students' ownership of course material. The sharing of colleagues' classroom and preparation experiences eventually led to a "rubric" of best metacognitive practices.

Process

In biweekly meetings, faculty shared written reflections, classroom successes, problems, and strategies. As questions emerged in the on-campus learning community, these could be shared with the cross-institutional learning community. Candid journal entries and genuine conversations strengthened awareness of new ways of presenting material and promoting students' active involvement in our courses. The camaraderie experienced at meetings encouraged all to resume the arduous yet rewarding attention-to-details needed when planning lessons.

The Academy enabled a "receptive environment" in which to discuss teaching challenges; teachers were actively involved in developing metacognitive skills in themselves and consequently, in their students. Listening to colleagues underscored the value of group work. The support of the group energized all to think through each course, each class in a new way. One professor of music began to assemble a cache of questions and activities that would help students to be actively involved in her courses.

Outcomes

Academy participants improved class participation and teacher effectiveness by both using and teaching metacognitive strategies such as: active listening; critical thinking; comparison and contrast; scaffolding and looping; group problem solving; reflecting on easily-confused words (e.g., affect, effect); creating a definition meaningful to the student; examining logic (or lack of logic) in a written piece or discourse; mapping; and creating scenarios for student reflection/collaboration.

Other metacognitive approaches such as asking questions that make students reflect on their class/test preparation; creative projects; reflection on class preparation; and structured discussions in class improved student AND faculty metacognition. In music, for example, the teacher developed a Q/R (quick response) strategy for music history; engaged students in "Where in the World" for World Music class; and challenged students to think of creative projects and to self-assess these projects.

Journaling, meeting/sharing with the group, and personal and group brainstorming were helpful strategies. Academy members met with good success in employing the flipped class.

The importance of faculty metacognition and the need to improve upon it was strengthened through this work. Collaboration served as a structured support, a constant reminder of the need to make metacognition central to course planning, execution, and assessment.

The Academy, made up of volunteer teachers who desired to learn more about metacognition and best practices, offered camaraderie, resources, and a small remuneration. The collaborative nature of the Academy allowed members to fully develop their understanding of metacognition and the advice/suggestions provided in the meetings became a springboard for changes adopted in classrooms – and beyond. One Academy member described the impact of this cooperative professional development:

> As I reflected, journaled, and collaborated with other faculty, I acquired fluency in finding ways to introduce and promote higher levels of thinking in my students. Creative thought became easier, habitual, and seemed to spill over to everything I was working on. (Doutt, 2015)

Another key development in metacognitive awareness grew out of conversations at meetings. It became apparent that best metacognitive practices included reflective planning, effective implementation of higher thinking skills while teaching the lesson, and reflection on the lesson. Members of the Academy worked together in creating a "Cross-disciplinary Rubric for Faculty Metacognition." This rubric has become a hands-on, concrete tool that is used in pursuit of higher thinking skills. Among Academy members, "the Rubric" (as it is affectionately known!) serves as a symbol of our collaborative efforts and is a source of inestimable pride.

Cross-Institutional Initiative: Building a Cross-Institutional Learning Community

A faculty learning community is a cross-disciplinary faculty and staff group of members who engage in an active, collaborative, program with a curriculum about enhancing teaching and learning and with frequent seminars and activities that provide learning, development, the scholarship of teaching, and community building (Cox, 2004). Research of 395 faculty at six universities indicates that faculty learning communities are highly effective in improving student learning and in changing beliefs and attitudes about teaching (Beach & Cox, 2009). Participation in FLCs deeply engages each community member in the reflection and evaluation of their teaching and their own learning (Desrochers, 2010).

Reflective practices encourage resiliency and resourcefulness in the face of uncertainty and develop habits of attention and analysis that can sustain higher education as it works to address the problems of society (Larrivee, 2000). It enables individuals to achieve greater flexibility and creativity by developing accurate perceptions and avoiding premature assessments (Mezirow, 1991). As individuals learn through reflection, they are able to enhance their overall personal and professional effectiveness, which in turn enhances student learning.

Teaching Challenge
This study explored two pedagogical concepts: building a cross-institutional faculty learning community via Skype and the impact of reflective journaling on teaching and learning.

Process
Meetings with one another and the faculty development expert provided the opportunity to explore effective methods of meeting remotely. Reflective prompts developed with guidance from the faculty development expert structured the practice of journaling and discussion. His advice regarding qualitative assessment of the journals guided our evaluation efforts. Working collaboratively with other faculty with the same outlook and mindset served to motivate and empower all.

Four faculty members from different disciplines and different institutions engaged in structured reflective journaling around the following questions:
1. What helped my teaching?
2. What hindered my teaching?
3. What did I learn about my teaching?

Each participant kept a reflective teaching journal and met biweekly via Skype to discuss insights and developments. Assessment methods included completion of a survey at the end of the project and coding and evaluation of reflective journals.

Outcomes

Positive outcomes were observed in both the process of reflective journaling and participation in a cross-institutional faculty learning community. Reflective journaling influences teaching by heightening faculty awareness in regards to teaching and learning.

Learning experiences that are actively engaging enable students to connect to content and elicit deeper learning, increased critical thinking, and stronger evaluation results (assignments, papers, tests). Examples of *engagement* include experiential learning (service and field trips), peer-to-peer and student-to-faculty collaboration, games and debate/discussion:

> I noticed a significant difference in my first class when I participated in the review game with the students and in the second class when I did not. WOW!

> So I must say what helped my teaching the most is the engagement of the students because of the hands on nature of the activity.

> Service projects conducted as part of a class, although preventing as much content being covered has payoffs in more students being engaged with the actual content being covered in additional semester classes.

Creating and implementing lessons that are *relevant* to students requires faculty to ask questions such as: How does this content apply to students' lives? What's the purpose? How can this serve them and society at large? Relevance must be intentionally communicated and experienced. Examples of relevant learning activities include guest speakers, YouTube videos, experiential learning (service and field trips), intentional connection to current topics, explicit application to career goals, and modeling:

> I learned that the best way for my student to understand the business cycle, unemployment, and inflation was to discuss it in terms of the current economic situation.

> Students got to see first-hand the impact on Valley Creek of housing development upstream of the Park (by visiting Valley Creek). I found the students asking me many more questions about storm water damage's impact to stream and human health and what they could do to prevent it!

Learning activities that give students *autonomy* foster ownership of their learning. Faculty can foster student ownership by giving students choices, topics, methods, objectives and assessments:

> I gave the class options as they planned their final project this week, based in part on advice from Dr. Jernstedt. They listed all of the issues we have discussed this semester, categorized them, and then evaluated which would be the most useful to cover. They then had to decide how to break up the work, based upon the students' interests and needs, and how to present their work to me and to their peers. They took ownership over this and decided what my criteria of grading would be, based on the goals of the project.

> Using authentic assessment allowed my students to decide how they would show me what they learned. They feel empowered and take ownership.

DISCUSSION

Taken together the four faculty narratives suggest that the strongest motivations for faculty engagement are the same for learners in general. Teachers, like learners, are motivated by mastery, autonomy and purpose (Pink, 2012). Teachers want to improve what they are doing; they want to feel that what they are doing makes a difference; and they want to be part of something larger than themselves. They are also highly motivated by the connection formed with others in the process of collaborative learning.

What these narratives also suggest, importantly, is that efforts to change behavior — whether individually or institutionally, take time. Faculty consistently report that studying their own teaching — whether redesigning their curriculum or implementing new engagement strategies and measuring results, required far more time than they had anticipated, but it was well worth the effort.

Reflection is a critical part of learning — on the part of learners (faculty) and the learning community (institutions). This requires all to bring their authentic selves to conversations, to become fluent in reflecting individually and collectively, and to keep focused on learning and learning to improve.

For example, when faculty engaged in the cross-institutional learning community in regular reflective practice about their teaching, they noted:

> … It allows me to think through and really know if I am meeting my teaching objectives. It allows me to think of ways to adapt when I am not, and celebrate and enhance when I am.

> Reflective journaling showed …. That I really do like it (teaching)! And I'm a much more creative, engaging, and risky teacher when I can recognize that."

Reflective journaling ..."allows me to do "research in action." When I look at my teaching this way it motivates and inspires me"

Faculty also appreciate being able to learn with faculty from other disciplines and institutions. In such a rich environment, this enables faculty to experience firsthand collaborative learning and complex problem solving. As one faculty notes, "This professional development opportunity was in fact an occasion for us to mirror what we were preaching: 'learning by doing' (Sheety, 2015)."

Consortium staff support for collaborative faculty professional development is a critical support to keep things moving. As faculty work to balance other responsibilities, consortium staff can provide administrative and coordination support to keep the project moving forward and to assist faculty in their engagement (Moy et al., 2014).

Institutional self-awareness is improved when project milestones and related data measures are clear, specific, and reported regularly. For example, this effort established a goal to expose through workshops and conferences 35% of full and part-time faculty to this initiative by the end of year two. Consortium staff delineated this into actual numbers of full- and part-time faculty for the project and an average per institution so that leaders had a very clear sense of the targets they individually and collectively needed to achieve from year to year.

By year one, the initiative was very close to hitting the 35% target among full-time faculty but was falling short in reaching part-time faculty. Because progress was reported to leaders each semester, they could then adjust their efforts to expose more part-time faculty. By the end of the second year, the initiative exceeded its 35% goals exposing 233 full-time faculty (82%) and 171 part-time faculty (40%) across seven institutions.

Faculty leadership played a critical role in broadening faculty exposure through workshops and in leading learning communities. Giving faculty leadership roles also strengthened their sense of ownership for its success. In most cases, faculty leaders researched their teaching while serving as workshop and learning community leaders. Stipend support, institutional leader praise and public acknowledgment of their leadership incentivized the work.

Ongoing coaching support by a faculty development expert provided a critical support for faculty as they tested new teaching approaches. As learners themselves, when faculty could receive regular expert feedback (every 4–6 weeks), this kept them motivated to engage in mastering their own continuous learning loop – strengthening their self-awareness of their teaching process, evaluating their intervention, and adjusting to meet their research goals. Faculty found that engaging in the scholarship of teaching and learning sometimes helped them meet teaching, research, and institutional responsibilities simultaneously. Engagement in this effort often led to professional development presentations and publications that served to improve their portfolios for promotion and tenure. Likewise, learning within the cross-institutional community was often shared within institutions benefitting other faculty facing similar challenges.

Leadership support advances wider adoption of evidence-based teaching approaches. Direct affirmation of faculty efforts, providing release from other institutional meetings to attend sessions with the faculty development expert, securing expedited review of institutional review boards when research involved students, giving faculty participants opportunities to present their work within institutional professional development workshops and letters of appreciation for tenure and promotion files all serve to reinforce faculty participation while building broader knowledge of evidence-based teaching approaches.

In institutions where these conditions and supports were present, and where leaders worked directly with a core of participating faculty to integrate this effort into existing professional development structures, faculty exposure to the project was significantly higher than in institutions where alignment and coordination efforts were less evident.

Collaborative professional development is an important, resource-efficient strategy for small institutions seeking to build institutional capacity in an environment of diminishing resources. It creates critical mass – enabling faculty who are often only one or two of their kind within departments, to find others working in their fields, and it can foster a safe environment for nurturing trustful relationships that lead to future innovations (Moy & Dunbar, in press).

Learning communities are an important vehicle for building and sustaining change and innovation (Kezar, 2015). Our experience suggests that this is a critical institutional strategy to build faculty capacity within and across colleges and universities.

A cross-pollination effect in collaborative professional development goes well beyond the individual – building shared learning, community and purpose across a department, an institution, a consortium and a discipline. This makes collaborative professional development both time and resource efficient. As institutional leaders reinforce and support initiatives through formal channels, faculty can spread informally through their many interactions with peers a contagious passion and renewed shared purpose that is both supportive and rewarding.

REFERENCES

Ambrose, S. A., Bridges, M. W., DiPietro, M., Lovett, M. C., & Norman, M. K. (2010). How *learning works: 7 research-based principles for smart teaching.* San Francisco, CA: Jossey-Bass.

Bailey, M. J., & Dynarski, S. M. (2011). Inequality in postsecondary attainment. In G. Duncan & R. Murnane (Eds.), *Whither opportunity: Rising inequality, schools, and children's life chances* (pp. 117–132). New York, NY: Russell Sage Foundation.

Beach, A., & Cox, M. (2009). The impact of faculty learning communities on teaching and learning. *Learning Communities Journal, 1*(1), 7–27.

Bissonette, T. (2011) Everyone's developmentally delayed, starting with us. *The Chronicle of Higher Education.* Retrieved from http://chronicle.com/article/How-Developmental-Delay-Holds/128585. Accessed on August 14, 2011.

Boettcher, J., & Conrad, R.-M. (2004). *Faculty guide for moving teaching and learning to the web* (2nd ed.). Phoenix, AZ: League for Innovation in the Community College.

Bransford, J. D., Brown, A. L., & Cocking, R. R. (Eds.). (2000). *How people learn: Brain, mind, experience and school.* Expanded Edition. Washington, DC: Commission on Behavioral and Social Sciences and Education, National Research Council. National Academy Press.

Brown, P. C., Roediger III, H. L., & McDaniel, M. A. (2014). *Make it stick: The science of successful learning.* Cambridge, MA: The Belknap Press of Harvard University Press.

Cox, M. D. (2004). Introduction to faculty learning communities. *New Directions for Teaching and Learning, 2004*(97), 5–23.

Desrochers, C. G. (2010). Faculty learning communities as catalysts for implementing successful small-group learning. In *Small group learning in higher education: Research and practice.* Stillwater, OK: New Forums Press. Retrieved from www.calstatela.edu/academic/aa/cetl/resources/FLC.pdf

Dill, D. D., & Morrison, J. L. (1985). Ed.D. and Ph.D. research training in the field of higher education: A survey and a proposal. *Review of Higher Education, 8*(2), 169–182.

Doutt, K. (2015). *The impact of cooperative professional development.* Unpublished manuscript.

Fade, S. (n.d.). *Learning and assessing through reflection: A practical guide.* Retrieved from http://cw.routledge.com/textbooks/9780415537902/data/learning/9_Learning%20and%20Assessing%20Through%20Reflection.pdf

Gault, B., Reichlin, L., & Román, S. (2014). *College affordability for low-income adults: Improving returns on investment for families and society.* Report, IWPR #C412. Institute for Women's Policy Research, Washington, DC.

Jernstedt, G. C. (2011). SEPCHE faculty development conference, May 11.

Kezar, A. (2015). *Scaling and sustaining change and innovation: Lessons learned from the Teagle Foundation's 'faculty work and student learning' initiative.* Retrieved from http://www.teaglefoundation.org/getmedia/f5560934-c4db-42e3-8e52-439bd7aa82f6/Kezar-Sustaining-Change

Larrivee, B. (2000). Transforming teaching practice: Becoming the critically reflective teacher. *Reflective Practice: International and Multidisciplinary Perspectives, 1*(3), 293–307.

Lawlor Group. (2012). *Trends for 2012: Five marketplace realities and how private higher education must manage them.* Retrieved from http://m.thelawlorgroup.com/january2012.html

Levine, A. (2005). *Educating school leaders.* New York, NY: The Education Schools Project.

Mangan, K. (2015). The challenge of the first-generation student. *Chronicle of Higher Education*. Retrieved from http://chronicle.com/article/The-Challenge-of-the/230137/. Accessed on May 18.

Mendoza, P. (2012). *Should I work or should I borrow? A counterfactual analysis on the effect of working while enrolled and the impact on baccalaureate completion* (Vol. 42). Washington, DC: National Association of Student Financial Aid Administrators.

Mezirow, J. (1991). *Transformative dimensions of adult learning*. San Francisco, CA: Jossey-Bass.

Moy, E., & Dunbar, D. A. (in press). Building faculty capacity for innovation. In *Pushing the boundaries of collaboration: What consortia can accomplish*. Upland, CA: Blackbird Press.

Moy, E., O'Sullivan, G., Terlecki, M., & Jernstedt, C. (2014). Building faculty capacity through the learning sciences. *Change: The Magazine of Higher Learning, 46*(2), 42–49. doi:10.1080/00091383.2014.896710

Pallof, R. M., & Pratt, K. (2000). Making the transition: Helping teachers to teach online. Paper presented at EDUCAUSE: *Thinking it through*. Nashville, TN. (ERIC Document Reproduction Service No. ED 452 806). Retrieved October 4, 2003, from ERIC Database.

Palloff, R. M., & Pratt, K. (2003). *The virtual student* (pp. 17–28). San Francisco, CA: Jossey-Bass.

Pink, D. (2012). *The surprising truth about what motivates us*. Retrieved from https://www.youtube.com/watch?v=KgGhSOAtAyQ

Schneider, C. (2011). The leap vision for learning. American Colleges and Universities.

Sheety, A., & Melton, L. (2013). High support and high expectations: Engaging adult learners in designing and planning the learning experience. Paper presented at the 16th IIRP World Conference. Bethlehem, PA.

Sheety, A., & Melton, L. (2014 March). How the interaction between cognition, behavior and emotions affects learning preference of adults in higher education. Paper presented at the SoTL Common Conference, A conference for the scholarship of teaching and learning, Savannah, GA.

Sheety, A. (2015). *In response to faculty professional development*. Unpublished manuscript, Cabrini College, Radnor, PA.

Sorcinelli, M. D. (2007). Faculty development: The challenge going forward. *Peer Review: Fall, 9*(4), 4–9. Retrieved from https://www.aacu.org/publications-research/periodicals/faculty-development-challenge-going-forward

Weimer, M. (2002). *Learner centered teaching*. San Francisco, CA: Jossey-Bass.

Yang, Y., & Cornelious, L. F. (2005). Preparing instructors for quality online instruction. *Online Journal of Distance Learning Administration, 8*(1), 1–16.

Zheng, L., & Smaldino, S. (2003). Key instructional design elements for distance education. *The Quarterly Review of Distance Education, 4*(2), 153–166.

CREATIVE CROSS-CULTURAL CONNECTIONS: FACEBOOK AS A THIRD SPACE FOR INTERNATIONAL COLLABORATIONS

Natascha Radclyffe-Thomas, Anne Peirson-Smith, Ana Roncha and Adrian Huang

ABSTRACT

As industries are increasingly globalized, our students' future workplaces require facility with cross-cultural collaboration, yet curricula often remain situated within the home culture. This chapter presents a qualitative case study on a collaborative project between students in London, Hong Kong, and Singapore. An overview of the process is given drawing on the experiences of the teachers and students involved, informing a discussion around the issues inherent in the internationalization of the curriculum. Tutors created a shared private Facebook group to connect London College of Fashion students with students at City University Hong Kong and LASALLE College of the Arts Singapore. Students worked on separate but aligned briefs that mirror contemporary working

University Partnerships for Academic Programs and Professional Development
Innovations in Higher Education Teaching and Learning, Volume 7, 243–266
Copyright © 2016 by Emerald Group Publishing Limited
All rights of reproduction in any form reserved
ISSN: 2055-3641/doi:10.1108/S2055-364120160000007023

patterns and allowed co-creation of educational experiences beyond the geographic and time constraints of working internationally, specifically addressing issues around global and local communications. The Facebook platform was used separately and collaboratively to support students' learning and the digitally mediated collaboration allowed for flexibility in when and how education took place, providing a third space for co-creation of learning: a global classroom.

Keywords: Cross-cultural; Facebook; international; learning; partnerships

This is indeed a special idea which can act as an exchange of ideas (without actually going on an exchange program) on a virtual platform which could be translated into concrete ideas in researches and essays (global classroom student participant).

This chapter presents a case study of a collaborative online international project developed between university tutors in London, Hong Kong, and Singapore. It explores the motivation behind an initial pilot collaboration – a global classroom between London and Hong Kong – and how that pilot informed a subsequent triangular collaboration with Singapore as a third partner. The pilot global classroom was run as an exploratory collaboration, and a case study methodology was adopted to record and analyze the experience for this and the subsequent extended collaboration (Yin, 2003). The initiative aimed to foster exchange of students' social and cultural knowledge to drive learning in an inclusive environment (Ryan & Hellmundt, 2005) using a blended pedagogical approach; the international collaboration was only one aspect of the course delivery, which was offered in addition to physical lectures, seminars and tutorials. The authors' aims aligned with each institutions' mission to provide creative education that fosters globally aware, technically competent young professionals, and failure to deliver on the learning outcomes for the collaboration would likely prejudice future initiatives, so student feedback was collected in each location. In total nearly 300 students participated in the two global classrooms and the case study provides an overview of the process; outlining the successes and challenges.

The authors engaged in extended online discussions before running a pilot initiative by introducing the collaboration into one assignment in their respective courses in Popular Culture (30 students) and Advertising (35 students) (CityU HK) and Fashion Forecasting and Brand Development (35 students LCF) in Semester A of 2013–14. Along with a content analysis of the group page and online activities, the impact of this project on teaching and learning was monitored and analyzed throughout using evaluative student feedback based on individual and team-based Wiki-style multi-modal self-reflections through summative student feedback forms, in addition to questionnaires, focus groups, and interviews with individual students, as well as the tutors' observations and reflections. Following a thorough review of the pilot, the second global classroom ran in Semester B 2014–2015 with 40 CityU students from the Fashion Communication course, 93 LCF Fashion Branding students and added an additional partner with 48 students taking a course in Fashion Media and Industries at LASALLE College of the Arts, Singapore. Feedback was collected from each partner involved in the second iteration and is reported on below. The tangible outcomes identified from all cohorts include: enhancement of professional and critical thinking skills; collaborative competencies; intercultural awareness and accommodation; communication competencies; independent learning skills; activated innovation; and creativity through the use of appropriate technology in blended educational spaces.

CONTEXT: MILLENNIAL STUDENTS IN A GLOBALIZED SYSTEM

With 340 million Twitter tweets daily and over one billion people on Facebook, the changes that social networks have made to our everyday lives are so evident that they can no longer be ignored or dismissed by universities as they structure communication, learning and access to knowledge. Social media engagement is part of students' lives; digital platforms are the source of informal education linking individuals with shared interests, but digital social networks have not been part of many formal educational experiences (Radclyffe-Thomas, 2008; Schuller & Watson, 2009).

Education theory shows that close interactions between faculty and students improve students' critical thinking, knowledge acquisition, analytic competencies, and intellectual development and furthermore that peer-to peer interaction is a predictor of student attainment (Junco, 2012). Students learn best when they are intrinsically motivated with personal agency and active involvement in their learning (Collins & Amabile, 1999; Csikszentmihalyi, 1999).

Mazur's flipped classroom concept highlights the benefits of peer-to-peer instruction and confirmed the throwing open of the academy doors (Lambert, 2012). The rise in digital technologies should enable greater student autonomy and facilitate collaborative work with access to unlimited information, skill-development tutorials and subject-discipline networks with students as "active co-producers" of knowledge where the learning process is a "participatory ..., social (process) supportive of personal life goals and needs" (McLoughlin & Lee, 2010, p. 31; Ulbrich et al., 2011). But despite digital-native rhetoric and progress towards more student-centered classrooms, many students do not recognize their own cultural capital and their role as active participants in their education. Furthermore, higher education institutions often fail to translate students' social media enthusiasm; institutions and individual faculty often remain resistant to crossing the boundary between academic and social spheres.

Although institutions often highlight the internationalization of the curriculum and the fostering of global graduates as key guiding policies, the practical means of how this internationalization or globalization may come about is often unclear. Putting to one side the argument that much internationalization has focused on the recruitment of international students, it has been generally understood that physically traveling and studying in another country is the optimal method of building awareness of other cultures. In certain subject disciplines, for example, modern foreign languages, it is customary for students to spend extended periods abroad with the intention that immersion in another culture will enhance both language learning and cultural awareness. Students on non-language courses are often encouraged to study or work abroad or participate in field trips with the same aim, albeit with a recognition that the effect of the exposure is likely to be reduced. Recent approaches to internationalizing the curriculum have changed the focus from sojourners to the majority non-mobile students and seek to introduce an international dimension to teaching and learning or "internationalizing at home" utilizing the affordances of digital technologies to facilitate virtual mobility or collaborative online international learning (COIL) (de Wit, 2013). Yet opportunities for working with peers in higher education institutions around the world are still limited for many students.

THE CASE STUDY

The Partner Institutions

City University Hong Kong (CityU) is a public research university founded in 1984 with a mission to "nurture and develop the talents of students and to create applicable knowledge in order to support social and economic advancement" (CityU, 2015). CityU's overall objective is to deliver student learning in an engaged and global manner by utilizing digital technologies for pedagogical purposes to deliver educational content in a more dynamic and flexible way aligned with students' learning needs and enhance their digital competencies to prepare them for professional life. CityU's Discovery Enriched Curriculum (DEC) aims to prepare globally aware, self-driven, technically competent, and creative young professionals. CityU students are predominantly Hong Kong Chinese learning in a second language context, yet each class would on average have three to four exchange students for one semester typically from Europe, North America, or Australia whose cultural perspective also added to the global classroom experience.

London College of Fashion (LCF) is a constituent college of the University of the Arts London, which is the largest art and design university in Europe and has approximately 36% non-UK students. LCF has recently been named as one of the top universities internationally for fashion education and one of the key strands of LCF's policy is to internationalize the curriculum to "develop curriculum which is culturally diverse, enriched by strong and focused partnerships with peer institutions across the world" (unpublished Strategic Plan 2010–2015). LCF has a higher proportion of non-UK students than the other colleges in the university, with students coming from all over the world to study in London, including a large number of students from South East Asia. LCF alumni work in all areas of the fashion industry worldwide.

LASALLE College of the Arts in Singapore is a leading tertiary institution in cutting edge contemporary arts and design education and practice. The college offers 30 undergraduate and post-graduate programs in art design, film, animation, fashion, dance, music, theater, arts management, arts education, art therapy, and art history. Its faculty is led by a community of award-winning artists, designers, educators and researchers, and their practice-led research sets LASALLE apart as an international center of excellence. Critically acclaimed alumni form the core of the cultural and creative sectors in Singapore and increasingly internationally. With an emphasis on contemporary practice and research, our teaching philosophy emphasizes idea generation and new interpretations of creative disciplines. Students' ideas and creativity will set them apart as they emerge as a reflective practitioner in the industry (Fig. 1).

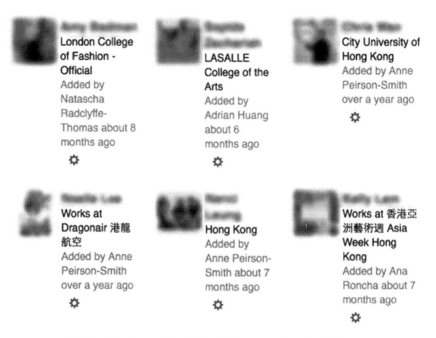

Fig. 1. Members of the Global Classroom Facebook Group.

OBJECTIVES

The aims of the global classroom can be summarized by the objectives set for the initiative to:

1. Make explicit the connection between the theories and concepts encountered in the classroom and professional practice by integrating all aspects of the learning experience in relevant professional fields in online, globally-based project work.
2. Provide an opportunity for students to practice individual problem seeking and solving techniques within the collective setting resonant of the workplace as individuals interact with team members to deliver the project brief.
3. Promote self and peer evaluation according to professional requirements using accessible and student-centered technology platforms.

4. Enhance collaborative and cross-cultural communication skills through active team based communication with peers and industry experts in real time settings that will be of benefit in the professional workplace.
5. Establish a unique tailored learning experience that will enable second language learners to work at their own pace and identify and adapt learning materials as needed for the project.

The pilot study emerged from a professional encounter at an international education conference where one of the authors presented a paper on the academic use of social media. Through mediated collaborations, the authors intended to acknowledge and raise the co-creation of learning using digital channels. The authors intended to create a space for students in different geographic locations to participate in directed work about fashion brands and foster informal communications around these, but also to enable in-country market research in unfamiliar cultures by promoting and encouraging students' participation outside of the set class tasks (Fig. 2).

Although the specific educational benefits of the collaboration that were envisaged could not be guaranteed and the authors were a little unsure how students would respond to the initiative, the overwhelming motivation was that it would be a worthwhile learning experience for students and staff alike.

Although the authors do not wish to endorse notions of "student as consumer" we do teach within subject disciplines that include analysis of consumer behavior and marketing communications where the concept of engagement and co-creation are well researched. Consumer engagement defines the relationship between brands and consumers grounded on the concept of social engagement: "whereby the consumer formulates and maintains a self-awareness of his or her membership within the community ... emphasizing the perceived similarities with other community members ... identification means that the consumer agrees ... with the community's norms, traditions, rituals, and objectives and promotes its well-being" (Algeshiemer et al., 2005, p. 20). Such interactions between brands and consumers have been greatly facilitated by digital interactive technologies (Leboff, 2011); consumer interactions or "co-creation" adding value to products and services as consumers' skills enrich the meanings and performance of brands, products and/or services (Prahalad & Ramaswamy, 2004). The concept of co-creation as theorized in the business world aligns with constructivist understandings of teaching and learning whereby peer interaction and active learning is believed to empower students, adding value to their educational experiences. This understanding underscored the

Fig. 2. Examples of Student Work Posted by Students in the Global Classroom Group and the Peer Feedback Received.

authors' objectives to empower students through building subject-discipline networks or communities of practice (Wenger, 1998).

The authors share a research interest in cross-cultural marketing communications and through the initial collaboration set out to devise project briefs for the respective undergraduate students in London and Hong Kong that would explore how transnational brands are promoted and perceived in different markets. Through curriculum mapping the authors decided to run parallel but separate briefs between our cohorts in London and Hong Kong with the intention to enhance the learning experience and student engagement with the subject content with global classroom partners so as to broaden student networks, expand use of technologies, and enhance cross-cultural communication. It also fully exercised English language competencies as a *lingua franca* in a cross-cultural, collaborative setting given that the CityU students are predominantly Hong Kong Chinese who are learning in a second language context.

The question of how to share learning resources between cohorts and how to capture student discussions and responses led to the decision to run the global classroom project as an online collaboration. Initial discussions focused on the relative merits of using internal or external platforms. Both institutions had their own VLEs but due to issues of access and perceptions of low student engagement with these institutional platforms it was determined that the public platform Facebook, to which all students were accustomed and had easy access, would answer the project objectives to enable asynchronous individual and collaborative learning, in-class and private study and to keep a record of interactions to inform our research. The authors were enthusiastic about the potential benefits the collaborations might have for our students' learning and their increased intercultural communication competence; however, the authors were also cautious about not over-stretching our students particularly in terms of workload, thereby affecting the learning outcomes and/or deliverables. Each of the two iterations revealed generally positive student responses, which in the interests of brevity are reported together in the emergent themes below (Fig. 3).

The pilot launched in Semester A 2013–2014 in the form of a private Facebook Group: the International Fashion Panel. The authors set up the Facebook group and administered the membership requests submitted by students in each location. One hundred students in London and Hong Kong were involved in the pilot study and were introduced to the group's shared online resources in asynchronous seminar sessions. Students worked on separate but aligned briefs that required them to analyze established fashion brands and propose an international brand extension; it was

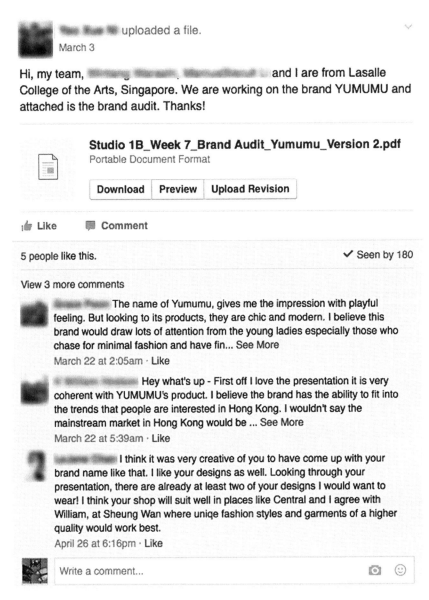

Fig. 3. Examples of Student Work Posted by Students in the Global Classroom Group and the Peer Feedback Received.

strongly suggested but not required that this would be into the markets represented by the partner colleges. Although there were minor differences in the project brief according to each partners' institutional requirements they followed the same basic outline which included an explicit objective to consider markets beyond those that are homogenous or too similar to the home culture (Killick & Dean, 2013) (Fig. 4).

As well as tutors posting relevant information and resources, students were directed to use the group prior to class to provide resources for later discussion, for example, to post marketing images and critiques of brand campaigns which they considered particularly innovative, controversial or problematic. Students were tasked with preparing local intelligence on their home market, for example, fashion hotspots, which they shared through the group. Students were thereby researching both their domestic market and the market they wished to enter. Students supplement secondary research sources by posting surveys and asking direct questions of their collaborators, for example, "Can any of the Hong Kong students tell me what the biggest cosmetic brands are in China?" Students shared their draft work to garner peer feedback on work in progress, and posted completed reports which served as useful comparisons between different educational systems. The tutors did not physically deliver to the students in the partner cohort but their presence in the group did engender a sense of co-teaching. It enabled the input of shared resources, and the Hong Kong tutor prepared a presentation on marketing in Asia with local knowledge and current examples which was delivered by the tutor in London as a supplement to the curriculum (Figs. 5 and 6).

As noted above, the authors had taken a cautious approach to the initial collaborative online international project, but the evidence from student and tutor feedback showed multiple complex learning outcomes had been achieved, many beyond our expectations. There was very little negative feedback on the global classroom, students having "voted with their mice" and not participated when and where they did not find value in the collaboration, however the authors felt that the slow start to the collaborative work may have been due to their desire to frame the collaboration as an academic one and hence having consciously avoided forced online socializing. On reflection this was felt to have been an unnecessary caution and an icebreaker introduction activity was devised for the next iteration. The CityU tutor had previously used Facebook in an educational context so was confident of its facility, but reported that both the frequency of posts and the level of dedicated engagement surpassed their expectations. The LCF tutor had previously used blogging with students but had no

April 30

hello guys. here is my thought on hk hotspots and topshop moodboard.
Thank you.

👍 Like   💬 Comment

✔ Seen by 124

Write a comment...

Fig. 4.   An Example of a Private Study Assignment Posted by a Student Prior to a
Seminar Discussion on International Fashion Marketing.

April 21 · Edited

Brand Extension: If I were to launch Adidas in London and Singapore, the following items are my considerations:

TARGET CUSTOMERS: Mainly youngsters and people who loving doing sports.
PRODUCT LINE: Focusing on football, basketball and running wear for men and women.
PRICE POINTS: Moderate high. Given that Adidas has a well-established international brand image and customer loyalty, offering products at high price would not lead to drop of sales, as I am confident customers wo...
See More

👍 Like   💬 Comment

2 people like this.   ✔ Seen by 142

Write a comment...   📷 ☺

Fig. 5. A Student Posts Draft Ideas About Their Project.

H&M report (Part A) Final.docx   Download
December 9, 2013 at 4:02pm · Latest version by

GE2105_PopCulture Assignment 3_A&FGroup Report.docx   Download
December 9, 2013 at 2:13pm · Latest version by

Adidas.docx   Download
December 9, 2013 at 9:56am · Latest version by

Uniqlo_Report.doc   Download
December 9, 2013 at 9:26am · Latest version by

Li-Ning (Part A).doc   Download
December 9, 2013 at 6:26am · Latest version by

Fig. 6. Files Uploaded onto the Global Classroom Facebook Group Which Acted as a Learning Resource for the Group Members.

experience – even personal – of using Facebook and was working in an environment that unofficially discouraged the use of external social media platforms, and although they reported the interaction was slow to get started they found the students' enthusiasm and the quality of outcomes impressive (Fig. 7).

An unexpected, but pleasing, outcome of the global classroom was that students from the first cohort remained members of the Facebook group after the duration of the formal collaboration and continued to use it informally to share relevant materials with classmates, and later to distribute surveys that supported academic courses they were undertaking which had no official link to the global classroom. This continued interaction, albeit at quite a low level, supported the sense that the authors were contributing to the establishment of a global community of practice. Following a review of the initial pilot study the authors felt confident to expand the scope of the collaboration and when a planned research trip to Singapore was arranged for Spring 2014, the London tutors invited the third partner college LASALLE College of the Arts Singapore to join the global classroom.

LASALLE had been involved in another online collaborative project the preceding semester preceding and this experience was useful both in terms of the planning and also with regard to collecting feedback from students involved in two different collaborative projects. Curriculum mapping resulted in a close match between courses and for the second iteration of the collaborative project; it was feasible to run the project between

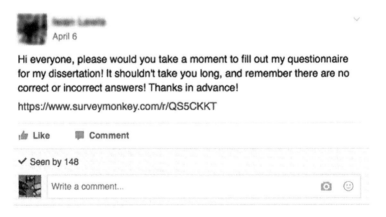

Fig. 7.   An Alumni of the Global Classroom Collaboration Uses the Group Page
to Disseminate a Questionnaire for Their Final Dissertation.

London, Hong Kong, and Singapore. With confidence established in the platform and process, all three partners decided to increase the depth of collaboration. Pedagogic aims for the global classroom were clarified to students from the outset as well as adding some more contact points and tightening up the specifics of the project timeline and deliverables. The second iteration was designed to produce more student-generated content and co-creation. The LASALLE tutor summed up their motivation for joining the global classroom thus:

> Our unwritten (till now) program ethos is to be "Asia-centric" with an international outlook'. We want graduates to be sensitive and well versed with the issues pertinent to development of the fashion industry in Singapore and the region, and also to be aware of the global nature of fashion business.

This notion of capitalizing on students' social and cultural knowledge to drive learning chimed well with each of the partners, as did the desire to engage students in their subject discipline at a global and local level. Initially, the students were given an icebreaker task asking them to introduce themselves and to share three places in the world that they would like to live and three companies for which they aspire to work. This task was undertaken "live" in seminars and followed up by an individual post to the group. This task served to kick off the global classroom with a low risk social interaction and also had the multiple benefit of the mindset of the student participants in a global frame, while at the same time enabling them to identify themselves and outline their career plans, which established stakeholdership in the group and also highlighted their commonalities given their shared demography. Students enjoyed reading these introductory posts and finding similarities and differences between the cohorts:

> Whilst reading the introductory posts from the international students it was interesting to see what brands they aspired to work for, some instantly recognisable and some not. This was a good indicator of what brands are popular within that segment and I was surprised at how many did not mention some of the big luxury fashion houses that were present on the UK posts.

> It has also helped me understand my peers at LCF and I was surprised by how many said they were interested in working for fashion magazines as this is something I have thought of in the past.

Overall, in terms of the outcomes of the global classroom experience, taking into consideration the students' experience from their actual online activity, course reflections, questionnaires and in-class interviews, the experience was a highly positive one in terms of teaching and learning for all of the parties involved as evidenced in these typical representative student responses:

> This was a truly great opportunity for me to understand how British fashion students perceive the everyday fashion brands that many people wear on the street globally and exchange my views with them.

> Having the link to the international fashion panel was such a useful tool for brand research; it was great to be able to get real up-to-date feedback rather than online statistics.

> We got useful feedback from the Hong Kong and LCF students, they willingly shared information regarding their fashion culture with us.

The generic critical competencies gained throughout the process of online engagement between the globally-based students were apparent; having to articulate ideas to a global audience raised the requirement to engage more deeply with the subject matter and think carefully about how those ideas were expressed:

> The exchange motivates me to produce work of a higher standard.

> This has stimulated my critical thinking even more .... I have to think about why I have such a decision, and explain it .... This also makes me think deeper on everything.

> To be able to see their work, and being able to compare ours was also helpful to critique our own work. We may not know much about the brands that they have chosen, therefore we are learning from the work that they have produced and it makes us think from that perspective when writing and editing our own.

Many students commented that the assignment had enabled them to reassess their assumptions in a broader way since they were being provided with multiple sources of information and opinions:

We were able to view the working style and creative processes by other colleges.

> ... the importance of cultural differences within the market place is one of the lessons I will take with me for a long time ... this term has been very beneficial in terms of me developing my understanding of international business, an essential skill for my future development .... (LCF student)

> I have learned a lot from the LCF International Fashion Panel Facebook site because of several reasons: 1) The content is so rich and it is based on different aspects of the industry so I have learned so much from others 2) I am able to know the cross-cultural opinions from different kinds of students ... 3) We can have detailed collaborative discussions using words and images.

Yet this was not just about acquiring knowledge for its own sake, and neither was it bound by the confines of the course syllabus, as many participants noted that they valued the potential to apply this knowledge to their own lives and to their future careers:

Most importantly, I can learn and obtain a lot of information about the marketing strategies in the fashion industry. I can apply them to other industries as well. After all I learn that marketing is listening that requires me to listen to the environment.

The global assignment and the choice of a social media site to engage the various student groups proved to be a very effective and responsive medium for facilitating collaborative work. Students described the Facebook group as "user-friendly" and "interactive."

To my surprise the Facebook site is very active and there are always people posting.

How people on the IFP interacted surprised me as they were active and responsive. Once I posted my moodboard for my assignment and someone commented on it within five minutes. She pointed out its weaknesses so I improved it

I have learned how useful it is to interact with other students from other countries and how easy it is to communicate. It is a good way to communicate with social media and interesting to see everyone's different views and opinions.

I'm always online and on Facebook so this is the perfect way for me to do an assignment as it fits so well with what I'm doing every day and it takes no effort to check into the International Fashion Panel.

SUMMARY

When compiling the feedback on the two iterations of the global classroom, the researchers conclude that the experience was successful beyond initial hopes and more than achieved the stated objectives. Students commented that the group enabled them to learn more about local business and gain exposure to international industry. In addition to achieving the specific discipline objectives, a standout finding was the transformational way students had used the global classroom as a self-reflexive space where they can explore their own and other's cultures and function as intercultural citizens (Byram, 2008), see their home culture as others might see it, and acknowledge their own cultural capital:

Not only did I learn the relationship between fashion and brand management and how media, marketing and cultural practices affect fashion communication, positioning and promotion, but also appreciating the cultural similarities and differences of Hong Kong, London and Singapore.

The experience is eye-opening as students from London and Singapore are experts of their own cities and their posts and comments are insightful, which just can't be replaced by performing Google search.

What I really understood from the panel was intercultural communication and support .... I discovered the beauty of people from two cultures working together voluntarily and giving assistance to each other when necessary.

Having an international group page was really good as we could share ideas and personally, Asian culture always brings me lots of interest. I hope there are more chances
for home students to know more about other cultures and studies.

KEY BENEFITS OF THE COLLABORATION

Tutors' feedback:
- Enhancement of professional and critical thinking skills
- Demonstration of collaborative competencies
- Increase in intercultural awareness and accommodation
- Independent learning skills and enhanced cultural capital (students developed local and international expertise)
- Demonstration of innovation and creativity
- Enhancement of (digital) communication skills

Students' feedback:
- Ease of access/use was crucial; preference for Facebook
- Appreciated regular posting of articles by tutors
- Appreciated constructive feedback on work from overseas students
- Gained insights into other cultures and ways of working/learning
- Exploration made fun
- Motivation to do better because work was viewed by overseas peers

CHALLENGES OF THE COLLABORATION

Undoubtedly, despite the overwhelmingly positive feedback from students in both iterations of the global classroom, challenges were encountered in this global teaching and learning experience. The main issues that emerged included cultural differences, time differences and varying institutional calendars and the administrative managerial realities of running this type of course. There was an initial hesitation for some students to sign up to Facebook and to communicate with strangers on social media but once the first posts were added, the collaboration quickly gained momentum. Because participation was not universal, that meant there was a risk that not all students would receive the same quality feedback.

Inevitably issues arose from the time difference between Asia and Europe and additionally each institution's differing academic calendars, nevertheless this mismatch does replicate the realities of the global workplace and reminds students that not all places, countries or cultures operate in the same way and hence personal work strategies have to be implemented to accommodate such differences. The administration of the global classroom suffered from the same time factors as above which also translated into extra workload for tutors who had to be mindful of participating and facilitating the collaboration. One unexpected bonus resulting from the tutors' participation was how posting relevant articles modeled the desired collaborative behavior and contributed to a sense of community with students commenting (Fig. 8):

> With articles that teachers are posting, students are able to see what teachers are interested in and also what they are following.

Fig. 8.   Example of a Tutor Posting Relevant Resources in the Global Classroom International Fashion Panel Group.

CLOSING COMMENTS

With our privileged position as academic gatekeepers we should challenge ourselves as to why we want to teach something, justify what the use is to students, and determine how to deliver our desired learning outcomes (Rogers, 1991). The need for fostering inclusive pedagogies and collaborative working practices across cultures is paramount as higher education institutions worldwide welcome more international students and faculty. The number of links higher education institutions have with peer institutions around the world has been used as a measure of their increased internationalization, but without embedding the practices of reflective learning, international collaborative projects run the risk of failing to impact participants' curiosity and cultural understandings (Byram, 2009). Social media can expand the classroom beyond its physical site into a virtual world with potential for students to work collaboratively across borders (Harris & Rea, 2009; Richardson, 2006). Globalization is a key feature of 21st century industry and being an effective team player is a highly valued skill in the global marketplace (McLean & Ransom, 2005), but merely focusing on delivering the requirements of a globalized workplace can be criticized as a reductive motivation for internationalizing the curriculum and denies the benefits for *all* students (and faculty) of developing a global outlook and an informed and critical global outlook (Killick, 2014). Thus universities can no longer operate without reference to the global environment (Brown, 2015) and have a responsibility in facilitating collaborative cross-cultural encounters that enable the exploration of disciplines in different locations. With these challenges in mind the authors advise fellow academics considering implementing collaborative cross-cultural learning initiatives to get started, to embrace the process and learn from the first iteration making improvements in subsequent ones.

In the case study discussed, participants combined familiarity and excitement through Facebook-mediated learning opportunities that allowed them to shape their learning experiences together. The assignment required students to share market information multi-modally in written English supplemented with images and this fostered cultural awareness of the differences and similarities of doing global business when working with multicultural partners in other geographic locations. That the networking took place through web-based applications and fostered online collaboration between the different partners demonstrated a clear representation of the digital habitats (Wenger, White, & Smith, 2009) we now inhabit. Collaboration with students and user (whether alumni or student) generated content are amongst the concepts explored through this project that set out to expand the boundaries of the classroom and provide a clear representation of the concept of communities of practice within a new environment, one within which the student experiences a discursive shift from traditional approaches to one where their subjective view and agency becomes a legitimate part of knowledge enquiry through critical engagement in an interpretative community (Peirson-Smith, Miller, & Chik, 2014)

The structure of the collaborative project is important but not dependent on the use of specific technologies, as some parties might believe. Technology provides new spaces for collaboration and interaction to occur, but successful educational outcomes still require specific and clear learning objectives and timelines. The key to setting up and managing a global classroom of this nature relies on a combination of the motivation amongst the tutors to make it work by being prepared to take a contained risk and being adaptive ensuring that the assignment is viable although it may evolve in unexpected, yet beneficial directions. In this case the global classroom operated where different cultures met (social-academic and international) and co-constructed their knowledge in a third collaborative inclusive space.

Table 1. Examples of Peer Feedback on Work Posted to the Global Classroom Facebook Group.

The audit was clear to follow and contained good visual stimulus, however we noticed the image quality was poor throughout. There was a good theme and text was clear to read and coherent. A good audit, nice job ☺

Hey guys! Your report is so beautiful! We are so impressed by your layout and how easy and engaging it is to read. The graphic elements and use of typography makes it really dynamic. What we would suggest is doing the product offering as a chart to make it better to navigate. Another thing that you could do is create a brand positioning map along with the paragraph to give a clearer visual perspective and comparison among its competitors. In terms of expanding into the London fashion market, Shoreditch would be the perfect place for your brand. It show cases many independent labels, that have a unique/quirky flare.

Wow – first of all the use of colors and font styles of your report interest me. I'm fond of using different colors to make things look lively. I think it was a great idea designing your presentation like that since it relates to your fashion brand bringing colors and energy to the fashion industry. I also think that your clothes would work well in Hong Kong because there are many teens in particular who are trying to find their own identity.

It was really creative of you to come up with your brand name like that and I like your designs as well. Looking through your presentation there are already at least 2 of your designs that I would like to wear! I think that your designs will work well in places like Central, Hong Kong and I also agree with ... in his post that unique fashion styles and higher quality garments of this type would work well in the Sheung Wan area of HK ☺

What I really understood was intercultural communication and support .... I discovered the beauty of people from two cultures working together voluntarily and giving assistance to each other when necessary.

Examples of co-creation of learning facilitated via the collaborative Facebook group:

• Facebook's "sharing" feature made it easy for tutors to post relevant articles from a variety of international and cross-disciplinary sources which were used to introduce theory, fashion information, and relevant data sources;
• Students could post responses to private study tasks that informed subsequent seminar discussions.

The authors created a series of brand boards illustrating the 4Ps of marketing as practiced by a selection of brands which target our students' age range and demography. The boards were uploaded to a Facebook album, and students worked in small groups during their seminars responding to the prompts and summarizing discussions in the comments section below each image thus recording those discussions for peers and tutors to respond to:

• Students could respond to tutor-set polls asking which specific topics they would like an industry guest speaker to respond to;
• Students could post links to surveys for their peers to complete regarding target customer behavior and the feasibility of their business plan proposals;
• Students could ask their classmates and international peers' opinions and conduct direct in-country market intelligence research.

REFERENCES

Algeshiemer, R., Dholakia, U. M., & Herrmann, A. (2005). The social influence of brand community: Evidence from European car clubs. *Journal of Marketing, 69*(3), 19–34.
Brown, S. (2015). *Learning, teaching and assessment in higher education: Global perspectives.* London: Palgrave Macmillan.
Byram, M. (2008). *From foreign language education to education for intercultural citizenship: Essays and reflections.* Languages for intercultural communication and education 17. Clevendon: Multilingual Matters.
Byram, M. (2009). Afterword, education, training and becoming critical. In A. Feng, M. Byram, & M. Fleming (Eds.), *Becoming interculturally competent through education*

and training. Languages for intercultural communication and education (pp. 211–213). Bristol: Multilingual Matters.

CityU. (2015) City University of Hong Kong (2015). *Vision and Mission.* City University Homepage. Retrieved from http://www.cityu.edu.hk/cityu/about/vm.htm

Collins, M. A., & Amabile, T. M. (1999). Motivation and creativity. In R. J. Sternberg (Ed.), *Handbook of creativity* (pp. 297–312). New York, NY: Cambridge University Press.

Csikszentmihalyi, M. (1999). Implications of a systems perspective for the study of creativity. In R. J. Sternberg (Ed.), *Handbook of creativity* (pp. 313–338). New York, NY: Cambridge University Press.

de Wit, H. (2013). COIL – Virtual mobility without commercialisation. *University World News*, 274. Retrieved from http://www.universityworldnews.com/article.php?story = 20130528175741647. Accessed on June 1.

Harris, A. L., & Rea, A. (2009). Web 2.0 and virtual world technologies: A growing impact on IS education. *Journal of Information Systems Education*, 20(2), 137–144.

Junco, R. (2012). Too much face and not enough books: The relationship between multiple indices of Facebook use and academic performance. *Computers in Human Behavior*, 28, 187–198.

Killick, D. (2014). *Developing the global student: Higher education in an era of globalization.* London: Routledge.

Killick, D., & Dean, L. (2013). Embedding internationalisation, and employability through graduate attributes. *Brookes eJournal of Learning and Teaching*, 5(1). Retrieved from http://bejlt.brookes.ac.uk/paper/embedding_internationalisation-2/

Lambert, C. (2012). Twilight of the lecture. *Harvard Magazine.* March–April.

Leboff, G. (2011). *Sticky marketing: Why everything in marketing has changed and what to do about it.* London: Kogan Page.

McLean, P., & Ransom, L. (2005). Building intercultural competencies: Implications for academic skills development. In J. Carroll & J. Ryan (Eds.), *Teaching international students: Improving learning for all* (pp. 45–62). London: Routledge.

McLoughlin, C., & Lee, M. (2010). Personalised and self regulated learning in the Web 2.0 era: International exemplars of innovative pedagogy using social software. *Australasian Journal of Educational Technology*, 26(1), 28–43.

Peirson-Smith, A., Miller, L., & Chik (2014). Teaching popular culture in a second language context. *A.* Pedagogies: An International Journal, 9(3), 250–267.

Prahalad, C. K., & Ramaswamy, V. (2004). *The future of competition: Co-creating unique value with customers.* Boston, MA: Harvard Business School Publishing.

Radclyffe-Thomas, N. (2008). White heat or blue screen? Digital technology in art and design education. *International Journal of Art & Design Education*, 27(2), 158–167.

Richardson, W. (2006). *Blogs, wikis, podcasts, and other powerful web tools for classrooms.* Thousand Oaks, CA: Corwin Press.

Rogers, A. (1991). Teaching adults. OU press.

Ryan, J., & Hellmundt, S. (2005). Maximising international students' 'cultural capital'. In J. Caroll & J. Ryans (Eds.), *Teaching international students: Improving learning for all* (pp. 13–16). London: Routledge.

Schuller, T., & Watson, D. (2009). *Learning through life.* Leicester: National Institute for Adult Continuing Education.

266   NATASCHA RADCLYFFE-THOMAS ET AL.

Ulbrich, F., Jahnke, I., & Mårtensson, P. (Eds.). (2011). Special issue on knowledge develop-
ment and the net generation. *International Journal of Sociotechnology and Knowledge
Development*, 2(4), i–ii.
Wenger, E. (1998). *Communities of Practice: Learning Meaning and Identity*. New York, NY:
Cambridge University Press.
Wenger, E., White, N., & Smith, J. D. (2009). *Digital habitats: Stewarding technology for
communities*. Portland, OR: CPsquare Publishing.
Yin, R. K. (2003). *Applications of case study research* (2nd ed.), London: Sage.

THE CARNEGIE PROJECT ON THE EDUCATION DOCTORATE: A PARTNERSHIP OF UNIVERSITIES AND SCHOOLS WORKING TO IMPROVE THE EDUCATION DOCTORATE AND K-20 SCHOOLS

Jill Alexa Perry and Debby Zambo

ABSTRACT

Since its inception at Harvard in 1921, the Doctorate in Education (EdD) has been a degree fraught with confusion as to its purpose and distinction from the PhD. In response to this, the Carnegie Project on the Education Doctorate (CPED), a collaborative project consisting of 80+ schools of education located in the United States, Canada, and New Zealand were established to undertake a critical examination of the EdD and develop it into the degree of choice for educators who want to generate knowledge and scholarship about practice or related policies and steward the education profession. However, programmatic changes in higher education can bring both benefits and challenges

University Partnerships for Academic Programs and Professional Development
Innovations in Higher Education Teaching and Learning, Volume 7, 267–284
Copyright © 2016 by Emerald Group Publishing Limited
All rights of reproduction in any form reserved
ISSN: 2055-3641/doi:10.1108/S2055-364120160000007024

(Levine, 2005). This chapter explains: the origins of the education doctorate; how CPED as a network of partners has changed the EdD; the use of bi-annual Convenings as spaces for this work; CPED's three phases of membership that have built the network; CPED's path forward.

Keywords: Education; doctorate; learning; partnerships; collaboration

ORIGINS OF THE EDD

The education doctorate (EdD) is almost 100 years old yet, since its inception it has been beset with misconceptions that have resulted in a degree known as a "PhD lite" (Shulman, Golde, Bueschel & Garabedian, 2006). Historically, such misconceptions are the result, in part, of how the degree came to be. In 1921, Henry Holmes, Dean of the newly established Graduate School of Education at Harvard College, created the EdD to "mark [the school's] separation from the faculty of Arts and Sciences" (Powell, 1980, p. 137) and to "train the [school] leaders" in administrative services and practical instruction (Powell, 1980, p. 144). Harvard's President Lawrence Lowell however, sought a research-intensive institution and required the addition of statistics courses and heave research dissertations.

At Teachers College, Dean William Fletcher Russell created the EdD to serve those working in practice. He offered course work that addressed "issues common to workers in the educational field," such as "educational administration, guidance, and curriculum and instruction" (Cremin, 1978, pp. 15−16). Additionally, dissertations included investigations of curriculum development and administrative and institutional reform issues (Cremin, 1978, p. 16). The University of Michigan offered the EdD to train practitioners as a direct response to the increase of "city, state, and federal officials in education [looking] increasingly to the university for manpower" (Clifford & Guthrie, 1990, p. 72). Between 1925 and 1940 many institutions saw the need to prepare practitioners. The result was an influx of young men seeking credentials to increase their administrative powers in schools.

Many academics have investigated the distinction between the EdD and PhD (Anderson, 1983; Brown, 1966, 1991; Clifford & Guthrie, 1990; Deering, 1998; Dill & Morrison, 1985; Freeman, 1931; Levine, 2007; Ludlow, 1964; Osguthorpe & Wong, 1993; Shulman et al., 2006) seeking to identify the type of students who enter and matriculate, their career ambitions, the number and type of courses taken during preparation, and the subjects of their dissertations. Yet these studies have yielded few definitive conclusions claiming the EdD is equal to the PhD, is less rigorous than the PhD, needs to be eliminated, or is fine just as it is (Perry, 2010). The reality is no academic study has been able to clearly delineate the EdD's purpose, impact, or distinction.

In 2006, Shulman, Golde, Bueschel and Garabedian argued for better distinction through collaborative action. They claimed, better understanding of the scholarship of practice and the scholarship of research would be essential to strengthen both the PhD in education and the professional practice degree in education (EdD).

FORMING PARTNERSHIPS TO ENACT CHANGE

Partnerships in education have been difficult to form, nurture, and sustain across the education field (Retine, 1996). An important first step to establishing collaborative partnerships is to acknowledge its aims, actions, and benefits (Cunnigham & Tedesco, 2001). The Shulman et al. (2006) call outlined this first step and as a result, the Carnegie Foundation for the Advancement of Teaching provided support for the creation of the Carnegie Project on the Education Doctorate (CPED) in 2007. The project was challenged to bring together several schools of education to collaborate and work together to nurture "proofing sites" where new EdD redesigns were to be considered, experimentation was to be undertaken, and evaluation was to occur. Ultimately, this network of partners was to affect the practices of all schools of education through outreach to the multitude of schools offering the EdD.

During the first year of the project, 25 schools of education started the work of rethinking the EdD, in a "grassroots" (Wergin, 2007) network, changing their programs, testing ideas locally, and sharing what they learn nationally at convenings (Perry & Imig, 2008). Convenings are held at various member institutions which allows for experiencing the contexts in which programs are nested. The term convening is meant to convey not only that these meetings are different from traditional conferences, but also that the central feature is coming together to discuss ideas programmatic changes and challenges surrounding the EdD. There are six key features that make a convening unique. Convenings are idea centered, combine various pedagogies for engagement, bring together multiple voices, provide space for unstructured conversations, hold high expectations for participation and offer a space for critical feedback.

Early convening discussions were shaped by two basic questions: *What are the knowledge, skills, and dispositions that professionals working in education should demonstrably have?* and *How do we prepare professionals to have them?* Answers to these questions were shaped by design-concepts that Shulman and his Carnegie colleagues found relevant in other professions: signature pedagogies, laboratories of practice and scholarship of teaching and learning, and capstone projects.

THREE PHASES OF CHANGE

Phase I: A Framework

Shortly after commencing, members realized that the graduate students they would be preparing come from different contexts, face different educational problems in their practice, and would need these differences to be addressed as they prepared to be transformational leaders in PK-20 settings. Thus, rather than aim for a single program model, the membership agreed that a framework would suit EdD design better as it would allow for CPED to have consensus but offer flexibility to honor the local educational context.

In October 2009, CPED Phase I faculty members convened and drafted such a framework which consists of (1) a common definition of the education doctorate, (2) the creation of common definitions of original and emerging CPED design concepts, and (3) the articulation of six working principles that guide practitioner-preparation program development.

Common Definition: CPED members composed a new definition of the EdD: "*The professional doctorate in education prepares educators for the application of appropriate and specific practices, the generation of new knowledge, and for the stewardship of the profession*" (Carnegie Project on the Education Doctorate [CPED], 2009). This definition underscores the belief that both practical and theoretical preparation are necessary to form the practitioner's habits of hand, heart and mind and to help them study and impact problems of practice. This definition also suggests that intentional preparation will transform current practitioners into *Scholarly Practitioners* (defined below) that carry the moral imperative to protect and guide the profession.

Working Principles: At the October 2009 convening, the membership developed a set of guiding principles that provide the foundation for EdD program development. Working together 49 faculty members representing 24 of the original 25 member institutions narrowed 35 statements of principles that came from their own EdD doctoral programs. After two days of collaborations, a set of six principles were defined. The principles state: The Professional doctorate in education:

(1) Is framed around questions of equity, ethics, and social justice to bring about solutions to complex problems of practice.
(2) Prepares leaders who can construct and apply knowledge to make a positive difference in the lives of individuals, families, organizations, and communities.
(3) Provides opportunities for candidates to develop and demonstrate.collaboration and communication skills to work with diverse communities and to build partnerships.
(4) Provides field-based opportunities to analyze problems of practice and use multiple frames to develop meaningful solutions.
(5) Is grounded in and develops a professional knowledge base that integrates both practical and research knowledge, that links theory with systemic and systematic inquiry.
(6) Emphasizes the generation, transformation, and use of professional knowledge and practice.

These principles were to be adopted and applied to member programs with the hope that future funding would allow for the testing and studying of how the principles improved CPED-influenced EdD programs.

Design Concepts: With the principles as a foundation, members set out to create design-concepts that would provide scaffolding upon which the principles could be enacted and would result in programs much different from research doctoral programs. Six design-concepts were defined at the June 2010 convening.

Scholarly Practitioner: The *Scholarly Practitioner* is a professional educator who, as result of attending a CPED-influenced EdD program, can blend practical wisdom with professional skills and knowledge to name, frame, and solve problems of practice; use practical research and applied theories as tools for change because they understand the importance of equity and social justice; disseminate their work in multiple ways; and are obliged to resolve problems of practice by collaborating with key stakeholders, including the university, the educational institution, the community, and individuals.

Focusing on the important roles of theory and practice both in preparation and in practice, CPED contends that EdD graduates will have the skills and abilities to be transformative leaders.

Signature Pedagogy: The second design concept is adopted from Lee Shulman's definition of *Signature Pedagogy* – a pervasive set of practices used to prepare scholarly practitioners for all aspects of their professional work: "to think, to perform, and to act with integrity" (Shulman, 2005, p. 52) – with the understanding that there exists multiple ways to reach these ends.

Inquiry as Practice: Different from traditional research preparation, Inquiry as Practice is the process of posing significant questions that focus on complex problems of practice. At the center of this skill is the ability to use data to understand the effects of innovation. As such, Inquiry as Practice requires the ability to gather, organize, judge, aggregate, and analyze situations, literature, and data with a critical lens.

Laboratories of Practice: Laboratories of Practice build upon models of preparation undertaken in other professions such as medicine and law. They are settings where theory and practice inform and enrich each other to address complex problems of practice and develop solutions that can be implemented, measured, and analyzed for the impact made. Laboratories of Practice facilitate transformative and generative learning that is measured by the development of scholarly expertise and implementation of practice.

Problem of Practice: Problems of practice are the persistent, contextualized, and specific issue embedded in the work of a professional practitioner, the addressing of which has the potential to result in improved understanding, experience, and outcomes.

Dissertation in Practice: The culminating project, called the Dissertation in Practice, is scholarly endeavor that impacts a complex problem of practice defines this ideal (CPED, 2010).

Together, EdD definition, the guiding principles and design-concepts offer member institutions the framework needed to redesign their Ed programs.

Shortly after implementing the framework, CPED set out to learn how schools of education were changing as a result of participation in this network of collaboration.

Phase II: Studying CPED's Change and Impact

In 2010, CPED received a $700,000 U.S. Department of Education Fund for the Improvement of Post-secondary Education (FIPSE) grant to study how 21 of its original member schools of education changed their EdDs. Specifically, the research project sought to use a multi-case analysis to document and evaluate

1. Change in the organizational structures of graduate schools to accommodate new professional practice degrees for school and college leaders.
2. Change in the signature learning processes, learning environments, and patterns of engagement of faculty and candidates in EdD programs that participate in CPED.
3. Fidelity to the set of guiding principles developed in Phase I of the initiative (2007–2009). And to
4. Disseminate lessons learned and best practices for the design and implementation of professional practice degrees.

A cross-case analysis of 21 CPED institution cases, conducted and written by 38 CPED faculty researchers, revealed the following claims and provides evidence as to how CPED members as partners changed at the institutional, programmatic, and individual levels.

CPED's Impact on Schools of Education

The cross-case analysis revealed that CPED had influenced schools of education in terms of policies, faculty positions, an understanding of the EdD, and as cachet, or branding. Below is an explanation of each of these.

Policies
Members noted that working as partners helped schools of education address both the internal and external problems they were facing. Internally, enrollment issues indicated changes were necessary. However, many institutions faced confusion between their EdDs and PhDs, as questions were being asked as to the quality, purpose, and distinction of EdD programs from PhDs. Faculty weren't clear and this led to little or no distinction in coursework or degree requirements. Coursework was disconnected from the needs of practitioner students and low-quality dissertations were being generated to satisfy capstone requirements. As a result, many institutions had large numbers of ABD (all but dissertation) candidates,

and faced competition for enrollment with nearby institutions. Schools of Education were overburdened, losing money, and not meeting the needs of their current students or attracting future students. Working with CPED to define the EdD's purpose became a means to establish policies and structures that pushed completion rates for lagging students, while better designing quality programs to attract and serve the needs of students who wanted to remain in the field and not work in academe.

Externally, institutions reported facing pressure from multiple sources. State-level governance wanted improvement in preparation of educational leaders; districts and organizations were asking for well-trained individuals and research partners; and practitioner advisory groups wanted programs that would provide them with strong leaders that could implement change. These pressures caused institutions to investigate their programs through self-studies and internal reviews. Some institutions found that students and graduates wanted programmatic changes specifically around the dissertation, one that would better help them gain leadership abilities. However, in a few cases, programmatic change was not agreed to by state legislatures and, as a result a traditional EdD program continued while a CPED-influenced program was created alongside it.

Although not all institutions made dramatic shifts in policies, it was clear from the cross-case analysis that these schools of education were faced with internal and external policy issues that needed to be addressed and CPED offered a means to begin conversations of change and, in some cases, instituted drastic policy shifts.

Faculty
Emerging from the data were two themes related to faculty – a change in their positions and their resistance to changes. First, although not present across all cases, was the hiring of clinical faculty to have a role in EdD programs and fill non-tenure track positions. Several institutions noted clinical faculty to be central to designing their professional preparation doctorate and teaching in their programs. These individuals were highly valued because of their strong connection to the world of practice and professional contacts combined with their university experience. They served as liaisons between the school of education and districts or educational organizations. Clinical faculty members were also given roles on dissertation committees serving as guides to help students apply research to solve problems in practice.

A second change in positions was the role of tenure-track assistant faculty members. In many cases, junior faculty members were hired into tenure-track positions with the intent of having them heavily involved in or even leading the change effort for the EdD program design. The data suggested that new tenure-track faculty were chosen to lead and be involved in programs because it was believed they would be invested in the institution and more open to change than some of the more established faculty members. Assistant faculty members were viewed as having more energy, ambition and a vision for change. A few interviewees from across a handful of institutions noted, however, that giving this kind of work to junior faculty members could be detrimental to their promotion and tenure as well as to the change process itself. Assistant Professors had little institutional knowledge (e.g., how to work around the system), voice, or resources to get things accomplished. In addition, they were encumbered with the responsibilities of the tenure process.

Faculty resistance was also found in the cross-case analysis. Seasoned faculty who resisted such changes in hiring practices, faculty roles, or program redesign faced difficulty. In some cases, faculty resisters held on to historical visions of the EdD, saw no use for change in their program's mission or coursework, or pushed back on ideas such as moving classes from weeknights to weekends. In other cases these faculty had challenges when they were not willing to work with new hires with fresh perspectives. In many cases resisting faculty were asked to leave programs and/or take on other responsibilities.

Resistance often resulted from the decision-making process and how the institution became involved in CPED. At some institutions the dean made the decision to join CPED without consulting with any faculty governance. Resistance also came from faculty members who were not chosen to serve as liaisons between CPED and their home institutions. Many cases revealed that those further away from the effort were less familiar with CPED's principles and design-concepts and, because of this, claimed they could not see any difference in the CPED-influenced EdD. At institutions where faculty members were part of the decision-making process, they were more knowledgeable about CPED's ideas and engaged in the change effort. In successful cases, it was noted that the key to working with resisters and implementing a successful re-design of the EdD was an early and inclusive engagement of faculty in various stages of their careers.

Understanding of the EdD Degree
As noted earlier, the need to distinguish and establish the EdD as a professional degree stemmed from the murky beginning noted in the above description of its origins. Historically viewed as a "PhD-lite" (Shulman et al., 2006),

administrators and faculty in schools of education were looking for ways to rebrand and give better identities to their programs. In addition, with districts and organizations asking for better training for their employees, it was revealed that traditional program timeframes and research preparation were not meeting the needs of current and potential students. Joining CPED presented the means for establishing the EdD as a professional degree; however, data revealed that because of the literature that was emerging at the time from the Carnegie Foundation's work on the PhD and on preparation in other professions (Golde & Walker, 2006; Shulman et al., 2006; Walker et al.,2008) in some cases faculty conversations began percolating before the CPED was formally created.

CPED offered a way to improve the quality of programs by making them intellectual but practical. CPED encouraged this way of thinking by supplying a language, a pathway, and framework for change. As a means to avoid the PhD-lite label, CPED members provided relevance to the EdD degree by paying attention to rigor, program quality, and the needs of practitioners.

Cachet or Branding
Upper administration viewed CPED as cachet in the form of name recognition and networking. The Carnegie Foundation for the Advancement of Teaching has a long history of success in reforms and deans had no reason to believe this project would be any different. Having the Carnegie name attached to the project was an advantage. Members saw value in having direct interaction with individuals who had experience in leading reform efforts in higher education. They found the ideas of Dr. Lee Shulman, President-Emeritus, and his Carnegie colleagues to be extremely useful and they valued CPED's leadership in arranging opportunities for them to interact at bi-annual Convenings with like-minded individuals. Such advantages brought ownership, legitimacy, and validation to reforming the EdD. Faculty and deans also viewed the initiative as one that was grounded in research that would both inform programmatic change and strengthen and distinguish the EdD.

A second form of cachet was the opportunity to network and partner with other schools of education around the United States who were grappling with the same issues. Though not a usual practice in higher education, faculty and deans who participated directly in CPED convenings expressed a sense of openness and validation as they tested their ideas and realized that they aligned with others. Having the opportunity to comfortably discuss the real issues facing the EdD degree, as well as programmatic problems and solutions, provided a kind of professional development that faculty had not had before.

In sum, CPED became a reform effort addressed challenges and quelled discontent by pushing change from the inside out. CPED offered deans and faculty at member institutions a guiding framework that helped distinguish their EdD degrees from their PhDs. The collaborative nature of Convenings engaged them in a respectable, national discussion about doctoral work, helped them see what others were doing, encouraged them to make changes, and confirmed their progress toward distinction. CPED provided answers to challenges that institutions were facing in a more constructive and flexible manner. Individuals formed partnerships and learned from and with each other at bi-annual Convenings and in beyond when they remained in contact with each other.

CPED's Impact on EdD Programs

The data revealed that involvement in CPED caused programmatic changes and because of these, EdDs now look different and are distinct from PhDs. CPED affected all aspects of program development from admissions, to courses, to their delivery, to support structures, and to the look and feel of the dissertation. However, even with these changes, program developers were able to use their own experiences, values, expertise and visions to design or redesign their programs. Programs did not become clones of each other (Shulman et al., 2006). How much, when, and how deeply members incorporated CPED's framework into their program varied based on where an institution was located and where a program was in the design or redesign process.

Program Design
When it came to programmatic changes, timing mattered. Data showed programs were at varying phases of development. The data reveal three stages of program design development. First, some EdD programs had been in existence for a long time but were indistinguishable from PhD programs. These programs were losing money, had overworked faculty, and had many ABD (all but dissertation) candidates. The administrators and faculty members in these programs recognized that they needed to redesign their programs and turned to CPED for answers. Second, some programs had just been granted approval and administrators and faculty members in these programs were just beginning the design process. These members wanted

guidance, ideas, models, and direction from CPED. Finally, other programs were clear and distinct. Faculty had already implemented changes and their programs were distinct and meeting students' needs. Faculty members in these programs wanted affirmation of their ideas and an opportunity to showcase their ideas. These programs became models for other institutions.

In successful programs, CPED's principles and design features were incorporated into the program's design. Articulating a vision of a scholarly practitioner and understanding these individuals as working professionals with professional knowledge helped members develop clear mission statements and goals. No matter where a program was in the design or re-design process, being a part of CPED helped administrators and faculty make programs more relevant to practice and working educational professionals.

Admissions
CPED affected admission policies by helping clarify the type of individuals appropriate for enrolling in EdD programs and what should be expected of them. Admission standards and policies sought to attract candidates working in PK-20 education or organizations that supported it, who had several years' experience and planned to remain in a work setting. The data also noted changing admission policies to admit a more diverse student body. Wanting to attract top working professionals, some institutions waived GRE requirements in lieu of more authentic demonstrations of professional knowledge and leadership. Some admission policies also required students to indicate a problem in practice that they intended to study and improve as part of their doctoral work. Different types of essays and writing samples, ones that focused on problems of practice or professional writing (versus academic writing), were changed requirements. Finally, a small number of institutions asked applicants to provide permission from their work contexts to ensure that their doctoral work an integral part of their everyday responsibilities.

Cohorts
Attrition rates had been a concern and as noted earlier, because of the confusion between the EdD and PhD there had been many students who had completed their coursework but not their dissertations. Investing time and money into a program and failing to graduate was a multifaceted problem for working professions. They wanted and needed a degree but at the same time needed structure that would support them as they pursued their degrees while employed full-time. A lack of post-coursework advising left working professionals without the contact they needed to remain engaged

and write their dissertations. To reduce attrition, CPED-influenced programs instituted cohort models that range in size from 12 to 150 students. In cohorts, students remain together and take courses together and, in many cases, are expected to finish together. Cohorts offered support and structure from program orientation through to dissertation defense. Additionally, at some point in most programs, students are broken into smaller groups (5–9 students) to facilitate faculty advising and offer closer monitoring. These groups have a faculty mentor and in some cases, this faculty member follows the group through to the dissertation phase and serves as their chair.

Cohorts were common across CPED members, but data demonstrated that the way cohorts were implemented varied widely from institution to institution. At some institutions faculty work to ensure that student cohorts form close bonds, but at other institutions cohorts are simply groups of students admitted together who take courses together. In most institutions students see cohorts as a means to learn from each other. Administrators and faculty equally see the cohort model as a means of personal and professional support, and also a means to eliminate ABDs.

Courses
Many institutions had students who hung around for 6–10 years post course work and never complete their dissertations. CPED-influenced programs wanted to address this by redesigning their programs to graduate students in two to four years. To accomplish this timeframe traditional PhD number of credits were reduced to 42–60 credits beyond the masters. This reduction did not symbolize less work, rather the dissertation process has become ongoing, included in the program timeframe and often begins in the first semester. Faculty members did this because they believed this time frame supports what they had learned from self-studies: practitioners had limited time and funds to commit to doctoral programs. However, the data showed that at several institutions, this quick completion time was a challenge for students. Being working professionals with family commitments, students noted troubles balancing these obligations with their doctoral study. At institutions where the short timeframe was successful, programs were cohesive, with courses building upon one another, and activities were related to students' professional lives and needs.

CPED-influenced programs that participated in the study require core/ signature courses that are taken in a sequential order along with electives (which in some, but not all, programs lead to principal or superintendent certification). A clearly laid out sequence indicates to students where they are headed and the time commitment of the program. Across CPED, both core and elective courses are offered in a variety of formats that support institutional logistics and the needs of busy, working professionals. Courses are offered face-to-face, in hybrid fashion, online, and by video-conferencing. As opposed to the early morning or afternoon courses offered to PhD students, courses in CPED-influenced programs take advantage of students' off time – evenings, weekends, summers. Courses also fit into professional schedules, by enabling students to meet online or monthly. Additionally, at some institutions courses are offered at students' work sites or in their districts so there is less travel time and offer an on-site laboratory of practice.

Aligned with CPED's principles, courses are designed to honor professional knowledge and practice, transform thinking, promote issues of equity and social justice, and connect theory and methodology to practice. At CPED-influenced programs courses and coursework are based on the needs of adult learners, encouraging students to be responsible for their own learning. Courses are enlightening, practical, and authentic; that is, grounded in the real world needs and experiences of practitioners. Examples of this can be seen in field-embedded classes, case analyses, and action research. Programs demonstrated that students learn in laboratories of practice (often their work setting) by doing and applying what they learn in their courses and reporting back through coursework. Courses are designed to scaffold learning and be closely tied to dissertation work. In many programs, dissertation work begins on day one, in course one. Students engage in lessons that can be applied to their contexts and in turn, begin to make changes, collect data, and write up findings early and consistently.

Courses in CPED-influenced programs are taught by a variety of individuals in varied combinations. At some institutions, only tenure-track faculty teach the EdD courses, whereas at others combinations of tenure-track and clinical faculty (sometimes graduates of the program) teach and sometimes, practitioners co-teach with faculty. At some institutions two courses are blended together and co-taught by faculty to provide interdisciplinary understanding.

Research Methods Courses
Historically, the perception of the EdD as PhD-lite resulted from less rigorous and weakened research methods courses and dissertation products. However, data show that CPED has influenced strong and concerted change in both the teaching of research and the development of dissertations. Even though students in CPED-influenced EdD programs typically

take fewer research methods courses than PhD students (12 hours compared to 18) rigor or quality are not sacrificed. Rather, methods courses in CPED-influenced EdD programs are targeted and useful to student's professional practice—teaching students to consume, use and do research.

Articulating the benefit of methodological knowledge, faculty members from the one institution said they wanted their students to become sound decision-makers and problem-solvers. Aligned with CPED's principles, developing students into problem-solvers was a common theme among faculty interviewed. To accomplish this goal, program content encourages students to apply what they learn to problems in their practice setting. When it comes to method courses, instructors provide understandable information in increments or, use a "just in time" approach. Examples of this include gap analysis, cycles of action research, and the research phases.

New Pedagogies

Because of CPED, programs created new pedagogies that focused on practitioner and adult learner interests and needs. These included:

- writing boot camps – to both improve students' academic writing and provide time for students to write academically
- modules – to allow online flexible learning times
- case-based learning – to develop thinking about authentic problems of practice
- project-based learning – to encourage collaborative efforts around problems of practice
- guest speaker colloquiums – to expose students to practitioners and academics who have addressed problems of practice
- international trips – to broaden students' perspectives of education and leadership.

Learning Environments

In CPED institutions learning environments vary; however, most are collaborative and constructivist in nature and designed to cross the university-practice divide. Even though some direct instruction and lecture still occurs, most environments are complimented with internships or laboratories of practice so students can learn from more knowledgeable others, with embedded field-work so students can learn from practice and with peer-to-peer collaboration to support learning.

Dissertations

Dissertations in CPED-influence programs vary but most are focused on problems of practice, which CPED defines as, "a persistent, contextualized, and specific issue embedded in the work of a professional practitioner, the addressing of which has the potential to result in improved understanding, experience, and outcomes" (CPED, 2009, 2013). In most CPED programs, dissertation work is embedded in coursework and begins early. Dissertations are the cornerstone of many programs and all coursework is linked to and enhance their development. Some programs still have traditional five or six chapter dissertations. However, variations do exist. For example, most dissertations are the work of an individual, but some programs encourage group products. Students write thematic dissertations, produce technical reports or evaluations for a client, write three research articles bound by an introduction and conclusion, produce a co-authored product, and write policy papers that offer the implications and alternatives of current policy initiatives in education. In most instances students report their findings back to their constituents.

Phase III: Expanding CPED's Influence

As a result of recruitment efforts, 34 colleges and universities joined the CPED initiative and launched a Phase II of the project. Phase II members joined CPED to get ideas, guidance and collaboration as a means to improve their programs. A third wave of members was admitted to the Project in 2014. Thirty-two institutions were admitted, including two from Canada and one from New Zealand. The application for the membership process asked applicants to outline their EdD program goals and related them to CPED goals and principles. In addition, responses to a survey given to these institutions indicated they had been following the Project's work and developing programs utilizing CPED principles and design concepts. Responses suggested three forms of influence – alignment of current program goals and core values with those of CPED; utilization of CPED principles as a launching point for redesign; and adoption of CPED principles into existing programs.

Consistent with learning from the FIPSE study, Phase III applications wanted to distinguish their programs and have opportunities to network with like-minded colleagues. Incoming members looked to the Project as a means to share, learn, and build a broader understanding of the education doctorate.

PAVING A NEW PATH FORWARD

From its inception, CPED has been more than just an intellectual exercise. It transcends the debate that took place over most of the 20th century and has become the first action-oriented effort aimed at producing definitions and frameworks for changing the status and purpose of the EdD. CPED has been able to do this by bringing together a group of universities working collaboratively to rethink and redesign the professional doctoral degree in education.

CPED has forged a new way to change programs and degrees based on Lee Shulman and his Carnegie colleague's initial challenge to schools of education to "reclaim" their education doctorates in a collaborative manner because they knew that no institution could do it without support. Arguing for a network of faculty that would engage in collaborative experimentation, CPED has asked faculty both locally and internationally to develop cohesive, outcomes-oriented, professional programs that prepare those who want to practice in and transform the field of PK-20 education. Eight years later, data show that this strategy was the best way to pave the path forward. CPED has had an impact at the institutional, programmatic, and personal level. It has changed the EdD and in the process changed the lives of administrators, faculty, and students. Although designed to be short-term, the CPED Project continues to grow, change, and develop programs that are distinctly designed for practitioners in education. Programs focus on the needs of working professionals, who in turn are changing the educational landscape of K-12 schools, community colleges, universities, and educational organizations.

Moving forward, the Project will continually adapt to maintain an organizational infrastructure that builds partnerships, networks members, advances its agenda, distributes resources, and expands its influence, making CPED the knowledge forum on the EdD. Partnerships like this are all too rare in higher education.

REFERENCES

Anderson, D. G. (1983). Differentiation of the Ed.D. and Ph.D. in education. *Journal of Teacher Education, 34*(3), 55–58.
Brown, L. D. (1966). *Doctoral graduates in education. An inquiry into their motives, aspirations, and perceptions of the program.* Bloomington, IN: Indiana University.
Brown, L. D. (1991). A perspective on the Ph.D.–Ed.D. discussion in schools of education. Paper presented at the American Educational Research Association.

Carnegie Project on the Education Doctorate. (2009). *Education Doctorate definition and working principles.* Retrieved from http://cpedintiative.org

Carnegie Project on the Education Doctorate. (2010). *Definitions CPED design concepts.* College Park, MD: Author.

Clifford, G. J., & Guthrie, J. W. (1990). *Ed school: A brief for a professional education.* Chicago, IL: University of Chicago Press.

Cremin, L. (1978). The education of the educating professions. Paper presented at the American Association of Colleges for Teacher Education.

Cunnigham, L. C., & Tedesco, L. A. (2001). Mission possible: Developing effective educational partnerships. *Journal of Higher Education Outreach and Engagement, 7*(1&2), 79–89.

Deering, T. E. (1998). Eliminating the doctor of education degree: It's the right thing to do. *The Educational Forum, 62,* 243–248.

Dill, D. D., & Morrison, J. L. (1985). Ed.D. and Ph.D. research training in the field of higher education: A survey and a proposal. *Review of Higher Education, 8*(2), 169–182.

Freeman, F. N. (1931). *Practices of American universities in granting higher degrees in education: A series of official statements* (Vol. 19). Chicago, IL: University of Chicago Press.

Golde, C. M., & Walker, G. E. (2006). *Envisioning the future of doctoral education: Preparing stewards of the discipline.* San Francisco, CA: Jossey-Bass.

Levine, A. (2005). *Educating school leaders.* New York, NY: The Education Schools Project.

Levine, A. (2007). *Educating researchers.* New York, NY: The Education Schools Project.

Ludlow, H. G. (1964). *The doctorate in education.* Washington, DC: American Association of Colleges for Teacher Education.

Osguthorpe, R. T., & Wong, M. J. (1993). The Ph.D. versus the Ed.D.: Time for a decision. *Innovative Higher Education, 18*(1), 47–63.

Perry, J. A. (2010). *Reclaiming the education doctorate: Three cases of proccesss and roles in institutional change.* Doctoral dissertation. University of Maryland, College Park, MD.

Perry, J. A., & Imig, D. G. (2008). A stewardship of practice in education. *Change, November/December,* 42–48.

Powell, A. G. (1980). *The uncertain profession.* Cambridge, MA: Harvard University Press.

Retine, N. L. (1996). Partnerships between schools and institutions of higher education. In R. Ackerman & P. Cordeiro (Eds.), *Boundary crossings: Educational partnerships and school leadership* (pp.31–40). San Francisco, CA: Jossey-Bass Publishers.

Shulman, L. S. (2005). Signature pedagogies in the professions. *Daedalus, 134,* 3.

Shulman, L. S., Golde, C. M., Bueschel, A. C., & Garabedian, K. J. (2006). Reclaiming education's doctorates: A critique and a proposal. *Educational Researcher, 35*(3), 25–32.

Walker, G. E., Golde, C. M., Jones, L., Conklin, Bueschel, A., & Hutchings, P. (2008). *The formation of scholars: Rethinking doctoral education for the twenty-first century.* San Francisco, CA: Jossey-Bass.

Wergin, J. F. (2007). *Leadership in place: How academic professionals can find their leadership voice.* Bolton, MA: Anker.

ABOUT THE AUTHORS

Rick J. Arrowood is Faculty at Northeastern University (Boston, MA) and is Visiting Professor, Swinburne University of Technology, Australia. At Northeastern, he serves as the Chair of the Nonprofit Management degree program. He focuses on teaching and research in nonprofit management, global leadership (domestically and abroad), and cultural diversity in the workplace as well as business, employment, nonprofit law, and ethics. His three decades of nonprofit experience widens his scholarly practitioner approach to teaching board leadership, financial management, human resources, workplace diversity, high performing organizations, and other management courses. He has taught leadership in Australia and Vietnam, as a visiting scholar in China, and as a guest lecturer in Russia.

Inese Berzina-Pitcher is Doctoral Candidate in the Higher, Adult and Lifelong Education program at Michigan State University, specializing in International Development. Inese has over 10 years of experience working in higher education. Her work and research focus on several areas of innovation in higher and adult education, such as new models of educator and education leader professional development programs, university internationalization, and university partnership building. She has been involved with different international projects, including coordinating the activities for the College of Education, MSU, and Azim Premji University partnership project.

Cathy Bishop-Clark is Professor of Information Technology began at Miami University in 1989. She has a bachelor's degree in Computer Science, a M.S. in Quantitative Analysis and a doctorate in Educational Foundations. Over the years Cathy has taught a variety of courses including liberal education computing courses for non-majors, a variety of software development courses, health information technology and systems analysis and design courses. Cathy's research has ranged from studying novice programmers to studying a variety of innovations in the computing classroom. At Miami, Cathy has been a faculty member in the department, an Associate Dean of the Middletown Campus, the chair of the CIT department, and is currently the Associate Dean of Academic Affairs at Miami University's regional campuses.

Patrick Blessinger is the Founder, executive director, and chief research scientist of the International Higher Education Teaching and Learning Association (HETL) and an adjunct associate professor in the School of Education at St. John's University (NYC). Dr. Blessinger is the editor-in-chief of two international academic journals and two international book series on higher education. Dr. Blessinger is a Governor's Teaching Fellow and a Fulbright Senior Scholar.

Wendy Bloisi has an international profile through her experience of teaching and research in Organisational Behaviour, Management, Human Resource Management and Research Methods in Germany, Thailand, Italy, Spain, Greece, Netherlands, China, Nepal, Sri Lanka, United Arab Emirates and Iran. Wendy is interested in making a difference through education.

Laura J. Carfang earned her Doctorate in Education from Northeastern University in Boston, MA, where she specialized in higher education administration. Her research focuses on internationalization, complex decision making models, and leadership. She currently is an Associate Director at the F.W. Olin Graduate School of Business at Babson College in Wellesley, MA, where she serves on the International Graduate Offerings Taskforce, and is an instructor in the undergraduate First Year Seminar program. Laura has extensive experience teaching abroad in Europe and Asia and serves as the regional board member and representative for the International Education Knowledge Community through NASPA: Student Affairs Administrators in Higher Education. Laura holds her M.A., from Middlebury College, and B.A., from Loyola University in Chicago.

Sherri Cianca is Associate Professor in the College of Education at Niagara University, Lewiston, New York, where she teaches STEM methods courses and courses on classroom assessment, and where she was instrumental in establishing a STEM concentration and STEM minor. Dr. Cianca attended the Ontario Institute for Studies in Education at the University of Toronto, receiving her Ph.D. from the department of math, science, and technology. Her research interests include STEM education, problem-based learning, culturally responsive teaching, and classroom assessment. Her interest in educating children of poverty has taken her on numerous occasions to Ethiopia where she conducted workshops and provided in-service training for teachers in Addis Ababa. Dr. Cianca's publications include articles and book chapters on constructivist-based teaching practices, middle school mathematics, WebQuests, cultures and philosophies, and she is currently writing a book on assessing common core learning in the STEM-based classroom.

Barbara Cozza is Associate Professor, Assistant Chairperson and Program Director for the Ed.D. in Instructional Leadership, in the Department of Administration and Instructional Leadership at St. John's University (NYC). Dr. Cozza's research targets school reform issues in the areas of curriculum, instruction, assessment, and leadership. She is senior editor for *The Journal of Applied Research in Higher Education*.

Beth Dietz is Professor of Psychology, Miami University. She has been with Miami University for 20 years. Her teaching interests include online distance learning, collaborative learning, and the use of technology to enhance teaching and learning. Her disciplinary research interests include small group behavior. She has published widely on the scholarship of teaching and learning. She also has interests in assessment and served as a faculty assessment associate at Miami University for the last 5 years. She has developed and conducted workshops on the scholarship of teaching and learning, online distance learning, and basic assessment.

Kathleen C. Doutt, IHM, D.M.A., is Professor of Music at Immaculata University. In addition to her work in music education, Sister Kathleen has had extensive experience as a pianist with soloists and ensembles and as a researcher in world music and metacognition. In spring 2012, through a grant funded by the Teagle Foundation, Sister Kathleen collaborated on a project to develop interdisciplinary faculty metacognition using the iPad. As a co-founder of Immaculata University's "Academy of Metacognition," Sister has received additional funding for advancing faculty metacognition: her collaborative work and research has yielded a rubric for cross disciplinary faculty metacognition.

David Dunbar† is Associate Professor of science at Cabrini University. His research interests include research discovery and science education. Dr. Dunbar's recent scholarship includes proteomics research of bacteriophages in collaboration with the Howard Hughes Medical Institute's national SEA PHAGES program, where he serves as a member of their national assessment team. David's other passion lies in exploring and measuring elements of undergraduate research experiences that contribute to strong engagement in undergraduate biology education. Dr. Dunbar holds a Ph.D. from Lehigh University in molecular biology and completed postdoctoral research with the Baserga Lab at Yale University.

Elizabeth Faunce is Associate Professor in the Business and Accounting Department at Immaculata University. Dr. Faunce teaches a multitude of classes in economics and finance to diverse student populations including traditional, adult learners, and online students. She has been actively involved in Teagle funded research projects focused on improving faculty metacognition since 2012 and serves as the Teagle convener at Immaculata for the Building Faculty Capacity Initiative. Elizabeth was a co-founder of the Immaculata "Academy of Metacognition" and firmly believes that this learning community has greatly enhanced her teaching and provided a better perspective of 21st century learners.

S. Giridhar is Registrar and Chief Operating Officer of Azim Premji University, a private, autonomous, not-for-profit University at Bengaluru, India, established by the Azim Premji foundation. Giridhar is one of the earliest members of Azim Premji Foundation, joining them in April 2002 after over 20 years of service in the corporate sector. At the Foundation, Giridhar led all the field programs as well as the research and advocacy functions before taking up his current role at the University. Giridhar writes regularly, drawing upon his experiences in the education sector and his articles have been published in the Wall Street Journal, Indian Express, The Hindu, Deccan Herald, Seminar magazine, FirstPost.com, etc. He has also co-authored a highly acclaimed book on cricket, "Mid-wicket Tales: From Trumper to Tendulkar" (SAGE Publications, 2014) that received high praise from critics, players, and the public.

Gerwin Hendriks studied Economics at Wageningen University. At the moment he works as Business Analyst at HU University of Applied Sciences Utrecht. His main areas of research interest include student success and student quality issues.

Leslie Hitch, Associate Teaching Professor, Northeastern University, and Visiting Fellow, Swinburne University of Technology, Australia, is faculty in the Northeastern Global Studies Masters and Higher Education programs in Boston and the Global Leadership Program at Swinburne. Her research is in faculty development focusing on the globalization of higher education. Prior to her faculty appointment, she was Director of Academic Technology Services at Northeastern; Vice President, Harcourt, Inc; Program Director, Simmons College; and director of executive education, Babson College. She holds a B.A. and MBA, Simmons College; Certificate, Management and Leadership in Education, Harvard School of Education; and an Ed.D. in Higher Education Administration, University of Massachusetts-Boston.

Adrian Huang is Lecturer in the Faculty of Design, LASALLE College of the Arts, Singapore, teaching across the BA Fashion Media & Industries and Diploma in Fashion programmes. With a background in designing, producing and retailing fashion apparel as well as the development of fashion training programmes for adult learners, his professional experience spans the conceptualization, making and marketing of fashion products, and the teaching of industry-specific skills and knowledge. He is currently completing his masters (MA Artist Educator) with LASALLE College of the Arts and his research interests include the development of creative processes in design education, fashion entrepreneurship and creative pattern cutting.

Rutger Kappe studied Industrial & Organizational Psychology at the Vrije Universiteit in Amsterdam. At the moment he works as assistant professor at the Inholland University of applied sciences and at the Vrije Universiteit. His main areas of research interest include learning and instruction, quality issues, competence based education, and foremost student success.

Doris Kiendl-Wendner is Chair of the Institute of International Management at FH JOANNEUM University of Applied Sciences in Graz, Austria. In this capacity her main responsibilities include HR management, HR development, quality assurance in teaching and research, curriculum development, internationalization, student counselling, teaching and research. She has obtained a JD in Law from the University of Graz, Austria, and a Master of Laws degree from the European University Institute, Florence, Italy. Her areas of research and teaching are primarily international business law and university management. From 2007 to 2014 she served as Vice Rector of FH JOANNEUM. Kiendl-Wendner is an expert on innovation in teaching and e-learning since she has established the center of quality in teaching at FH JOANNEUM which educates lecturers on methods of teaching in higher education. In addition, Kiendl-Wendner is a certified mediator and a board member of ENOHE (European Network of Ombudsmen in Higher Education).

Dominic Mahon, a native of London, England, Dominic has been working in the higher education sector since 2003. In that time he has taught in universities in the United Kingdom, Vietnam, Turkey, and Kazakhstan where he is currently based. With a background in Philosophy and Education, his current research interests are in the areas of measuring graduate attribute attributes, student motivation and the internationalization of higher education.

Anabella Martinez, Ed.D. in Higher and Postsecondary Education and MA in Student Personnel Administration from Teachers College, Columbia University; B.A. in Psychology from Universidad del Norte. Currently Assistant Professor, Department of Education and Director of the Center for Excellence in Teaching at Universidad del Norte. Fifteen years of administrative and teaching experience in higher educatión, leading programs and services focused on student and faculty development. Research interests include learning of research at the undergraduate level, as well as scholarly learning across the span of faculty careers.

Hazel Messenger is currently the MBA course leader at London Metropolitan University, overseeing provision in London and with partners in Sri Lanka and Nepal. She has extensive experience of partnership working and is particularly interested in the transformative potential of higher education.

Punya Mishra is Professor of Educational Technology at Michigan State University where he directs the Master of Arts in Educational Technology program. He is internationally recognized for his work on the theoretical, cognitive, and social aspects related to the design and use of computer based learning environments. He has received over $7 million in grants, has published over 50 articles and book chapters and has edited two books. Dr. Mishra is an award winning instructor who teaches courses at both the masters and doctoral levels in the areas of educational technology, design, and creativity. He is also an accomplished visual artist and poet. You can find out more about him by going to http://punyamishra.com/

Marjon Molenkamp studied Organizational Sociology at the Erasmus University in Rotterdam. At the moment she works as Institutional Researcher at Rotterdam University of applied sciences. Her main area of research interest is student success in metropolitan regions.

Elizabeth Moy is Executive Director of The Southeastern Pennsylvania Consortium for Higher Education (SEPCHE), a collaborative of eight colleges and universities in the Greater Philadelphia region. Ms. Moy has presented nationally and internationally on the role of consortia in enhancing institutional outcomes. She has facilitated numerous faculty development efforts employing the learning sciences and metacognition to expand evidence-based teaching practices, and has worked extensively with SEPCHE faculty to develop, study and assess undergraduate research experiences. Beth has a degree in English from the University of Texas at Austin and a masters degree in Social Work at Temple University.

Leslie Myers is Director of Teaching and Learning at Chestnut Hill, and an adjunct professor in psychology and communication. She has presented nationally and internationally on neuroscience and learning, work-life balance in academia and other topics. Leslie has been actively involved in Teagle funded research projects involving faculty development since 2011 and serves as a Teagle convener for the Building Faculty Capacity Initiative. She also spearheads a four-year leadership development program that utilizes metacognitive practices to encourage deep learning and critical thinking in at risk students. Leslie has a BA in education from Wittenberg University and a M.Ed in counseling from West Chester University. She is in the process of pursuing a Doctoral degree in Organizational Leadership.

Rachel Niklas has been teaching in international higher education for seven years. During this time, she has worked in Vietnam, Turkey, and Kazakhstan where she is currently a teaching fellow in EAP. She also has a background in Sociology and Psychology and is presently interested in the field of academic advising. She has presented at conferences in Turkey and England on levels of student motivation tying into feedback and has recently been exploring alternative modes of delivering student feedback for written work.

Iddah Aoko Otieno, Ph.D. was born and raised in Kenya. She is Professor of English and African Studies at Bluegrass Community and Technical College, Lexington, Kentucky. She is the founding Director of the Kenya Exchange Program, Bluegrass Community and Technical College – the first linkage with Africa within the Kentucky Community and Technical College System (KCTCS). She holds a B.Ed. (English) from Maseno University, Kenya, an M.A. (English) from Eastern Kentucky University, and a Ph.D. in Higher Education Policy (Comparative and International Education) from the University of Kentucky. Otieno is the editor of an *Anthology of Shorts Stories and Poems from East Africa* (2014). She is also an editorial board member of the Eastern Kentucky University's *Journal of Retracing Africa (JORA)* and a Co-editor of *Understanding Higher Education in Contemporary Africa: Traditions, Trends, and Triumphs* (2016).

Tom Otieno is Associate Dean in the College of Arts & Sciences and Professor of Chemistry at Eastern Kentucky University. His research involves the synthesis of various classes of transition metal complexes, determination of their physical and/or chemical properties, and the correlation of these properties with the structures of the complexes. In addition to numerous scientific publications, he has also published articles in the areas of academic leadership, faculty development, diversity, and university/K-12 partnerships.

Judith Parsons, IHM, Ph.D., is Associate Professor of philosophy at Immaculata University where she teaches an introductory survey course, ethics, aesthetics, and a course on the German phenomenologist, Edith Stein. Sister Judith has been an enthusiastic member of Immaculata University's "Academy of Metacognition" since 2013. Sister affirms that employing Academy activities such as journaling, interacting with colleagues, and intentionally using metacognitive strategies has made her a better-prepared, more confident, and empathetic teacher. Sister also credits the Academy with creating a vital community of teaching professionals who give credible evidence of a culture of lifelong learning on campus.

Anne Peirson-Smith is Assistant Professor in the Department of English, City University of Hong Kong, internship and projects co-ordinator and Programme Leader of the BA programme. In addition to having a professional background in public relations and branding she currently teaches and researches fashion communication and marketing, the creative industries, popular culture, public relations and branding at both undergraduate and postgraduate level and has published numerous articles and book chapters on these subjects. She has recently co-authored, Public Relations in Asia Pacific: Communicating Beyond Cultures (John Wiley, 2009) and Global Fashion Brands: Style, Luxury & History (Intellect Books, 2014). In addition, she is an associate editor of The Journal of Fashion, Style and Popular Culture (Intellect Publishers) and The Journal of Global Fashion Marketing. She is also on the advisory board of The Journal of Global Business and The East Asian Journal of Popular Culture (Intellect Publishers).

Jill Alexa Perry is Executive Director of the Carnegie Project on the Education Doctorate (CPED), an international consortium of universities collaborating to improve the Education Doctorate. She is also a Research Associate Faculty member at the University of Pittsburgh. Dr. Perry's research focuses on professional doctoral preparation in education, organizational change in higher education, and faculty leadership in higher education. Dr. Perry received a Bachelors of Arts in Spanish and International Studies and a Masters of Arts in Higher Education Administration from Boston College. She holds Ph.D. in International Educational Policy from the University of Maryland. She is a Fulbright Scholar (Germany) and a returned US Peace Corps Volunteer (Paraguay).

Natascha Radclyffe-Thomas is a University of the Arts London Teaching Scholar, Senior Fellow of the Higher Education Academy and currently Course Leader for BA (Hons.) Fashion Marketing at the London College of Fashion, University of the Arts London. Natascha has extensive international experience having taught fashion in the United Kingdom, Asia and the United states and has initiated several teaching initiatives including e-learning and international collaborative projects. Natascha's recent research looks at how issues such as culture, heritage, city-branding and social entrepreneurship manifest themselves in contemporary fashion marketing in Asia and the West. Natascha has published and presented papers internationally on research interests including creativity, pedagogy, cross-cultural communication, fashion branding, and marketing and also how issues around culture and communication manifest themselves in fashion education and practice. Natascha holds a Doctorate in Education and is on the editorial board of SPARK UAL's creative teaching and learning journal.

Ana Roncha is Post-Doctoral Research Fellow in Enterprise, Collaborations and Innovation at the London College of Fashion, University of the Arts London. Ana holds a Ph.D. in Design and Marketing Management for the Fashion Industry and lectures in the fields of fashion branding and strategic marketing. With over 10 years of experience creating high-impact strategic programs for international fashion, beauty and lifestyle brands, Ana has previously worked in house as a Brand and Marketing Communication Manager in the United States, United Kingdom and Portugal as well as on Branding and Communication Studios for brands such as Puma, L'Oreal, MoMa, Salsa Jeans, and Guy Laroche. Ana's research explores how innovation drives business development and value creation across SME's and leads to increased competitive advantage in the fashion sector. She has published in academic journals on the topics of strategic brand management, business model innovation for fashion and sustainability.

Thomas Schmalzer currently works as Senior Lecturer and Project Manager at the R&D centre of the Institute of International Management at FH JOANNEUM (University of Applied Sciences in Graz, Austria). Over the past years he was responsible for the acquisition, the coordination, as well as the overall management of over 50 R&D projects at the institute with a total volume of over 28 million EUR. His research areas cover entrepreneurship, innovation and internationalization of business, employability and competence-based education, regional development and cross-cultural differences. Thomas Schmalzer also works as a lecturer and trainer in economics, EU-Fundraising, as well as on international project and R&D management for companies and universities worldwide. He is the head of the Austrian team of the Global Entrepreneurship Monitor (GEM), the world's largest study in the field of entrepreneurship.

Alia Sheety is Associate Professor of education in the department of Educational Policy and Leadership at Cabrini University. Her primary areas of teaching are critical analysis of research, learning theories instruction and assessment. Dr. Sheety scholarly work includes exploration of adult learner preferences and the transition to online learning as cognition, behavior, and emotions integrate to support the learning process. Dr. Sheety completed her Ph.D. at Arizona State University and holds a master of art in Education and a master in business administration both earned at the University of Haifa, Israel.

Zuke van Ingen studied Business Administration. Currently he is working as Institutional Researcher at the Inholland University of Applied Sciences. His main area of research interest are student retention, drop-out, first year experience and graduation rates.

Jaap van Zandwijk studied Mathematics and Macroeconomics at Leiden University in Leiden (Netherlands). He has been working as a course manager in higher professional education. At the moment, he works as senior advisor at Leiden University of Applied Sciences. His main areas of interest are issues concerning student drop-out and student retention/success.

Digby Warren is currently Head of the *Centre for Enhancement of Learning & Teaching* [CELT] at London Metropolitan University. With over 20 years' experience of higher education development he writes, presents, and publishes on a range of developmental issues including diversity and transformational approaches.

Olof Wiegert earned his Ph.D. in Neuroscience from the department Biology at the University of Amsterdam. During his Ph.D. training he was chairman of the Ph.D. candidates Network of the Netherlands. Currently he is working as policy advisor and institutional researcher at the Amsterdam University of Applied Sciences. His main area of research interest is the dependence of student success and its possible predictors.

Domien Wijsbroek studied management, group interventions, organization development, and policy analysis. Worked in several universities and research institutes in the field of HR, management and management development. Became a lecturer at The Hague University of applied sciences. Currently employed as a researcher, working on finding some answers to this study success puzzle. Publications: mostly in Dutch in the field of study success. Some publications explore the relationship between language skills and study success in higher education.

Debby Zambo is Professor Emerita from Arizona State University and is currently working as the Associate Director of the Carnegie Foundation on the Education Doctorate (CPED). Debby received her Ph.D. from Arizona State University and, prior to her retirement, worked at ASU for 10 years as associate professor in the Division of Educational Leadership and Innovation in Mary Lou Fulton Teachers College. While at ASU Debby served as Coordinator of their Ed.D. program for two and a half years. Debby's research interests include newly designed Ed.D. programs and the application of educational psychology to educational practice. Since 2012, she has worked closely with Dr. Jill Perry, Director of CPED helping with various aspects of the organization including grant writing, convenings, and committees.

AUTHOR INDEX

SUBJECT INDEX